— HMS DARING —

# DARING CLASS
# DESTROYERS

# DARING CLASS DESTROYERS

by

Neil McCart

Previous Page: *HMS* Diana *shows off her classic destroyer lines.*                    *(Syd Goodman Collection)*

# CONTENTS

# ACKNOWLEDGEMENTS

I would like to pay special thanks to my old Commanding Officer of HMS *Ganges*, Captain John R. Gower DSC RN, of Aldeburgh, Suffolk, and my friend Tony Perrett of Gosport, Hampshire, for their help. Special thanks also to the staff of the Reading Rooms and the Special Production Teams at the National Archives, Kew, Surrey, for their help and assistance over a long period. I am also indebted to Vic Jeffery for his help with the RAN Darings. Thanks also to Steve Bush of *Maritime Books* for his help - and cups of tea. I must also pay special thanks to my wife Freda who, as always, has given me her full support and encouragement.

I would also like to thank the following for their memories of the Daring-Class destroyers: - Lt Cdr John Rodriguez Asti, Lima, Peru: Ian Cartwright, Berkhamsted, Hertfordshire: John Dent, Ipswich, Suffolk: Roy Emmington, Chatham, Kent: George Gardner, Archivist, University of Glasgow: F. J. Goodey, Tiptree, Essex: Frederick M. Hall, Wimborne, Dorset: Brian Hargreaves, World Ship Society, Tyne & Wear: Claire Harrington, Archivist, Mitchell Library, Glasgow: Richard Holme, Tunbridge Wells, Kent: Commander Ian Inskip RN, Cornwall: Charles Kitchen, HMS *Diana* Association, Broadstone, Dorset: Alfred Laws, Ashington, Northumberland: John Morris, Dalgety Bay, Fife: Dr Richard Osborne, World Ship Society, Nailsea, Somerset: Gordon Phipps, Burnham-on-Sea, Somerset: Jeremy Setford, High Wycombe, Buckinghamshire: Arthur Shadbolt, Hayle, Cornwall: Owen Simpson, Uley, Gloucestershire: John Solway, Friends of the National Maritime Museum, Greenwich, London: Keith Sowerby, Ferryhill, Co Durham: Bill Stanton, Brize Norton, Oxfordshire: Robert E. Stone, Cheltenham, Gloucestershire: Derek Taylor, Colchester, Essex: Ron Taverner, Horsforth, West Yorkshire: B. C. Whitaker, Leeds, West Yorkshire: Harry Whiteside, Pickering, North Yorkshire: Terence (Tug) Wilson, Paignton, Devon.

Documents Consulted at the National Archives:

    ADM 1 series - Reports of Boards of Inquiry.
    ADM 53 series - Ships' Logs.
    ADM 199 series - Reports of Proceedings.
    ADM 156 series - Courts Martial Records.

Miscellaneous References:

    *Daily Mirror* newspapers.
    *Daily Telegraph* newspapers.
    *Glasgow Herald* newspapers.
    *Navy News* - all issues 1957 - 1970.
    *Straits Times* (Singapore) newspapers.
    *Marine News*. Journal of the World Ship Society.
    *The Times* newspapers.
    Various Commission Booklets.

To the memory of Captain John Gower DSC RN,
Commanding Officer HMS *Diana* 1956-57, and HMS *Ganges* 1961-62.

# INTRODUCTION

Of all the Royal Navy's post-war destroyers, the class which epitomized the 1950s and 1960s was, without doubt, the Daring class. As part of the Admiralty's 1944 programme for modified Battle-class destroyers, it was originally intended that the new Daring class would comprise 16 warships. The first requests for tenders went out in January 1945 to four shipbuilding companies: Swan, Hunter & Wigham Richardson Ltd, at Wallsend-on-Tyne; John Brown and Co Ltd, at Clydebank; Messrs J. S. White & Co Ltd, at Cowes on the Isle of Wight, and Vickers Armstrong Shipbuilders. At that time, although the end of hostilities in Europe was in sight, no one could foresee an imminent conclusion to the war in South-East Asia and the Pacific.

However, on 14 August 1945, before any building work had started, the atomic bombs dropped on Hiroshima and Nagasaki brought a sudden end to the Second World War, and peace meant an inevitable reduction in the Admiralty's warship building programme. Every class of warship was affected by the cuts, from aircraft carriers down to auxiliaries, and the requirement for the "modified Battle-class" destroyers was halved. In the event, the eight destroyers of what became known as the Daring class were completed in two stages, with over two years elapsing between the completion of the first of the class, the name ship HMS *Daring*, and the last, HMS *Diana*, which did not leave Yarrow's shipyard until March 1954.

With a full load displacement of 3,600 tons, an overall length of 390ft, a beam of 43ft and a maximum draught of 17ft, the Daring-class destroyers were powerful ships with a main armament of six Mk VI 4·5-inch guns in fully enclosed twin turrets, two forward and one aft, controlled by a Mk VI, Type 275 radar director. Designed in the later years of the Second World War the guns overcame many deficiencies which had been experienced in the early years, and they were used extensively on destroyers and frigates right up to the early 1970s, with some 300 being manufactured. The guns were intended for automatic aiming and for a sustained high rate of fire. Ammunition was supplied from two magazines, each with a separate shell hoist, one for anti-aircraft shells and one for other projectiles, with a third hoist supplying the cartridges. They were designed to give a rate of fire of 24 rounds a minute, but in practice the complex automatic loading system was prone to breakdowns and the guns' crews often loaded by hand, keeping up a rate of fire of 12 to 14 rounds a minute. With an elevation of 45 degrees the guns had a range of 20,750 yards, and at an elevation of 80 degrees a range of 41,000 feet. For the first time in the Royal Navy an all-welded construction was used for the gun mountings, with the turret being supported by a cantilever structure which provided a circular gun bay clear of obstructions, which made for an easier transfer of ammunition to the revolving turret. In addition to the main armament the new destroyers were fitted with either four or six 40mm Bofors anti-aircraft guns, which were also radar controlled. As originally built they were also armed with ten 21-inch torpedo tubes, in two quintuple mountings, but these were never a success. For anti-submarine warfare they were fitted with a Squid triple-barrelled depth-charge mortar, which was located aft.

The main propulsion machinery was of an advanced design for the early 1950s, which had been developed by Parsons & Marine Engineering Turbine Research and Development Association (PAMATREDA), and consisted of two sets of double reduction geared steam turbines, each set driving one of the twin pro-

pellers. The superheated steam, at a temperature of 850°F and 650psi, was provided by either two oil-fired Babcock & Wilcox (*Daring*, *Decoy*, *Delight* and *Diana*), or two Foster Wheeler (*Dainty*, *Defender*, *Diamond* and *Duchess*), water-tube boilers. Altogether the machinery developed 54,000 SHP, giving them a maximum speed of 34·75 knots. In four ships of the class, *Decoy*, *Diamond*, *Diana* and *Duchess*, the electrical plant differed from previous ships of the Royal Navy in that it was an alternating current installation, operating at 440 volts, 3-phase, 60-cycles-per-second. The other four ships were fitted with the conventional direct current at 220 volts. Fitted with twin funnel uptakes, the forward funnel was built into the lattice mast, and the after funnel was small and narrow, which enhanced the appearance of these handsome ships, although at the design stage there had been some discussion about the appearance of the after funnel, and one proposed design shows a much wider and larger uptake, reminiscent of the single funnel of the Battle-class destroyers. Fortunately, this design was dropped at some stage prior to building.

Internally the Darings incorporated a number of innovations, including all-electric galleys, fluorescent lighting and a laundry. At the time of their construction the accommodation for both officers and ratings was described as being of a high standard, but in practice with complements of between 295 and 308, most of those who served in them considered them to be cramped and uncomfortable ships. Both senior and junior ratings ate, slept and lived on the messdecks, and there was little room for recreation. For officers conditions were a little better, but multiple berth cabins were extremely cramped and one officer remembers that he and two colleagues occupied a two-berth cabin, with him sleeping on a camp bed which left no room for anyone to move about the cabin. Nevertheless, despite the lack of comfort, those who served in the Darings look back on them with pride and Reunion Associations for all eight ships are strong and thriving, with great camaraderie among both officers and men.

For the Royal Navy of the early 1950s, however, the new class represented the ultimate in warship design, comprising eight powerful destroyers which were capable of carrying out duties normally assigned to light cruisers. Each of the Daring-class ships was in commission for less than 20 years, but during that time they saw the final transition from the big-gun era, to the age of the guided missile. During their early years of service at least one ship of the class operated with the Navy's last big 15-inch gun battleship, HMS *Vanguard*, and in their closing years they operated with the Navy's first guided missile ships, the County-class destroyers. As their Official Logs, which are preserved at the National Archives, proudly proclaim, they were originally classified not as destroyers, but as warships of the "Daring Class".

Neil McCart
Cheltenham, 2008

# Part One

# HMS DARING

## January 1952 - May 1971

*A good port side view of* Daring *taken in March 1952.*                    *(Portsmouth Royal Naval Museum)*

On 24 January 1945, the massive Red Army offensive reached the Gulf of Danzig to seal off East Prussia, and at the same time the first commercial shipping between Britain and France resumed the trade which had been cut off since May 1940. On the same day a letter was sent out from the Admiralty Contracts Department in Bath to Swan, Hunter and Wigham Richardson, the shipbuilders of Wallsend-on-Tyne. The letter opened with the sentence: 'I have to request that you will proceed forthwith with the construction and completion in all respects of two destroyers of the Battle class.' It went on to state that the two ships were to be built to a new design, and that: 'It is desired that the first vessel to be built by you

should be the prototype of the Class and should be progressed accordingly.' As wartime conditions still applied the Admiralty also instructed that: 'Your tender should be forwarded in due course, meanwhile the work should proceed without prejudice to the price.' Such was the urgency which still prevailed in the last week of January 1945.

On 15 August 1945, some seven months after the order had been placed and before any building work had begun, the Second World War came to an abrupt end and the order for the second of the two new destroyers was cancelled just as abruptly. The first order, however, was unaffected and some six weeks later, on 29 September, the first keel plates of HMS *Daring* were laid. With the war over there

*The Rock of Gibraltar provides the backdrop for this view of Daring taken in early 1952 when she was outbound for Malta.* *(Author's Collection)*

was now no urgency to complete and commission the ship, and four years elapsed before the destroyer was ready to take to the water. During those years, however, full advantage was taken of the advances in technology and this was reflected in the all-welded hull construction, the fully automatic and radar-controlled main armament, and the fluorescent lighting throughout the ship.

HMS *Daring*, from which the new class of destroyer took its name, was launched on Wednesday 10 August 1949, the ceremony being performed by Mrs Joan Hall, the daughter-in-law of Viscount Hall, the First Lord of the Admiralty, who had served in that political department in the pre-war Administration of Ramsay MacDonald, and in Attlee's post-war Government. It had taken four years to get *Daring* into the River Tyne, and with priority at the shipyards being given to commercial tonnage, another four years would elapse before she was ready to join the fleet.

In January 1951 fire broke out in one of *Daring's* transformer rooms, caused by an electrical short circuit. It almost proved fatal with four workmen being overcome by fumes and having to be rescued by the local fire service. Six months later, in the summer of 1951, the first key naval personnel travelled north to Wallsend to stand by *Daring*, and on 1 October that year her first commanding officer, Captain E. Hale RN, was appointed to the ship. He arrived on board in time to be present during the shipbuilder's trials which took place in the North Sea, off St Abb's Head, in early October 1951. Steaming through a good sea and with calm weather in light condition *Daring* attained a speed of 34.2 knots, and in deep condition a speed of 32.94 knots.

On 28 January 1952, some seven years after the order had been placed, the Captain Superintendent Contract Built Ships made his final inspection and immediately afterwards the ship was commissioned for trials. During the afternoon of the following day

the ship's company was brought up to full complement with the arrival of the main draft by special train from the Royal Naval Barracks at Devonport. They then had three days to familiarize themselves with the ship. Finally, after embarking stores, a quantity of ammunition for gun trials and carrying out final machinery tests and inspections, at 08.10 on 2 February *Daring* slipped her moorings and put to sea to carry out her final acceptance trials. At this stage she was still in the charge of staff from Swan, Hunter and Wigham Richardson, and the Wallsend Slipway and Engineering Company, her main machinery contractors, and was flying the Red Ensign from her masthead. Passing the entrance to the River Tyne at 0900, *Daring* set course north to carry out a two-hour full-power trial which was successful, and at 1312 that same day, in a position Lat 56°10.4'N/Long 02°13.5'W, Captain Hale accepted HMS *Daring* into the fleet. At the same time the Red Ensign was hauled down and the White Ensign was hoisted. That evening, after further tests and trials, *Daring* returned to the River Tyne to secure alongside the merchantman *Scottish Lion* at Swan Hunter's Quay. Next day, in the wardroom, a special commissioning service was held and during the following eight days *Daring* carried out various trials both in harbour and at sea. On 7 February she carried out radar and gunnery trials, with Firefly and Sea Hornet aircraft providing some realism for the radar and Bofors crews. This period of trials was frequently disrupted by poor visibility and heavy rain squalls, but fortunately the inclement weather did not seriously affect the schedule and on Tuesday 12 February *Daring* left the shipbuilder's yard, making her 49th passage through the Tyne pierheads, and set course for Rosyth and a four-hour fuelling stop. That same evening she left the Firth of Forth and, steaming by way of the Pentland Firth, set course for Devonport. Despite severe gale warnings being in force the weather during the passage was generally good, with both the sea and the wind abaft the beam, and the opportunity was taken to begin preliminary training at Action Stations, and to carry out other

important drills. At 0600 on Friday 15 February the destroyer passed the Eddystone Light, and two hours later she secured alongside Devonport Dockyard's No 1 Wharf where, the following day, she was joined by the Norwegian frigate *Narvik* (ex-HMS *Glaisdale*), to whose ship's company *Daring* acted as host.

As the first of the powerful new class of destroyer it was inevitable that she would attract a great deal of interest, and during her 18-day stay at Devonport there was a steady stream of VIP visitors to the ship. On 4 March she steamed east to Portsmouth where, for three weeks, she received further VIP and press visits. On 31 March she embarked a virtual army of press reporters and cameramen for the passage to Portland, during which the ship's company laid on an impressive display of gunnery with the 4.5-inch guns firing impressive broadsides at smoke targets and the Bofors guns firing break-up shot. The anti-submarine 'squid' mortar, the weapon which had rendered obsolete the depth charge, and whose existence had not long been made public, was fired with its projectiles landing well ahead of the ship. It was said that during the manoeuvres the fleet carrier *Implacable* signalled to Captain Hale, 'I hope she is better than she looks.' To which Hale replied, 'Design may be a bit Picasso, but she is a good ship at sea.' That evening *Daring* anchored off Portland, and next day began two weeks of intensive training as she began the first phase of her operational work-up, designed to get the ship's company into a state of full operational efficiency. On 10 April she returned to Devonport to give Foreign Service Leave. *Daring* was destined for the Mediterranean Fleet based at Malta, where she was to be leader of the newly formed Second Destroyer Squadron, and at 1415 on Wednesday 7 May, following the C-in-C Plymouth's Ceremonial Divisions, she sailed for Malta, via Gibraltar, arriving at her mooring in Lazzaretto Creek on 16 May.

*Daring*'s arrival at Malta heralded the start of an extremely busy six weeks, with the ship scheduled to complete her work-up exercises and drills, and

these got under way with C-in-C Mediterranean's Ceremonial Divisions. At sea she operated with other units of the Mediterranean Fleet, including the cruisers *Newcastle* and *Gambia*, the destroyers *Armada*, *Gravelines* and *Vigo*, the frigate *Opossum* and the submarine *Sanguine*. On Thursday 19 June *Daring* left her buoy at Lazzaretto Creek to rendezvous with *Gambia*, *Vigo* and the depot ship *Forth*, and for a time the flagship of the Mediterranean Fleet, *Glasgow*, for anti-aircraft exercises in local waters. During the course of the day *Daring* fired off large quantities of both 4.5-inch and Bofors ammunition. During the first dog-watch the Bofors guns were firing break-up shot when a round in M2 mounting became jammed. As attempts were made to clear the offending shell it exploded, killing Senior Commissioned Gunner G. W. Rossiter and Ordnance Artificer W. P. Murphy, both of whom received extensive gunshot wounds. That evening *Daring* anchored in St Paul's Bay and the following forenoon returned to her buoy in Lazzaretto Creek. On 21 June the funerals of the two men took place. It was not a good start to the commission.

On 24 June *Daring* put to sea to resume her work-up exercises, this time in company with the frigates *Opossum* and *Vampire*, and the submarine *Trump*. The exercises continued during the first two weeks of July, culminating on Tuesday 15 July when the ship underwent her sea inspection by the Flag Officer Second-in-Command (FO2), Mediterranean Fleet. In the third week of July *Daring* underwent a dockyard assisted maintenance period, which included some time in dry dock. On 29 July Captain Hale relinquished his command, and Commander V. J. St Clair Ford MBE RN, who had been Executive Officer in *Daring* since July 1951, took temporary command of the ship. During the period the ship was in dry dock local leave was granted, with some members of the ship's company taking the opportunity to stay at the Krendi Rest camp. By Tuesday 12 August *Daring* was out of dry dock and alongside the Canteen Wharf. Two days later she spent 48 hours at sea undergoing

machinery trials before returning to Grand Harbour to secure alongside the destroyer *Cheviot* at Club House Wharf. Three days later, during the forenoon of Monday 18 August, Commander St Clair Ford suddenly collapsed and died following a heart attack. His funeral took place two days later, after which Commander J. L. Rathbone DSC RN, who had just relinquished command of *Cheviot*, took temporary command of *Daring*.

On 26 August, with her maintenance completed, *Daring* left Malta to make a fast passage to the North African port of Tripoli where she embarked a special cargo of gold bullion, which was then given an equally fast passage back to Malta where it was unloaded. The first week of September saw *Daring* once again at sea, this time for the fleet's summer cruise under its new C-in-C, Admiral Lord Louis Mountbatten. After leading the fleet to sea in the depot ship *Forth*, the C-in-C transferred his flag to *Glasgow*. Also in company was the aircraft carrier *Glory*, the cruiser *Cleopatra*, the destroyers *Armada*, *Chequers*, *Chieftain*, *Chivalrous*, *Gravelines* and *Saintes*, the frigates *Loch Dunvegan*, *Loch Lomond*, *Meon*, *Mermaid* and *Vigo*, the C-in-C's dispatch vessel *Surprise*, the fast minelayer *Manxman* and the submarines *Sanguine*, *Sentinel* and *Sturdy* - a formidable array of warships. The exercises began in the Western Mediterranean with units of the French Navy, and for *Daring* they included a visit to Toulon, followed by more manoeuvres off the French coast. On Thursday 18 September, whilst *Daring* was at anchor off Golfe Juan, her new commanding officer, Captain P. D. Gick OBE DSC RN, joined the ship. Four days later, on the conclusion of the second phase of the exercises, *Daring* put into Naples to begin a four-day visit to the Italian port where, at 09.00 on 22 September, Captain Gick formally took command of the destroyer and Commander Rathbone left the ship.

There is no doubt that *Daring*'s first commission had got off to an inauspicious start, and inevitably this had had its effect on the morale of the ship's company, but under Percy Gick's inspired leader-

ship the atmosphere soon changed and, in the words of one rating, 'Daring became a vastly different ship.' The exercises continued with Daring acting as planeguard to the aircraft carrier Theseus and on 9 October she secured to a buoy in Malta's Grand Harbour. There were to be no runs ashore, however, for within hours Daring had been ordered to put to sea and to make for Port Said.

Leaving Grand Harbour during the afternoon of 9 October, Daring rendezvoused with the aircraft carrier Glory, which was bound for the Far East and the war in Korea. The destroyer was escorting her into the Red Sea and both ships were given a ceremonial 'send-off' by four units of the First Destroyer Squadron which steamed past with farewell signals flying. Three days later the two ships arrived in Port Said and on 13 October they steamed south, with Daring making her first transit of the Suez Canal. Next day, after acting as planeguard for Glory, Daring parted company and steamed on to Port Sudan for a three-day courtesy visit while the aircraft carrier continued her passage south. When Daring was opened to the public during the afternoon of 17 October, over 1,700 local people took the opportunity to visit her. Leaving Port Sudan the next day Daring steamed north to spend seven days at anchor in Port Suez, at the southern entrance to the Suez Canal. With Egyptian nationalist feeling against the British military occupation of the huge Suez Canal Zone bases running high, and with the corrupt, but pro-British, King Farouk having been deposed by a military coup, it was felt that a British presence should be maintained in the Suez Canal area. Steaming north on 29 October, Daring anchored in the Great Bitter Lake for 24 hours, with the ship's company being granted shore leave to the British base area at Fayid. Finally, on the last day of October Daring joined the cruiser Euryalus at Port Said and that afternoon the two warships sailed for Malta, arriving in Grand Harbour three days later.

For the rest of the year Daring remained in the Malta area, carrying out frequent exercises with the aircraft carriers Theseus and Ocean, and in mid-January 1953 she once again put in a high-profile appearance at Port Said, where the political situation following the overthrow of King Farouk was still extremely fragile. Although shore leave was granted to the ship's company until 2230, the security situation was such that armed sentries were posted at strategic points around the ship, and there was a tense atmosphere as Egyptian opposition to the presence of British military bases in the country showed no signs of abating. During the evening of 10 February one of the ship's sentries sighted a suspicious object in the water close to the ship and he opened fire. With a full-scale security alert in force the ship's divers carried out a thorough search of the ship's bottom and the area around the vessel, but fortunately it was a false alarm and at midnight, with the search completed, everyone was able to relax. Five days later Daring steamed down the Suez Canal to anchor in the Great Bitter Lake, off Fayid, where she spent three days before returning to Malta.

For Daring's ship's company March was an extremely busy month, with a major exercise in the Western Mediterranean and Atlantic Ocean, which included the aircraft carriers Eagle and Indomitable, the cruisers Glasgow and Euryalus and Daring's sisters Diamond and Duchess. The exercise, code-named 'Rendezvous', included shutting down the ship and pre-wetting as defence against nuclear fallout, and it ended at Malta on 21 March. Seven days later, having hoisted the flag of Admiral Lord Mountbatten, Daring put to sea for the day in company with Chequers to carry out a ceremonial steampast for the Yugoslavian leader Marshal Tito who was returning home in the training ship Galeb after an important State visit to Britain. On her return to Malta Daring remained long enough to de-ammunition and to land a large quantity of stores, before sailing for Gibraltar where, on 9 April, she began a two-month dockyard assisted refit. During this period the ship's company was accommodated ashore, and the ship herself was docked down in Gibraltar's No 2 Graving Dock. Although this period provided a break from

shipboard routine, the shore accommodation for ships' companies whose ships were in refit was far from ideal, and so there was a general sense of relief on 24 July when *Daring*'s company moved back on board and the ship herself was shifted to the detached mole. Two days later, at 1002 on Sunday 26 July, with the ship still being made ready for sea after her refit, *Daring* was ordered to sail to assist in the search for survivors following a collision in the Strait of Gibraltar between two small ships, the British steamer *Culrain* and a Spanish cargo vessel, the *Duero*. The collision had happened in dense fog, and the Spanish ship sank an hour later, giving her crew time to take to lifeboats. In the event *Daring* was able to slip her moorings at 1025 and set course for the scene, arriving an hour later to find thick fog still covering the area and, in the busy waterway, shipping passing dangerously close to the damaged British ship which had embarked *Duero*'s survivors. After transferring the 28 seamen from *Culrain* the destroyer returned to Gibraltar where they were disembarked.

Five days after her mercy mission, having embarked 11 passengers and three cars for the return passage, *Daring* sailed for Malta where she arrived on 3 August. Seven days later, in company with the destroyer *Saintes*, *Daring* left Grand Harbour to carry out exercises in local waters. During the forenoon of 11 August she anchored in St Paul's Bay, and there she remained until the next forenoon when she weighed anchor for another round of exercises and manoeuvres. No sooner had these begun, however, than a priority signal was received from the C-in-C ordering the ship back to Grand Harbour, and by 1230 she was secured to her buoy. It was then that the ship's company learned of massive earthquakes which had rocked the Greek Ionian Islands, killing hundreds, injuring many more and causing widespread destruction of property in towns and villages. One of the worst hit areas was the town of Argostoli on the island of Cephalonia (Kefallinia), which was described by the crew of a reconnaissance aircraft thus: 'All towns there have been destroyed, and the greatest

damage was in the south.' Meanwhile, in Grand Harbour, working parties urgently loaded tons of food, medical supplies, tents and equipment into every available space on *Daring*'s decks. Finally, at 1645, just four hours and 20 minutes after her arrival, and carrying four naval surgeons and 17 additional sick-berth attendants, she sailed for Cephalonia, anchoring off Argostoli at 0600 on 13 August, less than 24 hours after receiving the signal to return to Grand Harbour. Although she was the first vessel carrying aid to arrive at the stricken island, she was quickly followed by the Italian destroyer *Artigliere* and a small flotilla of LCTs.

As soon as *Daring* anchored, working parties were being detailed to clear roads in order that communications could be restored, and to recover bodies from wrecked buildings and fight fires. With severe tremors continuing to shake the islands it was difficult and dangerous work, but after three days great progress had been made and *Daring* was able to move south to the island of Zante (Zakinthos), where further relief work was undertaken and a number of refugees embarked. Finally, with a massive Greek and international relief effort under way *Daring* was able to leave for Patras, where she disembarked her passengers, before heading for Piraeus by way of the Corinth Canal, where she secured alongside during the late afternoon of 19 August. The following day, by way of a thank-you on behalf of the Greek Royal Family, she received a visit from the Duchess of Kent, her son Prince Michael and daughter Princess Alexandra. On 23 August *Daring* left Piraeus and, just over 24 hours later, she arrived back in Grand Harbour.

During the next two weeks *Daring* spent seven days at sea on day running exercises with the cruiser *Cumberland* and the submarine *Token*, but by 5 September 1953 she was on her way once again to Port Said. However, her guardship duties at Navy House Quay were interrupted by another series of Mediterranean earthquakes, this time on the island of Cyprus, which was starting to simmer with political unrest against British rule. During the night of 11 September severe earth tremors had rocked the

*Daring shown on 5 September 1953, leaving Grand Harbour for Port Said.* (World Ship Society)

western seaboard of the island, destroying homes and killing and injuring scores of people. Two days later, during the afternoon of Sunday 13 September, *Daring* was placed at immediate notice for steam and a 31-lorry supply convoy arrived from the Army base area at Fayid, loaded with army tents. For three hours working parties laboured in the hot and humid weather and on completion of embarkation, with tents piled up in every available inch of deck space, *Daring* left Port Said to make a fast overnight passage to Cyprus. Next day, after unloading the tents into lighters off the town of Paphos, she returned to Port Said where she remained until mid-October when she steamed, by way of Limassol, to Malta, arriving in Grand Harbour during the last week of October.

During the remainder of 1953 and during January 1954 *Daring* operated from Malta, carrying out exercises in local waters with the aircraft carrier *Glory* and the cruiser *Gambia*. She underwent FO2's harbour and sea inspections, and during the second week of February 1954, in company with

*Glasgow* and *St Kitts*, spent ten days operating off Cyprus in support of 40 Commando Royal Marines, who were carrying out amphibious landing exercises. With No 14 Squadron, Royal New Zealand Air Force, undertaking the role of enemy, *Daring* and *Glasgow* carried out a bombardment of Cape Arnanti in north-west Cyprus. On Tuesday 16 February, Captain E. A. Blundell OBE RN joined the ship by jackstay from *Glasgow* and four days later, after *Daring*'s arrival in Grand Harbour, he took over command of the destroyer from Captain Gick. For *Daring* herself there followed a three-week maintenance period, including ten days in dry dock.

It was mid-March before *Daring* was at sea again, this time carrying out planeguard duties for the aircraft carrier *Eagle*, and air defence exercises with the cruisers *Bermuda* and *Gambia*. By the end of March the squadron, including *Daring* and *Eagle*, had steamed west to Gibraltar in preparation for joint exercises with the French Navy, including the cruisers *Gloire* and *Montcalm*. Also taking part

were heavy bombers from RAF bases in Germany and carrier-borne aircraft from the US Sixth Fleet in the Mediterranean. Code-named 'Medflex Able' and 'Shield One', the exercises also included French and Italian submarines. They ended on 3 April 1954, when *Daring* and *Eagle* put into Toulon for a three-day visit. At 1030 on Tuesday 6 April *Daring* and *Eagle* left Toulon to carry out flying exercises in Italian waters, and at 0730 on Friday 9 April, whilst in the Tyrrhenian Sea, east of Sardinia, an urgent signal was received from the C-in-C Mediterranean ordering both ships to a position Lat 39°52'N/Long 14°16'E, to search for a missing BOAC Comet IV jet airliner.

The Comet IV, G-ALYY, had left London bound for Johannesburg at 15.00 on 7 April, and had land-

ed safely in Rome, where it was delayed at the city's airport for 24 hours while a fuel gauge was repaired. Then, at 0625 on 8 April, with a new crew of seven and carrying 14 passengers, it took off from Rome Airport bound for Cairo, where it was due to land that evening. Thirty-two minutes after taking off the pilot reported: 'Over Naples, still climbing' - then nothing more was heard. When it failed to arrive in Cairo it was listed as 'overdue', but in the early hours of 9 April it was posted as 'missing' and a full-scale air-sea search was initiated. As soon as the C-in-C's signal was received *Eagle*'s aircraft spotted wreckage floating in the sea in a position Lat 39°39'N/Long 14°43'E, about 30 miles north of Stromboli. By 1840 that day *Daring* had arrived at the scene of the crash, and at 2030

*Four of Eagle's Avenger aircraft fly over Daring as they began the search for the BOAC Comet 4 airliner which had crashed off Stromboli on 9 April 1954.* (Author's Collection)

two bodies were recovered. By 2300, with the search having been called off for the night, *Daring* had recovered large quantities of wreckage, including parts of the aircraft's fuselage and passengers' personal effects. Next morning at 0500, the search resumed, but it soon became clear that nothing of significance would be found and, taking up station astern of *Eagle*, *Daring* set course for Naples, where she arrived later the same day to disembark the bodies and wreckage. As this was the third Comet IV airliner to crash with the loss of all passengers and crew within the space of 12 months, the whole Comet fleet was grounded; subsequent investigations revealed that metal fatigue was the cause. By the time structural faults had been rectified Britain's lead in commercial jet travel had been lost to the USA's Boeing passenger jets.

For *Daring* the visit to Naples ended on 13 April and next day she returned to Malta where she remained until the end of the month. On 1 May, in company with *Eagle* and other units of the Mediterranean Fleet, *Daring* sailed to rehearse the next day's ceremonial meeting and steampast as the Royal Yacht *Britannia* arrived in Malta. The Queen and the Duke of Edinburgh were on a major Commonwealth tour which had been begun by air before they joined the chartered passenger liner *Gothic* in Jamaica on 21 November 1953. From there *Gothic* had sailed via Panama to Fiji, Tonga, New Zealand, Australia, Ceylon (Sri Lanka), and then to Aden, from where the royal party flew to Entebbe in Uganda. From East Africa they flew to Tobruk where, on 30 April, they embarked in *Britannia* for the two-day passage to Malta.

After the fleet rehearsal *Daring* remained at sea overnight, and Sunday 2 May dawned bright and sunny, but with strong winds. At 1030 the ship's company manned the upper decks and half an hour later, led by the cruisers *Glasgow*, *Gambia and Bermuda*, *Daring* and her sister *Delight*, together with seven other destroyers and two frigates, steamed past both *Britannia*'s port and starboard sides, firing a co-ordinated 21-gun salute as they bore down on the royal yacht at 25 knots. With lit-

tle slackening of speed both lines wheeled inward and passed *Britannia* a second time, within only half a cable of the royal yacht as officers and ratings gave three cheers. There then followed a fly-past, before the units of the Mediterranean Fleet escorted *Britannia* to Malta, entering Grand Harbour the following forenoon. During the rest of the month, apart from a short visit to Tripoli with the cruiser *Bermuda*, *Daring* remained in local waters.

On 5 June, together with *Bermuda* and her sister, *Daring* sailed for Cyprus where exercises and manoeuvres were carried out, before the three warships spent four days at Famagusta. During two of the four days the ships were opened to the public, and despite the fact that political agitation against British rule was coming to a head and later in the year would explode into riots and civil unrest which, in turn, would lead to insurgency, the three ships were a popular attraction. On 10 June *Bermuda* (Flag FO2 Vice-Admiral J. P. L. Reid), *Daring*, *Delight* and the frigate *Whirlwind* left Famagusta for an official visit to Lebanon where, after five days alongside in Beirut, President Shamoun of Lebanon embarked in *Bermuda* for a day at sea with the squadron. During the displays *Daring* put on an impressive show of gunnery, firing some 60 rounds from her main 4.5-inch armament. After disembarking the President off Beirut the four warships set course for Turkish ports where *Daring* paid official visits to Iskenderun and Izmir, Piraeus in Greece and the Italian naval base at Taranto. The final call was followed by a joint convoy escort exercise with the Italian destroyer *Artigliere* before *Daring* returned to Grand Harbour on 23 July.

During the forenoon of 9 August *Daring* left Malta to set course for Gibraltar and home, arriving in Plymouth Sound during the morning watch of Monday 16 August. Two hours later after Customs clearance, *Daring* steamed up harbour to secure alongside No 1 Wharf in Devonport's South Yard. She had been away for over two years and by 1100, within two hours of her arrival, the first long leave parties had left the ship. However, the commission

was not yet over and on 15 September she was once again at sea with her sister *Delight* and heading north for Invergordon and the North Sea where, with the cruiser *Jamaica*, the destroyers *Agincourt* and *Barrosa*, and Norwegian naval units, she undertook convoy escort exercises, with the RFAs *Olna* and *Brown Ranger* providing the merchant vessels. Code-named 'Morning Mist' and 'Polar Mist', and with only a 48-hour break at Tromsø, the exercises continued until the early hours of 4 October, when *Daring* set course for home, arriving at Devonport on 5 October. This time the destroyer remained in the dockyard for four months undergoing essential maintenance, and it was February 1955 before she put to sea again.

When *Daring* sailed from Plymouth Sound on 9 February she carried out several days of machinery trials, before joining her sister *Defender* for the passage to Gibraltar and major fleet exercises in the Atlantic and Western Mediterranean. As well as *Daring* and *Defender*, also taking part were *Delight*, *Bermuda*, *Scorpion* and *St Kitts*. On 1 March they steamed east for Malta where they joined units of the Mediterranean Fleet, including *Tyne*, *Apollo*, *Reward* and *Saintes*, for joint Home and Mediterranean Fleet exercises. There was a visit to La Spezia, during which the C-in-C Home Fleet, Admiral Sir Michael Denny, visited *Daring*, and on 10 March the combined fleets began further exercises. Three days later, however, *Daring* was withdrawn from the manoeuvres with serious damage to boiler room frames and next day she put into Malta. It soon became apparent that major dockyard repairs were required and on 1 April she left Malta, to secure alongside at Devonport five days later. On Friday 6 May, as *Daring* was being prepared to sail north to her builder's yard, there was an explosion in No 3 diesel generator, caused by leaking fuel. Although one rating suffered minor injuries, damage was superficial and eight days later the ship sailed for the River Tyne. Two days later she arrived alongside Swan Hunter's Quay at Wallsend, where she would remain for three months. *Daring*'s first commission, which had seen

more than its share of problems, was at an end.

During the four summer months of 1955 she lay alongside the Wallsend shipyard of Swan, Hunter and Wigham Richardson undergoing boiler room repairs, and on 3 August her new commanding officer, Captain H. R. Bromley DSC RN was appointed to the ship. On Friday 19 August, having been dry docked, the destroyer left the River Tyne and steaming south she set course for Devonport. After anchoring in Plymouth Sound during the early hours of 21 August she steamed up harbour the same forenoon to secure alongside the battleship HMS *Vanguard* at No 7 wharf in Devonport Dockyard. Next day her ship's company was brought up to strength with the arrival of 104 ratings from the Royal Naval Barracks and at 1440 that afternoon, in the shadow of the Royal Navy's last battleship, *Daring*'s recommissioning service was held on the forecastle. Nine days later she sailed to carry out a series of machinery trials before leaving Devonport on 19 September for Gibraltar and the Mediterranean, arriving in Malta's Grand Harbour nine days later.

During October 1955 and the first two weeks of November *Daring* carried out an intensive series of work-up exercises, often in company with *Saintes* and *Whirlwind*. By 22 November she was fully operational and that forenoon she sailed for Cyprus. Since *Daring*'s previous visit in June 1954 the political situation on the island had deteriorated rapidly. In December that year rioting had broken out in Nicosia and in Limassol, and within weeks a full-scale insurgency had erupted as Greek Cypriots called for Enosis, or union with Greece, which of course was opposed by the minority Turkish section of the population. By the autumn of 1955 British soldiers were being killed and a state of emergency had been declared. It was common knowledge that large quantities of weapons and explosives were being smuggled into Cyprus by sea, and *Daring* had been ordered to carry out patrols of the coastline in an attempt to prevent arms smuggling. However, with such a large area to cover and with the presence of large fleets of local fishing boats, and ships

*A dramatic aerial view of* Daring *during high-speed manoeuvres in the Mediterranean.*　　　*(Author's Collection)*

which were trading legitimately between Greece and Cyprus, the Royal Navy's arms blockade was virtually an impossible task. In the event it had only a minimal effect on General Grivas' EOKA guerrilla organisation. *Daring*'s first patrol lasted for four weeks, during which time she refuelled

from *RFA Brown Ranger* which had a semi-permanent anchorage in Famagusta Bay. She also anchored off Kyrenia, but owing to the situation ashore no shore leave was granted. To everyone's relief the patrol ended during the evening of 15 December, and on the following day *Daring* arrived

Daring *at Sliema Creek, Malta, in November 1955, sporting her enlarged funnel casing.*
*(Portsmouth Royal Naval Museum)*

in Beirut for a four-day visit. On 23 December the destroyer returned to Malta where Christmas and New Year festivities were held.

After leaving Malta on 23 January 1956 *Daring* and her sister *Defender* exercised with the cruiser *Birmingham* and other units, with short breaks at Aranci Bay, Sardinia, and at Cartagena in Spain. On 14 February *Daring* and *Defender* arrived in Port Said to oversee the withdrawal of the 2nd Battalion, Grenadier Guards, the last British fighting troops to leave Egypt following an agreement signed in October 1954, which one senior Army officer described as 'a protracted departure'. This provided for the complete withdrawal of British forces which had to be completed by 16 June 1956. Some British politicians were having difficulty coming to terms with Britain's reduced post-war role in world affairs, but with the rise in nationalist aspirations in Egypt the Army had been hard pressed to defend its own base areas from a restless, uncooperative and resentful local population. Part of the 1954 agreement provided for the retention of 700 British servicemen to maintain the Suez Canal base areas which, in the event of a foreign attack on

Egypt, could be reoccupied. In reality, however, it was clear that despite this 'face-saving' formula, no Egyptian Government would agree to a military reoccupation - thus the scene was set for a watershed in Britain's colonial history.

For *Daring* the guardship duties in Port Said were interspersed with patrols off the coast of Cyprus, and in the second week of March a visit to the Libyan port of Tripoli. The last weeks of March saw the destroyer operating in the Western Mediterranean, with a visit to Barcelona. In April she returned to Maltese waters for exercises with *Birmingham*, *Saintes* and *St Kitts*. On 8 May, with her sister *Decoy*, she returned to Port Said for guardship duties, but with the British military withdrawal almost complete and with Egyptian nationalist tensions having subsided, she remained for only two days before carrying out another patrol of the Cypriot coastline. It would be six months before she returned to Port Said as part of what a senior British officer described as, 'The strange British return to Egypt'. During the last week of May *Daring* took part in training exercises with Italian units off Sardinia, before steaming west for

Daring *at speed.* (MoD/Crown Copyright)

Gibraltar and onward to the UK, arriving in Devonport Dockyard during the forenoon of 6 June. On 26 July 1956, just over six weeks after the final British military withdrawal from Egypt, whilst *Daring* was high and dry in Devonport South Yard's No 2 dry dock, President Nasser of Egypt nationalised the Suez Canal Company. On the day after the announcement in London the Chiefs of Staff were summoned by Prime Minister Anthony Eden and told to prepare plans for the invasion of Egypt and the reoccupation of the military bases in the Suez Canal Zone. For over three months protracted negotiations were conducted, but in fact in collusion with Israel, which was always eager to expand its occupation of Arab land, the British and French Governments planned a massive invasion of Egypt on two fronts.

In the short term these plans did not affect *Daring*'s assisted maintenance period at Devonport, and during August she lay alongside No 4 basin in the North Yard. On 4 September, however, the maintenance work was completed and next day she ran machinery trials in the Channel. Three days later *Daring* was undergoing weapons training off Portland with the cruiser *Glasgow*, and by the middle of the month she was on intensive training exercises in the North Sea, in the area of the Moray Firth. Also present were *Glasgow* and *Defender*. There was little time for recreation as the ships carried out convoy escort, anti-aircraft, anti-submarine and bombardment exercises. On Wednesday 17 October the intensive training was relaxed when *Daring* set course for Bremen to make a five-day visit to the German port. Meanwhile, in the Mediterranean a large invasion force was slowly gathering at Malta, and on the troubled island of Cyprus, and on 24 October *Daring* left Bremen to rendezvous with *Defender* and make a fast six-day passage to Malta, where she arrived alongside Grand Harbour's Boathouse Wharf during the morning watch of 31 October. There followed an eight-hour pause for refuelling, and at 1500 *Daring* and *Defender* left Malta to join the Anglo-French invasion fleet bound for Port Said.

As part of a secret agreement signed at Sevres, France, it had been decided that on 29 October Israel would invade Egypt across the Sinai Desert to positions close to the Suez Canal, following which Britain and France would deliver an ultimatum calling upon Egypt to allow the massive Anglo-French military invasion force to reoccupy the Suez Canal Zone bases they had evacuated only four months previously, thereby ensuring the canal remained open to shipping. In fact there was never any danger to the Suez Canal for at Sevres the Israelis had agreed to halt their offensive well short of the waterway. The Protocol of Sevres had hampered military moves, for in order to maintain the pretence of being self-appointed 'peacemakers' it meant that the Anglo-French invasion fleet could not sail until after the ultimatum had been delivered to Egypt. It was assumed correctly in London and Paris that Nasser would reject the ultimatum, thus giving Eden the moral justification for the invasion. The opening moves of the Suez campaign began at 1630 on 29 October when, without any prior declaration, Israel began its assault on Egyptian forces in Sinai. After initial setbacks the Egyptian Army recovered well, and it was only with the aid of the French Air Force that the Israeli advance began to go to plan. The joint British and French ultimatum to Egypt was delivered in the early hours of 30 October and, as expected, it was rejected, leaving the way open for British air attacks on Egyptian airfields to begin.

At sea on board *Daring* three hours after leaving Grand Harbour, Captain Bromley spoke to the ship's company and told them that they were part of the escort for the Anglo-French invasion force, and that *Daring*'s role, with her sister *Defender*, was to provide a planeguard and anti-submarine screen for the aircraft carrier *Bulwark*. With the Fleet Air Arm attacks on Egyptian targets beginning in the early hours of 31 October *Daring* took up station some four cables astern of the carrier. During the whole period of the Suez operations the destroyer provided *Bulwark* with her vital screen and close defensive support, and she continued to do so after the

humiliating ceasefire which, under financial and diplomatic pressure from the United States, Eden was forced to order at midnight on 6 November. For *Daring* the ceasefire made little difference to operational requirements, and with *Defender* she continued to provide support to the carrier force. On 11 November, *Daring* entered Port Said for the last time to secure alongside the depot ship *Ranpura*, but six days later she returned to sea to carry out planeguard duties for the fleet carrier *Eagle*. *Daring*'s part in the Suez operations ended on Saturday 24 November when she returned to Grand Harbour.

A week after her return to Malta *Daring*'s new commanding officer, Captain G. I. M. Balfour DSC RN joined the ship, and the following day he took command. *Daring* remained in the Mediterranean until September 1957 when, with *Defender*, she returned to home waters and Devonport to give leave and to undergo maintenance. In October that year she took part in NATO exercises in the

Western Approaches and in the North Sea. The exercise was commanded by the C-in-C, Home Fleet, Admiral Sir John Eccles, who flew his flag in the depot ship *Maidstone*, with the Royal Navy being represented by a strong carrier force, including *Eagle*, *Ark Royal* and *Bulwark*. Also taking part were the cruisers *Gambia* and *Sheffield*, as well as *Daring* and her sisters *Dainty*, *Defender* and *Delight*, and six frigates.

In mid-January 1958, following Christmas leave, *Daring* left Devonport as part of the Second Destroyer Squadron to rendezvous with her sister *Dainty*, the cruiser *Ceylon* and other units of the Home Fleet, including *Maidstone*, now wearing the flag of the new C-in-C, Admiral Sir William Davis. The Home Fleet squadron which assembled off Portland was a powerful force, and it also included *Bulwark*, *Bermuda* and *Daring*'s three sisters *Dainty*, *Defender* and *Delight*. From the Third Destroyer Squadron were HM Ships *Camperdown* and *Barfleur*, and also joining the force were the

*Daring* steams up the Hamoaze to Devonport Dockyard on 30 September 1957, during service with the Home Fleet. *(Author's Collection)*

frigates *Troubridge* and *Ulster* and the submarines *Tiptoe* and *Turpin*. The exercises which followed were conducted jointly with the Royal Canadian Navy, including the carrier *Bonaventure*. They began in the Western Approaches and continued across to the Western Atlantic Ocean right up to the end of the month, when the fleet dispersed to begin its spring cruise programme in the Caribbean. *Daring* and the other units of the Second Destroyer Squadron visited Nassau and Bequia Island, south of the island of St Vincent, and took part in joint exercises with US naval units, during which *Daring* paid a short visit to the US base at Guantanamo Bay, Cuba. By 20 February *Daring* was secured alongside *Maidstone* at Port of Spain, Trinidad where, on the depot ship's spacious decks, C-in-C's Ceremonial Divisions were held. The final Caribbean visit for *Daring* was to Union Island for recreational leave before she rendezvoused with other units and steamed north to Bermuda and the naval base at Ireland Island. In mid-March, after carrying out maintenance at Bermuda, the whole force steamed north to Halifax, Nova Scotia, carrying out further exercises which were completed with a four-day visit to the Canadian port before they set course for home. The eastbound transatlantic passage took the form of a convoy escort exercise, with *Bulwark*, *Bonaventure* and *Maidstone* taking the role of merchant vessels. The exercises concluded on the last day of March at the Isle of Man's Fleshwick Bay. On 1 April *Daring* weighed anchor and set course for Devonport, arriving during the forenoon of the next day. It was the end of the destroyer's second eventful commission and ahead lay an eight-month refit.

During her refit at Devonport Dockyard *Daring* became a familiar sight alongside No 4 basin, or in No 8 dry dock. At just before midnight on 27 November there was a fire in A engine room, caused by steam pipe lagging which had been ignited by welding equipment earlier in the day, and which had smouldered unnoticed. Fortunately, it was soon under control and extinguished. By the end of December 1958 conditions on board were

returning to normal, and on Monday 12 January 1959 the destroyer's new commanding officer, Captain C. P. Mills CBE DSC RN, joined the ship. Eight days later, on 20 January, the ship's company moved back on board from shore accommodation at HMS *Drake*, and at 14.30 the same afternoon, in the middle of a torrential thunderstorm, HMS *Daring* was commissioned for service with the Mediterranean Fleet.

Six days after recommissioning *Daring* began her post-refit trials in local waters, and during February 1959 she returned to the dockyard for further adjustments to her machinery. During March the work-up began in earnest and continued up to the end of May, having been interrupted by further dockyard work and seasonal leave. During this period *Daring* operated with *Bermuda*, *Troubridge* and *Venus*. On 29 May, with her work-up completed, *Daring* paid an 18-day visit to Portsmouth before, on Sunday 14 June, sailing for Malta. Pausing only briefly at Gibraltar she arrived in Sliema Creek on 21 June and two days later took part in a major amphibious exercise, code-named 'Whitebait', which also included units of the US Sixth Fleet. Led by *Birmingham* and the aircraft carrier *Centaur*, the Royal Navy was also represented by *Defender* and *Saintes*, while the US Navy's contribution included the aircraft carrier *Intrepid* and the cruiser *Canberra*. On conclusion of the exercises in late June there was little spare time for *Daring*, and on 3 July she left Malta to carry out a Cyprus patrol, during the course of which she also exercised with *Birmingham* and *Battleaxe*. The patrol was broken for a two-day visit to Athens, and it ended on 29 July when she returned to Sliema Creek. As well as *Daring* the Second Destroyer Squadron in the Mediterranean also consisted of *Dainty*, *Defender* and *Delight*, with Captain Mills as Captain (D) of the Squadron. Within a week of her return to Malta *Daring* led the squadron to sea for exercises with *Birmingham* in local waters, which also included a Regatta Day at Augusta. *Daring*'s next visit was to the picturesque harbour of Monaco, where the Alpes-Maritime

form an impressive background and luxury yachts an impressive foreground. On board one of the latter was the former Prime Minister Sir Winston Churchill who, according to the signals, was most impressed with *Daring*'s smart appearance.

After returning to Malta and undergoing a short self-maintenance period, *Daring* and other units of the fleet took part in further training exercises and manoeuvres, which were followed by visits to Venice and the ancient walled town of Dubrovnik, the latter at that time being part of Yugoslavia. In mid-October, in company with *Birmingham*, *Comet* and her sister *Dainty*, *Daring* steamed west to Palma and to Port Mahon, Minorca, the latter visit being marred by two days of torrential rain. This was followed by the most unusual visit of the deployment, to Tunis, which was the venue for a large international trade fair. The return to Malta at the end of the month meant a great deal of hard work for the ship's company as they prepared the ship for Flag Officer, Flotillas' (FOF) harbour and sea inspections. The successful completion of the inspections did not, however, mean a respite for her and in mid-November she and the Second Destroyer Squadron, together with the frigates *Eastbourne*, *Whitby* and *Zest*, and later in the month the aircraft carrier *Victorious*, operated from the Italian naval base at Taranto, when the Italian Navy led the exercises in the Ionian Sea. The highlight of this period of operations came during the first week of December with a six-day visit to Civitaveccia, the port which serves Rome. Christmas was spent at Sliema Creek, Malta, but no sooner were the festivities over than *Daring* was at sea again for training exercises with other units of the squadron, and the destroyers *Battleaxe* and *Crossbow*. During the afternoon of 31 December the exercises were brought to an end when one of *Crossbow*'s boiler tubes burst, severely scalding one of the boiler room crew. As she was left without power, tugs towed her back to Grand Harbour, and the injured man was transferred to *Daring* for a high-speed return to Malta where he was rushed to hospital.

The new year of 1960 saw *Daring*, together with *Crossbow*, *Delight*, *Zest*, and the submarine *Otter*, carrying out exercises off Malta and, for *Daring* and *Crossbow*, this included a visit to the Algerian port of Bone (Annaba). It was the first visit by Royal Navy warships since the late 1940s, and there was a civic reception at the Town Hall for the ships' officers. It was also an opportunity for Captain Mills to lay a wreath at the memorial to British servicemen in the English cemetery. *Daring* left Bone on 11 January and arrived in Grand Harbour the next day, and soon afterwards began a six-week dockyard assisted maintenance period, which included two weeks in dry dock.

*Daring*'s last days of the commission in the Mediterranean were spent in Maltese waters, taking part in 'Exercise Marjex', with the cruiser *Tiger* and other units of the fleet. On 14 March 1960 she left Sliema Creek to steam east for Gibraltar, calling on the way at the Algerian port of Djefwa. At Gibraltar she rendezvoused with units of both the Home and Mediterranean Fleets, and was visited by the C-in-C Home Fleet and the First Sea Lord. During the morning of 25 March FOFH (Home) hoisted his flag in *Daring* before she slipped her moorings to rendezvous with *Tiger*, *Dainty*, *Battleaxe*, *Solebay*, *Teazer* and *Llandaff* to take part in 'Exercise Dawn Breeze V', during the course of which she would make her passage home. Six days later, during the forenoon of Friday 1 April, having completed the busy foreign service leg of the commission, *Daring* secured alongside Devonport Dockyard's No 7 wharf.

Having undergone her routine maintenance in Malta, *Daring* remained alongside at Devonport just long enough for the ship's company to take leave which was due, and on 2 May 1960 she made the passage to Portland for anti-submarine exercises with *Crossbow*, *Chichester*, *Dundas*, *Ulster* and the submarines *Sentinel* and *Talent*. A weekend visit to Portsmouth was followed on 11 May by a six-day visit to the Hanseatic City of Bremen where, with *Crossbow*, *Talent* and *Thermopylae*, she was welcomed alongside the Europehaven by a German military band and a large number of towns-

people. The friendliness and open hospitality of the German people was much appreciated, with visits being organised to the local motor works and brewery, and when the ships were opened to the public over 4,000 visitors passed over *Daring*'s gangway in the course of one afternoon. After leaving Bremen the group made its way into the Baltic Sea, via the Kiel Canal, to Helsinki where *Daring* secured alongside the Lansisatama Quay in the city's main dock area. Once again the hospitality of the local people was almost overwhelming, with invitations flooding in - ranging from a dance for 500 sailors to a tennis party for four. Once again there were organised visits to local tourist attractions, including the fortress of Suomenlinna, built by the Swedes in 1784 on one of the five interconnected islands at the harbour mouth, to protect the city from seaborne attack. Another notable trip for some was to the local brewery which included generous 'free samples'. A number of *Daring*'s ship's company sampled the hot steam and icy cold water Sauna bath, an unusual experience for Britons in those days.

On 26 May, however, the foreign visits ended and *Daring* left Helsinki for Scottish waters off Campbeltown where, with the submarine *Amphion*, she carried out three weeks of sonar trials. During this period she spent Whitsun weekend alongside in Greenock, and a weekend at Scapa Flow, but most evenings were spent secured to a buoy at Campbeltown, leaving the following morning for more trials. During the third week of June, in company with *Centaur*, *Delight* and *Battleaxe*, she took part in anti-submarine exercises off Scotland's north coast, and spent most of the time stalking the submarine *Talent*. The exercises ended in Rosyth on 24 June and after a weekend break *Daring*, *Centaur*, *Dainty*, *Blackpool* and *Defender* took part in a storm-tossed 'Exercise Fairwind V' north of the Shetland Islands which, for *Daring*, ended on 2 July with a two-day visit to Bergen and a five-day visit to Horten in Oslofjord, before she returned to Devonport for summer leave and to take part in Navy Days.

On Monday 8 August 1960, *Daring* left Devonport to steam north to Icelandic waters for fishery protection duties. With Britain and Iceland in dispute over the quantities of cod which were being caught in the rich waters of the Arctic Ocean, the Royal Navy had been called upon to protect British trawlers and *Daring*'s first patrol, which was largely uneventful, lasted for three weeks. On 26 August *Daring* was relieved by *Crossbow*, but before returning to Rosyth she was diverted to the North Cape to provide medical assistance to the trawler *Northern Gem* before returning to Rosyth. After a break of four days *Daring* left the Firth of Forth to rendezvous with *Gambia*, *Defender* and *Apollo*, to carry out anti-submarine exercises with *Truncheon* and *Undine*. In mid-September the group was joined by *Hermes* for 'Exercise Fallex 60' which took place in Arctic waters. *Daring*'s involvement ended on 2 October, when she returned to Devonport for a two-week maintenance period. On 18 October she sailed for Arctic waters once again, to begin a second Fishery Protection Patrol in stormy northern waters. Once again the patrol was largely uneventful, and on 7 November the destroyer paid a 12-day visit to Chatham, which concluded with a Sea-Day for 70 Reservists and WRNS. This was followed by a five-day visit to Rotterdam, and an exercise off the Scilly Isles with *Gambia*, *Defender*, *Zest* and *Blackpool* which, appropriately for *Daring*, was code-named 'Lastex'. It was to be the last time for more than six years that the destroyer would operate at sea with other units of the fleet, for she was to be plaed in Reserve at Devonport. The exercises off the Scilly Isles were followed by a visit to the French naval base at Brest and, on 9 December, a visit to the South Wales town of Newport. The commission was drawing to a close and during the forenoon of Thursday 15 December, with her paying-off pennant flying, she returned to Devonport Dockyard. No sooner were all the berthing wires in place than the first long leave parties were leaving the ship and at the end of December, with de-ammunitioning and de-storing complete, *Daring* was moved into

No 5 basin. At 0930 on 19 January 1961 a short paying-off service was held on board and next day the remaining members of the ship's company moved to shore accommodation at HMS *Drake*, and *Daring* herself passed into dockyard hands. During the commission she had steamed 64,000 miles.

For six years, under the supervision of a small care and maintenance party, HMS *Daring* lay alongside the non-tidal basins at Devonport Dockyard. Indeed, as many will remember, during the early 1960s she had become a 'fixture' in the dockyard. In January 1963 her small complement was increased to a long refit party, for in June 1959 it had been announced that the *Daring*-class destroyers would be modernised. Originally the proposals included arrangements for the extension of the forecastle to increase the length of the ship in order to incorporate a machinery control room, a helicopter landing platform and hangar, two Seacat (GWS 21) guided missile launchers, an air-conditioned Operations Rooms, air-conditioned and all-bunk messdecks and up-to-date radar systems. However, as is often the case where defence spending is concerned, these ambitious plans were subsequently cut back severely and in the event the only real modernisation carried out was to the living accommodation, with Junior Rates getting Centralised Messing with a dining hall which operated on a self-service cafeteria system. Although about half the ship's company had bunks for sleeping, the remainder continued to use hammocks, and generally the standard of habitability was below that of more modern ships.

On 1 August 1966 *Daring*'s last commanding officer, Commander J. de Beaufort Suchlick RN, was appointed to the ship and gradually, as the refit progressed, the ship's company numbers were increased. In the bitterly cold December of 1966 *Daring*'s ship's company moved back on board from shore accommodation in HMS *Drake*, and on 16 December, for the first time in six years, the ship was towed from No 4 basin and secured alongside the sea wall at No 7 wharf. Three days later, at 1045 on Monday 19 December, the ship's company

mustered on the forecastle for the Commissioning Ceremony. Finally, at 0845 on Wednesday 4 January 1967, *Daring* slipped her moorings and put to sea to carry out the first of many post-refit trials. For two months the ship continued her trials, but on 14 March, with all her machinery and armament functioning correctly, she was able to steam east to Portland to begin the first phase of her work-up, which included a weekend break at Portsmouth. No sooner was the work-up under way, however, than it was rudely interrupted.

On Monday 27 March, whilst *Daring* was lying alongside at Portland beginning a week of harbour drills and at 24 hours' notice for steam, an urgent signal was received ordering the ship to prepare immediately for sea. *Daring* was to become involved in the highly publicised drama of the oil tanker MV *Torrey Canyon* which, during the early hours of Sunday 19 March, had gone aground on Seven Stones Reef, between Land's End and the Scilly Isles. The tanker, which was loaded with 120,000 tons of crude oil, had been on passage from Kuwait to Milford Haven, and for a few days after the grounding it was thought the vessel might be salvaged intact. It was not long, however, before large quantities of crude oil started leaking from the wreck and with the assistance of prevailing south-westerly winds started drifting towards the Cornish coast, threatening both the area's wildlife and the busy summer tourist season. The Government decided that in order to minimize the pollution the wreck of *Torrey Canyon* would have to be destroyed, and 'Operation Mop Up' was put into action, initially with Fleet Air Arm Buccaneer bombers using the stranded wreck as target practice and to hopefully set fire to the fuel.

On 27 March, as soon as *Daring* received the signal, the engineers began the job of raising steam, and the Regulating Office set about recalling liberty men which, as leave did not expire until 0730 the next morning, was not an easy task. In the event, despite the fact that she was at 24 hours' notice, at 0222 on 28 March, just over four hours after receiving the first signal, *Daring* slipped her moorings

and put to sea. By 1430 that afternoon she had reached her patrol area off Wolf Rock and had taken up her duties as safety ship, which involved keeping unauthorised shipping clear of the wreck area which was about to be bombed by the Buccaneers from Lossiemouth. Within 15 minutes of *Daring*'s arrival she had to divert a Polish cargo ship, MV *Wrozka*, from entering the 'sealed' area. Inevitably, when the Fleet Air Arm began their bombing runs the Soviet trawlers in the area, all bristling with radio and radar aerials, jostled for the best positions to witness the spectacle. During *Daring*'s 59-hour patrol of the area around Seven Stones Reef most watchkeepers on board had to stand longer watches than usual as it had not been possible to recall all liberty men, but by the afternoon of 30 March she was back alongside her berth at Portland.

During April and May 1967 *Daring* continued her work-up from Portland, and the gruelling round of exercises and manoeuvres was broken only by short visits to Portsmouth and Cherbourg, as well as a 48-hour enforced stay alongside at Portland when contaminated feed water was found in the ship's distilled water tanks. Despite all the emergencies and delays, however, on Thursday 8 June *Daring* successfully completed the final inspections of the work-up, and within 24 hours she had returned to Devonport to give foreign service leave and to prepare to sail for the Far East Station, which was to be the first foreign leg of her General Service Commission.

At 0900 on Monday 17 July 1967, *Daring* left Devonport to set course for Gibraltar on the first stage of her passage east, arriving alongside the south mole some three days later. Despite strained relations between the British and Spanish Governments over the status of Gibraltar, many members of the ship's company were able to enjoy the fiesta just over the frontier in La Linea, and one member of the ship's company actually got married during the 50-hour stay, but had to make do with an 18-hour honeymoon. In June 1967, following the Six Day Arab-Israeli War and the subsequent closure of the Suez Canal, ships sailing to and from the

Far East had to make the passage by way of Cape Town, and *Daring* was one of the first Royal Navy warships to be so affected. When she left Gibraltar during the forenoon of 22 July she was bound for Simonstown, and with RFA *Wave Chief* in company she was scheduled to make the passage without any refuelling stops. Five days later, however, a sick rating on board meant that the destroyer was forced to divert to Freetown in Sierra Leone where, on 28 July, she anchored for three hours so that the patient could be transferred to hospital ashore. Two days later, during the forenoon of 30 July, the equator was crossed and the event was duly marked with full ceremony. On Saturday 5 August *Daring* arrived at Simonstown naval base where, after the long, 19-day passage south, the break was made even more welcome by the warm hospitality of the local people. Most of the ship's company made the short, picturesque journey to Cape Town, and for a few there was the privilege of an invitation 'up country'. As had happened at Gibraltar, one of *Daring*'s complement was married, this time it was the navigating officer who married his South African fiancée whom he had met in the UK.

After leaving Simonstown *Daring* steamed into the Indian Ocean and set course for the Mozambique Channel where she would carry out her first Beira Patrol, the United Nations' oil blockade of Rhodesia after that country's illegal Unilateral Declaration of Independence. Two days after leaving South Africa *Daring* officially joined the Far East Station where she became the leader of the Fleet's First Destroyer Squadron, relieving the frigate *Llandaff* off Beira on 17 August. The Beira Patrol had been in existence since December 1965 and for the ships' companies deployed the main preoccupation was beating the monotony of long, hot days at sea under the searing Indian Ocean sun as their ships slowly steamed along the patrol lines, or sat at anchor. Often inter-departmental and inter-ship tournaments were organised, including pulling and sailing regattas, deck hockey, tug-of-war, and for some the more sedate uckers championships. As a reward there was the much-coveted 'Beira

Bucket' to be fought for - a highly painted but battered zinc dhobi bucket. During the clear, balmy evenings there was always a good supply of the latest films to be shown at the popular, but makeshift, quarterdeck or forecastle outdoor cinemas. For *Daring* the first patrol ended on 26 August when she was relieved by *Cavalier* and four days later she secured to buoys in Kilindini Harbour, Mombasa.

Anyone who has visited this East African port will have memories of an idyllic Indian Ocean holiday resort, with beautiful golden beaches which were protected from predatory sharks by a natural coral reef about a mile offshore, making it perfectly safe for sunbathing, swimming and snorkelling. Some preferred the bars and clubs of Kilindini Road, including the infamous Casablanca Bar, and for the more adventurous there were safari trips to nearby game reserves at Voi. For everyone on board the visit was all too brief, and on 9 September *Daring* sailed for her second Beira Patrol where she relieved the frigate *Gurkha*. During this period there were exercises and manoeuvres with *Troubridge*, and *Daring* was even able to lend some movie films to the Portuguese frigate *Alvares Cabral*. The monotony of the patrol was broken on 25 September when, having been relieved by the frigate *Phoebe*, *Daring* made an informal four-day visit to Diego Suarez in Madagascar. Sports matches between teams from *Daring* and the French Navy garrison ended in a diplomatic 'draw', with *Daring* winning the rugby match, and the French side the soccer. After the pleasant change of scenery *Daring* steamed south once again and having taken over from *Phoebe*, she continued her Beira Patrol.

On Sunday 15 October *Daring* was relieved by *Barrosa*, and after a three-day stopover in Kilindini Harbour she sailed, by way of Gan where she embarked essential stores and refuelled from the resident, but static, RFA *Wave Victor*, for Singapore. On 1 November she arrived in the Malacca Strait where she exercised with *Cavalier*, before finally arriving alongside Singapore Naval Base during the afternoon of 3 November. For the

ship's company there was an opportunity for rest and relaxation while the ship was taken in hand by the dockyard for a maintenance period. On 20 November they moved into shore accommodation at HMS *Terror*, whilst *Daring* moved into the large floating dry dock. The spacious, airy accommodation of *Terror* provided excellent recreational facilities, including a nine-hole golf course, a large swimming pool and the Armada Club which, it was said, served the iciest-cold 'Tiger Tops' (a pint of local Tiger beer topped with lime juice or lemonade), and the break was much appreciated by all on board. On Friday 15 December, with the refit almost completed and with the ship back alongside the sea wall, the ship's company moved back on board. Five days later *Daring* sailed to carry out her post-maintenance trials but returned to the naval base two days later, just in time to celebrate Christmas.

At 0800 on 27 December, with the Christmas festivities over, *Daring* left Singapore to set course for Hong Kong, where she arrived on New Year's Eve to take over duties as the colony's guardship. In 1967 Hong Kong had suffered some civil unrest which had spilled over from the political turmoil in China itself. Fortunately, during *Daring*'s 18-day stay Hong Kong was quiet, but on three separate days the destroyer carried out amphibious exercises in local waters. On 18 January 1968 she left Hong Kong for the US Navy's exercise areas at Subic Bay, which included a period of weapons training and a run ashore to the infamous town of Olongapo, close to the US Naval Base. By the end of January, however, she had returned to Hong Kong and resumed her duties as the colony's guardship. Once again *Daring*'s stay in the colony was quiet and on 5 February she carried out a 24-hour patrol with the colony's Police Force, which was designed to stop the flow of illegal immigrants from China.

At 0900 on Sunday 11 February *Daring* left Hong Kong to set course for the Subic Bay exercise areas, and to begin her passage to Australian ports which, for the ship's company, was to be the highlight of the commission. Steaming by way of the Sulu and

Daring *in the summer of 1968, in the final weeks of her operational career.*        *(Author's Collection)*

Celebes Seas, on the morning of 17 February she secured alongside Stoke Hill Jetty, Darwin, to embark fuel, fresh water and stores, but there was no time for shore leave and only five hours after her arrival she slipped her moorings and set course along Australia's northern coast, bound for Brisbane. Two days later *Daring* made her passage of the Torres Strait, passing close to Prince of Wales Island before setting course for the inner route of the Great Barrier Reef, a scenic part of the passage which will be long remembered by all those who served in the destroyer at the time. During the forenoon of 24 February *Daring* secured alongside Brisbane's Hamilton Wharf for a memorable five-day visit. In addition to the overwhelming hospitality from the people of the city, with Captain D's harbour and sea inspections looming, there was also a great deal of work to be done, but despite the intensive painting and polishing the destroyer's ship's company was able to host a party for children

from a local orphanage. At 0915 on 29 February, to a chorus of complaints that the visit had not been long enough, *Daring* steamed back down the Brisbane River to set course for Sydney, where she arrived the following day.

On her arrival at Sydney *Daring* joined other units of the Far East Fleet, including *Triumph*, *Devonshire*, *Dido*, *Euryalus* and *Zest*, which had been involved in a major exercise in Australian waters. Once again, however, the time alongside meant a great deal of hard work for *Daring*'s ship's company before the harbour inspection on 4 March. Next day the destroyer sailed in line ahead with the other units for her sea inspection, before taking part in joint manoeuvres and exercises in Jervis Bay, following which *Daring* was detached to Melbourne. Arriving alongside the North Pier of Williamstown Dockyard during the afternoon of 8 March, with the help of *Triumph*'s Fleet Maintenance Group, *Daring* began a 17-day assisted maintenance peri-

od. The visit coincided with 'Moomba' festivities in Melbourne which, roughly translated from the native aboriginal language, means 'let's get together and have fun'. Many members of the ship's company were able to take local leave, while on board no fewer than four Beauty Queens visited the ship, one of whom, Miss Philippine Islands, supervised the daily issue of rum.

Leaving Melbourne on Monday 25 March, *Daring* set course for the 3,000-mile passage to Mauritius, via King Island in the Bass Strait, whose inhabitants had requested that a Royal Navy unit pay them a visit. The destroyer anchored in Naracoopa Bay for two hours, but a heavy swell prevented all but one of the ship's motor boats making it to shore, where the First Lieutenant was able to exchange greetings with local dignitaries. After leaving the island *Daring* rendezvoused with *Cavalier* and *Troubridge*, before all three ships headed for Mauritius.

The long, 13-day, non-stop passage to Port Louis was spent carrying out exercises and manoeuvres in the Indian Ocean, refuelling from RFA *Plumleaf* which had sailed south from the Persian Gulf to meet them. Finally, during the afternoon of 7 April *Daring* secured to buoys in Port Louis Harbour. The island of Mauritius, which had seen both French and British colonial rule, had been granted independence just three months previously and at the time of *Daring*'s visit inter-communal strife had resulted in riots, but the dusk-to-dawn curfew which was in place did not mar the ship's company's enjoyment of the island's beautiful beaches. *Daring*'s stay in Port Louis lasted for just 48 hours,

after which the destroyer sailed for Mombasa, arriving in Kilindini Harbour on 13 April.

After carrying out a 14-day maintenance period, on 27 April *Daring* left Kilindini Harbour to start another series of Beira Patrols, where she relieved *Cavalier* and acted as consort to *Aurora*. Twelve days into the patrol *Daring*'s commanding officer was taken ill, and the First Lieutenant, Lt-Commander D. Penreath, assumed command. Two days later Commander Suchlick was transferred to *Aurora* for the journey home to RNH Haslar.

*Daring*'s deployment east of Suez came to an end in mid-July, following her passage home by way of South Africa. Her arrival in Devonport coincided with the Government's announcement of sweeping Defence cuts, included in which was the news that the Daring-class destroyers were to be phased out earlier than had originally been planned, and that *Daring* was to be withdrawn from operational service in the last weeks of 1968. This gave the destroyer just three more months of active service, and having given leave she sailed for Gibraltar where she spent a month as the guardship. Her final operational duty was to accompany *Cleopatra* and the submarines *Ambush* and *Narwhal* to the Swedish capital Stockholm for British Week. By mid-October, however, she was back at Devonport where she was decommissioned and laid up at a buoy in the Hamoaze, where she remained for two years during which time she provided a supply of spares for her sister ships which remained in service. In May 1971 she was sold to shipbreakers, and on 15 June that year she arrived at Blyth where she was broken up.

### HMS *Daring*
### Commanding Officers

| Name: | Date Appointed: |
|---|---|
| Captain E. Hale RN | 17 May 1951 |
| Commander V. J. St Clair Ford MBE RN | 29 July 1952 |
| Commander J. L. Rathbone DSC RN | 20 August 1952 |
| Captain P. D. Gick OBE DSC RN | 22 September 1952 |
| Captain E. A. Blundell OBE RN | 5 February 1954 |
| Captain D. H. R. Bromley DSC RN | 3 August 1955 |
| Captain G. I. M. Balfour DSC RN | 19 November 1956 |
| Captain C. P. Mills CBE DSC RN | 12 January 1959 |
| Commander J. de Beaufort Suchlick RN | 1 August 1966 |

# Part Two

# HMS DIAMOND

## February 1952 - November 1981

The order for the second of the Daring-class destroyers, like the first, went out on 24 January 1945 from the Director of Navy Contracts, this time to the Clydebank shipbuilding firm of John Brown & Company Ltd. The first keel plates were laid on 15 March 1949 and initially building work proceeded quickly, with the launching ceremony taking place on 14 June 1950. From this point, however, work slowed down and it would be another 20 months before HMS *Diamond* was completed. On 12 October 1951, her first commanding officer, Captain C. B. Alers-Hankey DSC RN, was appointed to the ship.

By the end of January 1952 *Diamond* was nearing completion and on 29 January the officers and men who had been standing by the ship began the task of embarking and stowing naval stores and equipment. Five days later one of their number, Petty Officer Roy Emmington, left Glasgow by train armed with over 100 cap tallies bound for the Royal Naval Barracks, Chatham, from where he would escort to the ship the first draft of 120 ratings. During the afternoon of 5 February the Superintendent Contract Built Ships made his final inspection of *Diamond*, after which the officers and men who had been standing by moved on board. That same afternoon Roy Emmington and his draft left Chatham for the overnight train journey to Clydebank. They arrived on board at 0720 on Wednesday 6 February. One and a half hours later, at 0900, the ship was Commissioned for the first time, and later in the day a second draft of ratings joined from Chatham. Next day, at 0910, *Diamond* slipped her moorings and set course downriver for the Firth of Clyde and a day of machinery trials. After several hours of full-power trials off the Skelmorlie measured mile, at 1530 that day *Diamond* was accepted into service from John Brown and Co Ltd, and the White Ensign was hoisted. A short time later she secured along-

side Customs House Jetty, Greenock, where she spent the weekend. During the forenoon of Sunday 10 February, following Ceremonial Divisions, a Commissioning Ceremony was held.

*Diamond*'s trials began in earnest on Monday 11 February, and for seven days she carried out day running exercises from Greenock, but on 22 February, sailing by way of the Irish Sea, she set course for Chatham. Two days later she arrived off Sheerness and on 25 February entered Chatham Dockyard where the final draft of ratings joined the ship, bringing her complement up to full strength.

Diamond *alongside her fitting-out berth at John Brown's shipyard, Clydebank.* (via Dave Scoble)

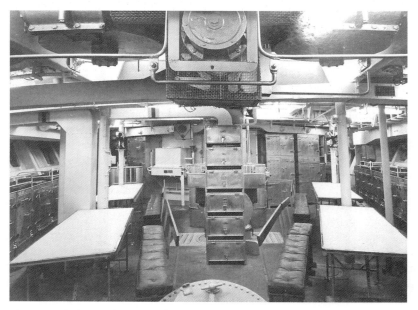

*A seaman's forward messdeck on board Diamond, which would have been identical in all eight ships of the class.* (via Dave Scoble)

*The small, but well-equipped sickbay.* (via Dave Scoble)

*The wardroom. Some 40 years later the only thing which will still be recognisable in today's warships is the flower-patterned upholstery.*
*(via Dave Scoble)*

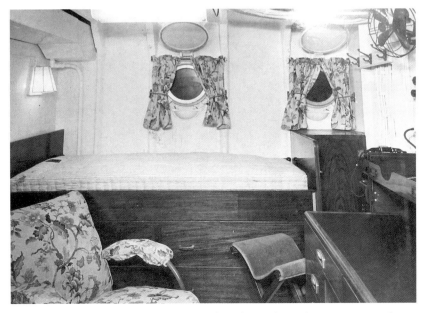

*An officer's cabin on board Diamond. Judging from the size it was almost certainly for one of the Heads of Department.* *(via Dave Scoble)*

*An excelllent view of* Diamond*'s forward superstructure and funnel, with the forward torpedo tubes to the right of the photograph.* *(via Dave Scoble)*

*A starboard view of* Diamond *in the firth of Clyde during her builder's trials.* (Syd Goodman Collection)

Like her sister *Daring* at Devonport, during her time alongside, *Diamond* attracted a lot of VIP visitors and in mid-April she was the star attraction at the port's Navy Days, with some 17,000 people visiting the ship. On 23 April, however, work began in earnest and *Diamond* sailed to begin a work-up period at Portland, operating with the aircraft carrier *Indefatigable*, the minelayer *Apollo* and the destroyer *Agincourt*. In June *Diamond* steamed north to the Clyde area, and for two months she took part in torpedo-firing trials in Loch Long and Loch Goil, with various types of new torpedo propellers being tested. In addition she undertook tests on a new propeller for the Daring-class ships, this being fitted in the dry dock at Alexander Stephens & Sons, Govan.

On 26 June she anchored off Douglas, Isle of Man, for a five-day visit and that Saturday she was opened to the public. By mid-afternoon, however, with strong winds blowing, the 391 members of the public who had braved the extremely choppy boat

ride out to the ship were hastily taken ashore again, but that night, with the ship at anchor and the ship-to-shore boat service suspended, seven officers and 152 ratings were stranded ashore in Douglas. Fortunately they were able to rejoin the ship the following morning and *Diamond* returned to Loch Long to continue her trials. During the last week of July *Diamond* returned to Chatham to give seasonal leave, and during this period her trial propellers were replaced.

On 5 September 1952 *Diamond* left Chatham bound once again for the waters of the Firth of Clyde where, with the submarine *Tireless*, further noise trials were carried out on different propeller designs. On 25 September, in Glasgow's No 2 dry dock, yet another set of propellers was fitted and the tests continued into October. On 17 October *Diamond* arrived at Portsmouth Dockyard where, in B lock, her original propellers were replaced and for the ship's company there was a welcome ten-day break alongside South Slip Jetty. At the end of

*A fine aerial view of* Diamond *at sea in the Mediterranean during the early years of her career.*

*(Author's Collection)*

October, however, it was back to work and after three days of radar trials in the Solent area, *Diamond* steamed north to Invergordon to join other units of the Home Fleet for major exercises. Other vessels taking part included *Eagle*, *Vanguard*, *Swiftsure*, *Barrosa*, *Corunna*, *Agincourt* and *Venus*, together with units of the Sixth Frigate Squadron and the submarine *Tireless*. The exercises began on 17 November, and *Diamond* operated in close co-operation with the cruiser *Swiftsure*, acting as her lee lookout, steaming some five cables ahead of her. It was a role she would frequently perform during the subsequent months. On this occasion *Diamond* and *Swiftsure* were detached on 27 November, and three days later they arrived off Sheerness, to steam up harbour on 1 December.

It was during this period of *Diamond*'s career that a light-hearted incident occurred, which is remem-bered by Roy Emmington: 'Captain Alers-Hankey almost always carried out daily rounds of one department, and on one Saturday the galley flat was chosen. To back up the galley staff extra sweepers were sent in and the galley was cleaned from top to bottom, including the rather dusty electrical cable trays overhead. As they were being conscientious-ly cleaned the fine layer of dust which covered them fell onto the trays of egg custard tart which had been laid out prior to serving. The Chief Cook on being informed of the "disaster" calmly pro-duced a large tin of multi-coloured desiccated coconut which he sprinkled on top of the dust layer. The whole ship's company enjoyed the sweet which accompanied lunch that day.'

On 20 January 1953 *Diamond* left Chatham to rendezvous with *Swiftsure* and to steam round to Portland to join other units of the Home Fleet

before setting course for Gibraltar. This time, as well as *Diamond* and *Swiftsure*, the exercises included *Manxman*, *Broadsword*, *Crossbow*, *Venus*, *Virago*, *Ursa*, *Agincourt* and *St James*, together with *Vanguard*, *Indomitable*, *Cadiz* and *Daring*. Following the exercises *Diamond* operated from Gibraltar with *Swiftsure* and *Crossbow* until mid-March, when she sailed for Lisbon where, after joint exercises, she was escorted up the River Tagus by the Portuguese frigates *Diego Gomez* and *Nino Triesto*. By 26 March, however, she was back at Chatham and in No 5 dry dock where she underwent a five-week maintenance period.

On 4 May 1952, with seasonal leave having been taken and maintenance work finished, *Diamond* left the dockyard to secure at a buoy off Sheerness. Three days later, having embarked the First Sea Lord, Admiral of the Fleet Sir Rhoderick McGrigor, she sailed for a weekend visit to Rotterdam where

the First Sea Lord visited NATO Chiefs of Staff. For *Diamond* the visit lasted just 52 hours before she moved down the coast to visit Ostend where she re-embarked the First Sea Lord and Lady McGrigor for manoeuvres with *Vanguard* and *Aisne*, before disembarking the guests at Dover and steaming on to Portland to join other Home Fleet units for exercises, before *Diamond*, *Duchess* and *Swiftsure* left for the Thames Estuary and Gravesend as part of the ceremonies and festivities for the Queen's Coronation. On 4 June the three units steamed round to Spithead where, with *Daring*, *Defender*, *Decoy* and *Duchess*, she took part in the Coronation Fleet Review. With the Queen's Review of the Fleet taking place on Monday 15 June, next day in company with *Swiftsure*, *Apollo*, *Duchess*, *Defender* and *Decoy*, *Diamond* left Spithead to begin a tour of home ports. *Diamond*'s first call was Aberystwyth, followed on 21 June by Glasgow, which was a fleet-

*An excellent working shot of* Diamond's *bridge whilst at sea. The cramped and exposed conditions are well illustrated in this photograph.*                                        *(Jeremy Setford)*

Diamond *at anchor for the Spithead Coronation Review of June 1953.*
*(Maritime Photo Library)*

ing 24-hour stay, before steaming for Belfast and finally, on Tuesday 7 July, Cardiff, where she spent four days alongside the Alexandra Dock. Leaving South Wales on 11 July *Diamond* rendezvoused with *Battleaxe* and *Crossbow* for manoeuvres which took them via Loch Ewe and Sullom Voe back to their base ports, and on 21 July *Diamond* returned to Chatham. Seven days later there was a change of command when Captain R. I. A. Sarrell DSO RN took over from Captain Alers-Hankey.

During August 1953 *Diamond* remained alongside at Chatham undergoing maintenance, while her ship's company took their seasonal leave. Navy Days that year took place during the first weekend of August, and during the three days she was opened to the public *Diamond* received some 20,000 visitors. By Wednesday 2 September, however, she was once again ready for sea, and she sailed to join her sister *Decoy* and to set course north for anti-submarine exercises and manoeuvres off Invergordon with *Eagle*, *Vanguard*, *Crossbow*,

*Duchess* and the submarine *Trespasser*. While she was on her way up the North Sea one of her young boy seamen was taken ill with suspected poliomyelitis and *Diamond* made an emergency call at Rosyth where the patient was quickly transferred to hospital. Sadly, as was common in those days, the boy died from the disease and on 6 September a memorial service was held on board. *Diamond* was to spend the whole of September in northern waters, and for most of that time she took part in the major fleet exercise, code-named 'Mariner', which also included *Eagle*, *Vanguard*, *Sheffield*, *Battleaxe*, *Swiftsure*, *Decoy*, *Duchess*, *Crossbow*, *Scorpion* and *Trespasser*, in the waters off Iceland.

During the evening of Tuesday 29 September, with the ships some 80 miles south of Iceland and having been at sea for six days, *Diamond* was one of six ships providing an anti-submarine screen for *Vanguard* and *Swiftsure*. The eight vessels formed 'Task Group 219.9', they were west of Iceland and

had 'darkened ship'. The weather was fine, but it was a very dark and cloudy night with a north-easterly wind and a moderate swell. The force was under the command of FOF (H), Rear-Admiral J. W. Cuthbert in *Swiftsure*, and at 19.55 the Task Group altered course and, with *Swiftsure* as guide of the fleet, *Vanguard* was steaming some 1,000 yards astern of the cruiser. *Diamond* was in screening station No 2, which was one of the ahead stations in a position 20° on *Swiftsure*'s port bow at a distance of 3,800 yards. At the time the Task Group was steaming at ten knots and was not zigzagging. At 2152 the group was ordered to reverse course, which in *Diamond*'s case involved a turn of 180° to port, so that she would once again be on station 20° and 3,800 yards from *Swiftsure*'s port quarter. However, shortly after the order was given those on *Swiftsure*'s bridge saw that *Diamond* was, in fact,

about a mile ahead and crossing the cruiser's bow to starboard, and at the same time she appeared to be altering course to starboard. On board *Swiftsure* Captain Bratt ordered navigation lights to be switched on, the wheel to be put over to 'Port 20' and two short blasts to be sounded on the siren. As the wheel order had no appreciable effect, Captain Bratt ordered 'Midships - Starboard 30', followed by 'Stop both engines'. However, within 30 seconds of the first order of 'Port 20' *Diamond* slammed into the cruiser's starboard side, just abaft the bridge.

Although the destroyer's bow did not penetrate far into the cruiser's side, being arrested by the lower part of *Swiftsure*'s armoured belt, the force of the collision dislodged a number of five-gallon drums of paint and white spirit, of which 98 were stored in the destroyer's forepeak, and threw them

*The triangular-shaped hole in* Swiftsure's *starboard side shows the extent of the damage caused by* Diamond's *stem.* (Ken Kelly)

into *Swiftsure*'s dental surgery. Within seconds of the impact there was a violent flash and a fire of intense heat, fuelled by the white spirit and paint, broke out in both the surgery and in what remained of *Diamond*'s forepeak. Although the collision caused no casualties, in *Swiftsure* the fire spread rapidly to the adjacent Master-at-Arms office, the sickbay and the Leading Stokers' messdeck, giving off thick black smoke and causing 40 casualties, most of whom suffered superficial burns. In the event the fire spread to *Swiftsure*'s bridge super-structure and to the officers' cabins and took some four and a half hours to extinguish. As to the visi-ble damage, a large V-shaped hole could be seen, extending from upper deck level to the top of her armoured belt.

As most of the paint and white spirit from *Diamond*'s forepeak was deposited in *Swiftsure*'s dental surgery, the flames from the fire which broke out in *Diamond*'s damaged forepeak licked around the forward end of the destroyer's bows, which was crumpled back to No.4 bulkhead. Fire parties were soon on the scene and the blaze was extinguished in about eight minutes, and there were no casualties on board the destroyer.

Although both ships were able to steam at reduced speed, it was 2155 before *Diamond* got under way again, and escorted by *Battleaxe* she set course for the old wartime anchorage of Hvalfjord, close to Iceland's capital of Reykjavik. *Diamond* anchored at 1830 on 30 September and was secured alongside *Swiftsure*'s undamaged port side, after which repair parties immediately got to work on the wrecked forepeak. Next day both *Diamond* and *Swiftsure* refuelled from RFA *Wave Master*, and at 1600 on Friday 2 October the two damaged ships, escorted by *Decoy*, left Hvalfjord to make a slow, four-day passage to Chatham. Finally, at 1145 on 6 October *Swiftsure* led *Diamond* into the anchorage at Sheerness, and on the following day they steamed upriver to Chatham Dockyard. For *Diamond* it meant two months laid up in dry dock whilst a new bow section was fitted, but for *Swiftsure*, although a modernisation refit was start-ed it was never completed and the collision effec-tively ended her operational career.

After spending almost three months in Chatham Dockyard's No.8 dry dock, it was Thursday 21 January 1954 before *Diamond* put to sea again to carry out post-refit trials off Portland. For much of the time the trials were carried out in severe weath-er conditions, and on occasions in thick snow bliz-zards which swept down Channel. On 5 February, in company with her sister *Duchess*, she set course for Gibraltar where, for the rest of the winter, she operated in warmer waters and milder weather con-ditions. In late February, with *Decoy* and *Duchess*, she accompanied the fleet aircraft carrier *Eagle* to Oran, and in mid-March she took part in combined Home and Mediterranean Fleet exercises, which also included the battleship *Vanguard*, the aircraft carriers *Eagle* and *Indefatigable*, the cruiser *Superb* and the depot ship *Maidstone*, which also doubled up as a merchantman for convoy escort exercises. On 1 April *Diamond* returned to Chatham to under-go maintenance and to give seasonal leave.

It was mid-June before *Diamond* put to sea again, and she set course for northern waters where she joined the battleship *Vanguard* and other units for Home Fleet exercises. She also made visits to the Scandinavian ports of Oslo, Stavanger, Copenhagen and Stockholm, and in mid-July she joined *Vanguard* for a convoy escort exercise which began at Harwich and ended in Lyness. On 30 July she returned to Sheerness and secured to No 3 buoy for 12 days, before steaming upriver to Chatham Dockyard where she was paid off. On Monday 30 August 1954 Captain T. L. Eddison DSC RN, took over command from Captain Sarrell and *Diamond* herself was prepared for her second commission. Next day the bulk of *Diamond*'s ship's company was drafted to the Royal Naval Barracks at Chatham, with some going on to the carrier *Glory* and others to the destroyer *Virago*. It would not be long before *Diamond* was operational once again.

At 1300 on Tuesday 31 August 1954, just over two hours after her old ship's company had left the ship, the main commissioning draft of men marched from the barracks to join *Diamond* in No.3 basin at Chatham Dockyard. Shortly afterwards the ship

Diamond *at sea off Portland, with an RFA in the background.* *(MoD/Crown Copyright)*

was recommissioned and nine days later she sailed for Gibraltar and Malta where, on 16 September, she joined the Mediterranean Fleet.

*Diamond*'s first two weeks on the Mediterranean Station were spent day running on shakedown exercises, and in October she took part in major fleet exercises, which also involved *Centaur*, *Glasgow*, *Bermuda*, *Duchess*, *Decoy*, *Chevron*, *Charity*, *Comet*, *Constance*, *Wakeful*, *Whirlwind* and *Roebuck*, as well as the Pakistani destroyers *Tippu Sultan* (ex-HMS *Onslaught*) and *Taimur* (ex-HMS *Chivalrous*), in the Malta exercise areas. On Friday 15 October the fleet carried out demonstrations for the Emperor of Ethiopia who was embarked in the cruiser *Gambia*. The manoeuvres ended with a high-speed steampast, after which the emperor continued to the UK in *Gambia*. On 9 November *Diamond* arrived at Port Said to take over duties as the Royal Navy's guardship for the Suez Canal Zone. It was an area where the British military presence was becoming increasingly resented by the Egyptian people, and events were moving slow-

ly towards the Suez Crisis of 1956. *Diamond*'s stint as guardship was broken by visits to the British base area at Fayid, where she anchored opposite Admiralty House in the Great Bitter Lake, and to the Jordanian port of Aqaba, where leave was granted and some members of the ship's company were able to visit the ancient ruins of Petra. *Diamond*'s duties at Port Said ended on 30 November when, at 1400, she steamed past de Lessep's statue at the end of the harbour breakwater and set course for Malta to begin a four-week self maintenance period, which included the Christmas and New Year holidays.

The start of 1955 saw *Diamond* leave Grand Harbour during the morning of 4 January to rendezvous with *Jamaica*, *Decoy* and *Duchess* for weapons training in the local exercise areas, followed by a passage to the French naval base at Algiers for a six-day visit, before returning to the Malta area for more fleet exercises. On 5 February she visited Palermo before taking part in a major combined Home and Mediterranean Fleet exercise

code-named 'Febex', which also included the two carriers *Albion* and *Centaur*, the cruisers *Glasgow* and *Jamaica*, as well as *Decoy* and *Duchess*. In addition to acting as planeguard for *Albion* during flying operations, and as a convoy escort, *Diamond* along with other units tested their procedures for passing through nuclear fallout, including pre-wetting. This was followed in March by 'Exercise Sea Lance', which ended with visits to Naples and Toulon, before *Diamond* returned to Malta on 6 April.

The destroyer's duties during April 1955 included amphibious landing exercises with a detachment of 30 Royal Marines who were landed on the beaches of North Africa close to Tripoli, then recovered the following day and returned to Malta. On 19 April the FO2 Mediterranean, Vice-Admiral J. P. L. Reid, carried out his harbour and sea inspections before, on 22 May, in company with *Sheffield* (flag C-in-C Mediterranean, Admiral Sir Guy Grantham), *Decoy*, *Diana* and *Duchess*, *Diamond* left Grand Harbour for training exercises and visits to ports in the Eastern Mediterranean. On 26 May the fleet visited Istanbul, and on re-entering the Mediterranean the force was joined by *Battleaxe* and *Scorpion* before the fleet dispersed to various ports. *Diamond* visited Alanya in Turkey, and Beirut before calling at Marmaris on 15 June where the whole fleet reassembled for three days, during which the Fleet Regatta was held. On 19 June, with the regatta and prize-giving over, the fleet put to sea to join an Indian Naval squadron, but *Diamond*'s foreign service was almost over, so she returned to Malta and on 24 June she began her six-day passage, via Gibraltar, to Chatham. On 1 July, after spending the night off Sheerness, she steamed up harbour and into Chatham's No .3 basin where she would undergo a three-month refit.

On 7 October 1955 *Diamond* put to sea again, and after a short work-up at Portland the destroyer steamed north to Scotland's east coast where, acting as planeguard to the aircraft carrier *Eagle*, she took part in a major fleet exercise code-named 'Phoenix 1'. The exercise kept *Diamond* in northern waters until the end of October, with a short break at Rosyth fol-

lowed by a visit to Wilhelmshaven. On 13 November the destroyer put into Devonport, where she secured alongside HMS *Vanguard* which was about to become part of the Reserve Fleet. *Diamond*'s visit to the West Country naval base was brief, and on 14 November she sailed for Portland and ten days of exercising with *Eagle*, for whom she again acted as planeguard. By 24 November she had returned to Chatham for maintenance and leave.

On Friday 13 January 1956, with seasonal leave and maintenance work completed, *Diamond* sailed from Chatham to rendezvous with *Duchess*, *Aisne* and the aircraft carrier *Ocean* to carry out a convoy escort exercise, with *Ocean* and RFA *Tidereach* taking the role of merchant ships. The exercise ended with a six-day visit to the picturesque Spanish port of Vigo, before *Diamond* returned to home waters where, on 2 February, she secured alongside the nineteenth-century battleship *Warrior* at Milford Haven, where the old warship was being used as a fuelling hulk. There then followed a week on the gunnery range at Aberporth in Cardigan Bay before she returned to Chatham to prepare for the end of the commission. During the afternoon of 10 February, as she was entering the South Lock at Chatham Dockyard, she collided with the sea wall, splitting one of the forward fuel tanks, which meant an unexpected three weeks in dry dock.

During the forenoon of Tuesday 21 February 1956, there was a change of command for *Diamond* when Captain M. G. Haworth DSC RN took over from Captain Eddison, and three and a half hours later, at 1240, the ship was recommissioned. It was a bitterly cold day and after the ceremony in the drill shed at Chatham Barracks the new ship's company, led by the Royal Marines Band, marched down to the ship which was undergoing her scheduled docking period. On 16 March, with the work completed, *Diamond* left Chatham to return to the Mediterranean where she would begin the foreign leg of her General Service Commission. Her arrival in Grand Harbour on 6 April coincided with the long build-up to the Suez crisis. In Egypt the implacable hostility of the local people to British

bases on the Suez Canal had led to an agreement to withdraw all British troops, and the evacuation of the bases was due for completion at the end of June that year. Initially, all that would be required of *Diamond* would be to 'show the flag' at Port Said. During her first weeks on station, however, she carried out work-up exercises with *Eagle*, *Birmingham*, *Decoy* and the submarine *Tally Ho*.

In addition to the withdrawal from Suez Britain had another colonial problem in the Mediterranean on the island of Cyprus. There, EOKA's bloody guerrilla war for Independence from Britain and union with Greece had been dragging on since 1954 and, with no end in sight, the Royal Navy had the thankless task of patrolling the island's coastline in order to prevent the smuggling of arms and ammunition. However, the unstoppable momentum of the insurgency in Cyprus bore witness to the difficulties involved. On 2 June *Diamond* left Malta to begin her first patrol of the commission, during which she stopped, boarded and searched a number of suspicious vessels. Landing parties assisted the Army as they carried out sweeps of the mountainous areas as they searched for insurgents. During this period recreation was confined to brief 'hands to bathe' periods most afternoons, and when the ship anchored off Paphos the Royal Marines of 40 Commando provided excellent hospitality. During the time spent at anchor tight security measures were enforced, with the ship's divers engaged on regular searches of the underwater hull. On 19 June the patrol was broken with a four-day break in the Lebanese port of Tripoli (now Trâblus), after which the ship returned to the coast of Cyprus. On 6 July, with the patrol completed, *Diamond* set course for Port Said, where she anchored in the harbour during the morning watch. At midday a make-and-mend was granted and soon afterwards the first liberty men were landed, with all leave expiring at 2359. However, now that the Egyptian authorities had seen the last British garrison withdrawn some three weeks earlier, they were flexing their muscles and at 1500 they curtailed shore leave for *Diamond*'s ship's company. Despite this setback the destroyer remained at Port Said for a further 24 hours, during

which time the 'gulley gulley' man performed on the forecastle and there was some lively, but good-natured haggling with the traders whose bumboats crowded round the ship. *Diamond* left Port Said on Sunday 8 July, returning briefly to Cyprus before reaching Grand Harbour on 13 July.

During the evening of Thursday 26 July, while *Diamond* lay moored to her buoys in Grand Harbour, momentous events were unfolding in Egypt. In Alexandria's Liberation Square, during the course of a speech to a vast and enthusiastic audience, President Nasser proclaimed his government's decision to nationalise the Suez Canal Company, and to place the joint British and French company under Egyptian control. The stage had been set for one of the watersheds in Britain's postwar colonial history.

Less than 24 hours after Nasser's announcement the Chiefs of Staff in London were ordered by the Prime Minister Anthony Eden to prepare plans for the military reoccupation of the former Suez Canal Zone bases, which meant the units of the Mediterranean Fleet would have to start intensive training exercises almost immediately. In early August *Diamond* began daily naval gunfire support training, and later in the month she acted as plane-guard for *Eagle* and *Bulwark* as the two carriers underwent intensive flying training. In early September *Diamond*'s main armament was in action once again as the destroyer bombarded the naval gunnery ranges at Filfa, off Malta. During the protracted three-month build-up to the Suez invasion there would be few opportunities for relaxation, but later in the month *Diamond* was granted a 48-hour break at Sicily's Porto Empedocle on the island's south coast and, on 28 September, at Toulon, which was followed by a joint Anglo-French amphibious training exercise.

*Diamond*'s period of intensive training at sea ended on 12 October when she returned to a very crowded Grand Harbour to carry out maintenance and to undergo her Admiral's Inspection. The inspection date had originally been set for 29 October, but as that was also the day most of the naval task force would sail for Suez the date was

brought forward and Admiral Holland-Martin was very favourably impressed with the ship. Finally, during the morning of 29 October, with the Israelis launching their pre-arranged attack on Egypt in the Sinai that same afternoon, the naval task force left Grand Harbour. *Diamond* sailed at 0735 to rendezvous with *Duchess*, *Barfleur*, *Jamaica* and *Eagle*, for whom she acted as planeguard during the long period at sea off Port Said.

During the passage east it quickly became apparent that helicopters were going to play a vital role in the Suez Campaign, and those from the three carriers regularly hovered over the destroyer's quarterdeck to make deliveries of fresh bread and mail. On 1 November, with *Eagle*, *Albion* and *Bulwark* in position some 50 miles off the Egyptian coast, aircraft from the three carriers began their attacks on Egyptian airfields. During this phase of the operation *Diamond* acted as escort and planeguard to all three carriers. Once the invasion itself got under way during the early hours of Tuesday 6 November, *Diamond* and *Duchess* joined the assault convoy and screened ahead as it approached the beaches of Port Said. During the latter stages of the approach *Diamond* led the landing craft, most of which were carrying the Royal Marines of 40 Commando. Finally, at 0400, when she was just a mile from shore and in very shallow water, *Diamond* stopped broadside on to the beach and, as the landing craft made their final approach, she carried out a beach bombardment. That afternoon she retired to an offshore anchorage, and the following day she investigated a number of unknown radar contacts. At 0810 on 8 November *Diamond* anchored just outside Port Said Harbour, and at 1130 the next day, with the ship at Action Stations, she weighed anchor to steam into harbour where she secured alongside the depot ship *Forth* 15 minutes later.

By this time strong American diplomatic pressure and hostile world opinion had brought the Suez Campaign to an abrupt end and the fighting had stopped pending the arrival of a United Nations force. However, Port Said was still a very dangerous place and *Diamond* was ordered to embark 25 foreign nationals, including six women and two children. Twelve were US citizens, six were Dutch and the remainder were Greek. At 1300, with her passengers safely aboard and accompanied by *Duchess*, *Diamond* sailed for Malta. It was said that during the two-day passage to Malta the destroyer's wardroom took on the appearance of a youth hostel, complete with camp beds. For *Diamond*'s ship's company, however, the arrival in Malta afforded a six-day break, and it was 17 November before she sailed for the return passage to Port Said. This time she remained in the devastated Egyptian port for only two days before putting to sea to act as planeguard for *Eagle* and *Bulwark*. On Tuesday 27 November, with the British and French troop withdrawal well under way, *Diamond* left the area to begin a second Cyprus patrol.

*Diamond*'s patrol of the Cypriot coast lasted for 19 days, during which there was some limited shore leave at the Army bases in Limassol and Dhekalia. On 17 December she returned to the waters off Port Said to oversee the final British troop withdrawals from Egyptian soil. At 1700 that day, with the last British and French troops having embarked in their transports, the ill-fated and ill-advised 'Operation Musketeer' was over, and at 2145 that evening *Diamond* took station astern of the troop convoy and escorted it to Grand Harbour, where it arrived four days later. With the harbour full to overflowing *Diamond* was accommodated in Sliema Creek, but on Tuesday 1 January 1957 she left Malta to rendezvous with *Decoy* and *Duchess* before setting course for home. Steaming by way of Gibraltar *Diamond* arrived off Sheerness during the late evening of 9 January and after spending the night at anchor she moved upriver into the Medway where it was said that de-ammunitioning was completed in record time. Finally, at 1100 on 11 January *Diamond* arrived in Chatham Dockyard where, as she secured alongside, families were waiting to greet the ship.

For ten weeks after her arrival home the workmen of Chatham Dockyard, in the words of one ship's company member, 'tore the ship apart', and it was to be the first week of April before conditions returned to normal; it was mid-April before the refit

Diamond *at anchor in May 1957.*                    *(Portsmouth Royal Naval Museum)*

was completed and *Diamond* was ready for sea again. On 16 April she left harbour to carry out two days of post-refit trials in the North Sea before returning to Chatham for a further ten days in dock-yard hands. By the end of the month, however, she had sailed for Portland to carry out her work-up period which took her through to mid-May. On Friday 17 May *Diamond* left Portland Harbour to rendezvous with *Duchess* and *Corunna*, and to set course for the North Sea where, off Spurn Head at 1930 next day, the three destroyers took over from the Trinity House vessel *Patricia* as escort to the royal yacht *Britannia*. The Queen and Duke of Edinburgh had set out earlier in the day for a State Visit to Denmark and the escort remained with *Britannia* until the forenoon of 21 May when they arrived alongside Langeline Quay, Copenhagen. There then followed a four-day stopover in the Danish capital, during which time the ship's company ensured a full attendance for trips to the Carlsberg and Tuborg Breweries. The royal visit to

Denmark ended during the early evening of 25 May when, with her three escorts, *Britannia* left Copenhagen and set course for Invergordon, where the Queen was to make her first visit to units of the Home Fleet. During the three-day event members of *Diamond*'s and *Duchess*' ships' companies combined to attend Ceremonial Divisions on board *Ark Royal*. The visit ended on Wednesday 29 May when the Home Fleet ships steamed past the royal yacht, after which, escorting *Ark Royal*, *Diamond* and *Duchess* set course for the United States.

The three ships had been chosen to represent the Royal Navy at the International Naval Review at Norfolk, Virginia, which was being held as part of the Jamestown Festival commemorating the first permanent settlement sent out from London by the Virginia Company, which landed on the continent of North America on 6 April 1607. The naval review was to be the highlight of the festival, but the outward bound crossing for *Diamond*, *Duchess* and *Ark Royal* was marked by severe Atlantic

weather, which curtailed the review rehearsals. When the three ships were some 150 miles north of Bermuda they sighted *Mayflower II*, the purpose-built replica of the original pilgrim ship which was also bound for the Jamestown Festival. Led by *Ark Royal* the three units steamed in close to give the tiny wooden sailing ship three cheers, and the following day the three ships arrived in Norfolk Navy Yard. Three days later they steamed out into Norfolk Roads to take up their review positions. The Review took place on 12 June when the US Secretary of Defence, Charles P. Wilson, embarked in the cruiser USS *Canberra* which, closely followed by her sister USS *Boston*, steamed between the lines of international warships to a simultaneous gun salute from all units present. Next day *Ark Royal*, *Diamond* and *Duchess* returned to their berths in the Navy Yard where they opened to the public for three days.

Leaving Norfolk during the morning of 17 June *Diamond* and *Duchess* detached from *Ark Royal*, which was bound for New York, and set course for Bermuda where, after embarking stores and fuel at Ireland Island naval base, they secured alongside at Hamilton. For the ships' companies of both ships the three-day stopover in Bermuda, with its beautiful beaches, was a pleasant break, but on 21 June the two ships set course for home waters. The transatlantic crossing was uneventful, and during the early evening of 28 June the two destroyers secured alongside Liverpool's Princes Pier. On Monday 1 July, with *Duchess* having left for her base port, *Diamond* was shifted to No 2 graving dock at Birkenhead to be fitted with trials propellers before, on 12 July, leaving for the Firth of Clyde where she would carry out seven days of noise tests, before leaving the area and steaming south to the Channel. Rounding Land's End during the early hours of 21 July, next forenoon *Diamond* secured to buoys in the Pool of London, off Tower Bridge Pier, for a three-day visit to the capital. The final passage of the commission came at 1000 on 25 July when, with families embarked, *Diamond* left the Pool of London to make the short passage down the River Thames to Chatham, where she arrived during the afternoon watch. Her arrival marked the end of the commission.

In the summer of 1957 Navy Days at Chatham was held during the first week of August. When *Diamond* opened to the public over 12,000 people took the opportunity to visit the ship which was lying in the dockyard at No 3 basin. Later in the month, on Tuesday 27 August, there was a change of command when Captain J. A. C. Henley DSC RN took over from Captain Haworth, and next day the ship recommissioned.

On 5 September *Diamond* left Chatham to join her sisters *Decoy*, *Diana* and *Duchess* off Portland, and two days later all four units set course for Gibraltar and Malta and service with the Mediterranean Fleet. Arriving in Sliema Creek on 16 September, *Diamond*'s first weeks on station were spent with her three sisters as well as *Birmingham*, *St Kitts* and the submarine *Sanguine*, carrying out work-up exercises. On 17 October Rear-Admiral Sir Charles Madden hoisted his flag in *Diamond* when he went to sea for the day to watch the destroyer, accompanied by her sister *Duchess*, being put through her paces. *Diamond*'s first 'foreign' visit of the commission came on 23 October when she put in to Tripoli for five days, followed by six days at Civitaveccia in Italy. After spending Christmas at Malta *Diamond* sailed for Cyprus (where the insurgency was in its third year) to carry out a long, eight-week patrol of the island's coast. These duties were interrupted by a brief stopover at Haifa before *Diamond* returned to Cyprus to continue her patrol which involved the stopping and searching of suspicious vessels. It finally ended on 18 February and two days later she arrived back in Sliema Creek.

On 3 March *Diamond* was back at sea and exercising with the aircraft carrier *Eagle*, to whom she once again acted as planeguard, and units of the US Sixth Fleet which included the carriers *Saratoga* and *Essex*. Local exercises culminated in the NATO exercise code-named 'Marjex', which for *Diamond* was followed by visits to Taranto, Ancono and Venice, then in the last week of March she returned to Grand Harbour to undergo a three-week mainte-

nance period. This gave the ship's company the first real prolonged relaxation period of the commission and it was 21 April before *Diamond* sailed again, this time to act as planeguard to *Ark Royal*. During the weeks that followed *Diamond* remained with the aircraft carrier and on 19 May, during 'Exercise Medflex Fort' in the eastern Mediterranean, a Sea Venom ditched into the sea soon after launching. *Diamond* was quickly on the scene and her seaboat rescued the pilot, but unfortunately the observer did not escape from the aircraft and was lost. Next day, with serious civil unrest in Lebanon, *Ark Royal* and *Diamond* stood by off the coast in case British nationals had to be evacuated from the country. Fortunately, no intervention was necessary and both ships remained in the vicinity of Cyprus where *Diamond*'s ship's company enjoyed some limited recreational leave. On 7 June she returned to Malta's Lazzaretto Creek where she secured alongside the depot ship *Ranpura*.

*Diamond*'s stopover in Malta was short and on 11 June she sailed for another patrol of the Cypriot coast, where the checking and searching of fishing boats and small merchantmen was interspersed with periods at anchor off Akoritiri, Limassol or Dhekalia. On Saturday 14 June, in company with *Diana*, she anchored in Dhekalia Bay where once again the ships' divers were kept busy making frequent searches of the underwater hulls. This was the situation during the forenoon of Tuesday 18 June when *Diamond*'s divers were searching *Diana*'s hull while the latter's divers searched beneath *Diamond*. At 1045 however, it was realised that one of *Diamond*'s divers, Able Seaman R. J. Warburton, was missing and a full-scale search was quickly organised. In the event it was 0500 the next morning before the missing man's body was found and taken to the British Military Hospital ashore. Next day both *Diamond* and *Diana* patrolled the coast and later that afternoon *Diamond* hove to off Limassol to embark the body of Able Seaman Warburton before getting under way again. An hour later, at 1915, with the ship some nine miles off Cape Gata Light, the funeral of AB Warburton took place and his body sadly committed to the deep. In the days that followed *Diamond* joined *Eagle* and *Sheffield* for joint exercises off Cyprus, before returning to Malta on 4 July.

*Diamond*'s foreign service was coming to an end, and at 0900 on 5 July 1958, together with her sisters *Decoy* and *Duchess*, she left Sliema Creek and Malta for the last time of the commission. It would be three years before she returned to the island. Once clear of the harbour they set course for Gibraltar and the passage home, arriving off Sheerness on 11 July. Three days later she steamed up harbour to Chatham Dockyard to undergo an eight-week maintenance period, during which seasonal leave was taken.

In the first week of August, at Chatham's Navy Days again, *Diamond* was a popular attraction, but as soon as the event was over she was shifted into No 5 dry dock for hull maintenance. The dockyard work was finally completed on Monday 8 September, and next day she left Chatham to serve the last four months of her commission as part of the Home Fleet. After rendezvousing with *Birmingham* and *Duchess* she sailed north to take part in 'Exercise Shipshape', a convoy escort exercise through the Pentland Firth and down the west coast of Ireland, before reaching Brest and finally Portsmouth on 26 September. During October she operated off the south coast, with visits to Newport in South Wales and Rotterdam. On 20 October, in company with *Birmingham*, *Decoy*, *Diana* and *Duchess*, *Diamond* sailed for Gibraltar and exercises in the Western Mediterranean which, on 3 November, included a four-day visit to the Spanish city of Seville, entailing a six-hour passage of the River Guadalquivir. As she left the Spanish port she grounded briefly, but, fortunately, no serious damage was sustained and she returned to Gibraltar.

On 25 November *Diamond* left Gibraltar to steam north for the bitterly cold and stormy waters off Iceland, where British fishing trawlers were defying a 12-mile territorial waters limit which Iceland had imposed round the island. This first 'Cod War' did not escalate into the more serious disputes of the early 1970s, and during *Diamond*'s two-week

patrol, carried out in company with *Llandaff*, there were no major incidents with the Icelandic gunboats. On 12 December *Diamond* went to the assistance of the Grimsby trawler *Northern Dawn*, one of whose crew members had died on board. With a very heavy sea running, launching the destroyer's seaboat was out of the question, and in the event the man's body had to be floated across to the destroyer on a liferaft, after which *Diamond* sailed south for Grimsby where, three days later, the body was landed. Next forenoon the destroyer arrived off Sheerness and later in the day she steamed up harbour to Chatham Dockyard. At noon the next day, Wednesday 17 December, *Diamond* paid off and was taken over by the dockyard for a 14-month refit.

During the long period when *Diamond* was laid up at Chatham a limited amount of modernisation work was carried out to her cramped accommodation, with her torpedo tubes being removed and replaced by additional deckhouses, which were given over to messdeck accommodation. However, despite this improvement *Diamond* and her sisters remained crowded and uncomfortable ships. On 21 November 1960, her new commanding officer, Captain H. H. Dannreuther RN, was appointed, and he was soon joined by key members of the ship's company. In mid-January 1961, *Diamond* ran a week of trials in the North Sea and just over two weeks later, on Tuesday 7 February, was recommissioned.

*Diamond*'s new commission began in earnest on Sunday 12 March 1961, when the C-in-C Nore inspected the ship's company at Ceremonial Divisions, and next day *Diamond* moved out of the dockyard to a buoy off Folly Point. During the rest of March and into April the ship ran trials and work-up exercises in the North Sea and Channel. These were concluded on 29 April when the ship was inspected by the Flag Officer, Sea Training. During May and June *Diamond* operated in home waters, from Portland and Rosyth, and on 18 June joined *Hermes*, *Bermuda*, *Battleaxe*, *Diana* and *Duchess* for 'Exercise Fairwind' off Scotland's east coast. This included a visit to Sundsvall in Norway and

ended with two days in Kiel before, on 5 July, she returned to Chatham.

*Diamond*'s stopover at her base port lasted just long enough for the ship's company to take seasonal leave before she sailed for the Mediterranean on 24 July, spending three weeks undergoing maintenance at Gibraltar en route and visiting Benidorm and Majorca, before arriving in Sliema Creek on 31 August 1961. The destroyer's arrival on the Mediterranean Station coincided with a much quieter period in that part of the world. Relations with Egypt had improved greatly and the Suez Canal, despite predictions to the contrary, was running as efficiently as ever. Cyprus, having gained its independence, was no longer in the grip of a vicious insurgency. During September *Diamond* exercised with *Lion*, *Battleaxe* and the depot ship *Ausonia*, which included a five-day visit to Limassol where shore leave was granted without security restrictions. During October there were visits to the Greek island of Thasos and exercises with the cruisers *Lion* and *Tiger*, and in November anti-submarine training with *Sea Devil*.

During the autumn months *Diamond* continued to operate in local waters off Malta, and in early September visited Naples before acting as plane-guard to *Ark Royal*. In mid-December, with other units of the fleet, *Diamond* took part in 'Exercise Spanex III', with the cruiser *Blake* and Spanish naval units, with Christmas being celebrated back in Sliema Creek. No sooner were the festivities over, however, than *Diamond* was back at sea undergoing weapon training with the frigates *Scarborough* and *Ursa*, with a visit to Genoa. This period of training set the pattern for the weeks which followed, with only a six-day visit to Piraeus in the second week of March to interrupt the training programme. On Monday 26 March 1962, however, with her sisters *Diana* and *Duchess*, *Diamond* left Malta to steam home by way of Gibraltar, arriving in Chatham Dockyard on 6 April.

Having undergone essential maintenance and with the ship's company having taken seasonal leave, on 3 May 1962 *Diamond* left Chatham to begin the final phase of the commission with the

Home Fleet. Training began off Portland in company with *Battleaxe* and *Duchess*, and moved round the coast to the Irish Sea before the ships returned to Portland. On 20 May, in company with *Bermuda* and *Duchess*, *Diamond* left Portland to steam north for the Baltic where official visits were made to Stockholm and Helsinki. These were followed on 7 June by a gathering of the Home Fleet at Rosyth, and a period of intensive training in the North Sea, involving *Centaur*, *Bermuda* and *Duchess*. This took them as far north as the Arctic Circle, culminating at the end of the month with a visit to Bergen. After leaving Norway *Diamond* steamed to Rosyth and, sailing from the Firth of Forth on 4 July, returned to Chatham where she secured alongside in the dockyard basin. It was the end of her fifth commission and ahead lay a four-month refit.

In the second week of November *Diamond* put to sea again to carry out machinery trials, but it was not long before plummer block trouble meant a return to Chatham. It was 1 December before she

sailed again to complete her trials. These continued through most of December, and included a pre-Christmas visit to Copenhagen. On Wednesday 2 January 1963, with the holiday period over, Captain J. D. Cartwright DSC RN relieved Captain Dannreuther, and at 0900 the next day *Diamond* was recommissioned.

After carrying out further trials and undergoing a work-up period at Portland, during March 1963 *Diamond* operated from Portsmouth, and returned to Chatham in early April for maintenance. Meanwhile, at the Admiralty, it had been announced that two additional escort squadrons were being formed, the first consisting of *Plymouth*, *Dido*, *Diana*, *Cambrian* and *Salisbury*, to serve on the Far East Station where Britain was embroiled in the 'Confrontation' with Indonesia; the second, consisting of *Rhyl*, *Lowestoft*, *Diamond*, *Caprice*, *Agincourt* and *Aisne*, was destined for the Mediterranean. However, at noon on Thursday 2 May, shortly before *Diamond* was due to leave

Diamond *leaving Portsmouth in March 1963.*                    *(Portsmouth Royal Naval Museum)*

Chatham, pieces of metal were found in the starboard main engine gearbox. It was immediately apparent that this was a deliberate act of sabotage and that repairs, as well as being costly, would take several weeks. During the whole of May and June the dockyard was employed on removing and repairing the damaged gears. It was not until Wednesday 10 July that *Diamond* was able to sail for two days of main engine trials before leaving for Malta. There was a further delay of five days at Gibraltar, where the destroyer was dry docked, but finally on Monday 22 July she arrived in Sliema Creek and officially became part of the Mediterranean Fleet.

One of *Diamond*'s first duties after arriving in Malta was to show the flag in far-off Aden, on whose borders with Yemen a civil war was raging. The involvement of Egyptian troops and sabre rattling by President Nasser had led to fears that Aden and the South Arabian Federation might be invaded. *Diamond* left Malta on 1 August and two days later she began her Suez Canal transit, arriving in Aden on 7 August. Throughout the years of colonial rule few British servicemen have ever enjoyed their time in the fetid heat and barren environment of Aden where, after only a few minutes ice-cold lager turned lukewarm, and where the only recreation to be found was in the bars and on the scorching beaches of the service clubs or in the duty-free shopping at Steamer Point. Fortunately for *Diamond*'s ship's company the visit was limited to three weeks and during the final weekend the destroyer steamed out to the island of Perim, the former coaling station situated in the Bab al Mandab, some 140 miles west of Steamer Point. During the 28-hour visit *Diamond* put on an open-air cinema show for the local people, before returning to Aden for a further four days.

*Diamond* left Aden on 28 August to return to Malta, transiting the Suez Canal on 2 September and arriving in Sliema Creek three days later. During the rest of the month she operated from Malta with *Hermes*, *Agincourt*, *Lowestoft* and *Rhyl*, and in the second week of October she began a

Diamond *alongside Portsmouth Dockyard in November 1967.* (T. Ferrers-Walker)

four-week self maintenance period, at the end of which she operated with *Lion* in the Eastern Mediterranean. She visited Beirut and Limassol, and at the end of November steamed west to Gibraltar for exercises and manoeuvres with units of the Home Fleet. During this period she ventured out into the Atlantic Ocean, paying a short visit to the Spanish naval base at Cadiz, before returning to Malta for Christmas and the New Year.

In the first week of January 1964 *Diamond* exercised in local waters, and in February she took part in a major multi-national NATO exercise, code-named 'Early Bird', which ended with a visit to the Italian naval base at Taranto where the C-in-C Mediterranean, Admiral Sir John G. Hamilton, hoisted his flag in the destroyer for the passage to Athens for the funeral of King Paul of the Hellenes. After leaving Taranto during the forenoon of 11 March *Diamond* made a transit of the Corinth Canal, before anchoring in Piraeus Bay the next day. Later that afternoon, with the Admiral ashore, *Diamond* returned to Malta to prepare for her sea inspection by FO2 Mediterranean. This took place later in March, and involved exercises with *Lowestoft* when they bombarded towed targets. It was followed by a little relaxation, with visits to Monte Carlo and Barcelona. *Diamond*'s overseas leg of her general service commission ended on 22 May at Chatham, when she returned for leave and for maintenance.

It was in late June 1964 when *Diamond* left her home base to begin the final operational months of the commission, and the first few weeks were spent day running from Portsmouth with other units of the 23rd Escort Squadron, including *Lowestoft* and *Salisbury*. During this period *Diamond* took part in a series of 'Sea Days' during which displays and weapon demonstrations were given to Members of Parliament, senior officers of all three services and students from the staff colleges. On Thursday 25 June, *Diamond* left harbour during the forenoon, and together with *Salisbury* and other units she carried out weapon and manoeuvring demonstrations until mid-afternoon. Whilst returning to harbour, however, and exchanging stations with *Salisbury*,

the two ships collided. Although damage to *Diamond* was minimal, the frigate suffered more serious damage, but fortunately there were no casualties and both vessels were able to secure safely alongside.

In the second week of July, in company with *Lowestoft* and *Rhyl*, *Diamond* steamed north to the Firth of Clyde to carry out anti-submarine exercises with the submarines *Cachalot* and *Porpoise*. During this period the destroyer was day running from Rothesay and Londonderry. In August, *Diamond* and other units of the Home Fleet, including *Lion*, *London*, *Carysfort*, *Agincourt*, *Corunna*, *Aurora*, *Dundas*, *Eskimo*, *Galatea*, *Leander*, *Londonderry*, *Lowestoft*, *Murray*, *Pellew*, *Puma*, *Relentless*, *Rhyl*, *Salisbury* and *Wakeful*, assembled at Portsmouth for ten days of conferences, social occasions and sporting events. At this time the C-in-C Home Fleet flew his flag in HMS *London*, and on 31 August the fleet made a ceremonial departure from Portsmouth. For *Diamond* this meant a return to northern waters with *Lion*, *Rhyl* and *Dundas*, for exercises off Scotland's east coast, which also included a visit to Stockholm, and a convoy escort exercise round Scotland's north coast.

By the autumn *Diamond*'s commission was drawing to a close, and in October she made her final foreign visits to Amsterdam and Bordeaux before returning to the Clyde in mid-November for anti-submarine exercises with *Finwhale* accompanied by *Salisbury*, *Rhyl* and *Chichester*. For *Diamond* the exercises ended at Portsmouth on 4 December when she secured alongside South Slip Jetty for de-ammunitioning. Three days later she sailed for Chatham where, during the afternoon of 8 December, she secured alongside No.3 basin. Five weeks after her arrival, as preparations were under way to take the ship in hand for a major refit, rumours began to spread that *Diamond* was to be scrapped. Her sister *Defender*, which had been laid up in Chatham Dockyard for over four months, was shifted alongside and two days later, at 1000 on Thursday 14 January 1965, *Diamond*'s ship's company marched to the naval barracks for the former's commissioning ceremony before marching back to

their new ship. At 1130 that day *Diamond* was paid off. At the same time that her White Ensign and Union Jack were lowered, in *Defender* they were hoisted. *Diamond*'s ship's company had transferred ships, and *Diamond* herself faced a period in reserve, followed by a modernisation refit which would keep her out of service for two years, not the scrapyard as had been rumoured.

During *Diamond*'s long lay-up at Chatham some modernisation work was carried out, but a plan to fit all the Darings with Seacat missiles was dropped. In the early summer of 1967 the destroyer was readied for sea, and on 31 July her new commanding officer, Commander M. F. Parry RN, was appointed. Just over two weeks later, at 1130 on Saturday 19 August, *Diamond* was recommissioned and ten days later she began a series of trials from Sheerness. These were followed by a further period in dockyard hands before, on Wednesday 22 November, she carried out her post-acceptance trials in the North Sea and Channel. Despite some machinery problems during the late evening of 24 November which left *Diamond* drifting without power for an hour and a half, the trials were concluded next day and the destroyer secured alongside Portsmouth Dockyard's North Corner Jetty. During the afternoon of 26 November there was a minor setback when fire broke out in B boiler room, but this did not prevent the ship from continuing her trials and after these ended on 14 December she made a visit to Amsterdam.

After spending Christmas and New Year at Chatham, on Monday 8 January 1968 *Diamond* began a busy three-month shake-down and work-up period at Portland. This finally ended on 9 April when the ship set course for visits to Esjberg, Stavanger and the German naval base at Friedrikshaven. It was 18 May before she returned to Chatham for docking and maintenance, prior to leaving for the Far East Station. On 9 July, having treated the families of the ship's company to an afternoon at sea, *Diamond* put into Portsmouth Dockyard where, that evening, a fire broke out in A boiler room and the City Fire Brigade was called. Again, the incident did not seriously disrupt

*Diamond*'s schedule and on 11 July she put into Devonport Dockyard, leaving three days later to join the aircraft carrier *Hermes* for the passage, via Simonstown, to the Far East. With Israel having invaded Egypt the previous year, all ships sailing between the UK and the Singapore naval base were routed round the Cape of Good Hope, which *Diamond* and *Hermes* reached on 31 July. It was *Diamond*'s first visit to the Cape, and as she had always maintained close links with De Beers Consolidated Mines, a party from the ship was invited to Kimberley as guests of Mr Harry Oppenheimer to watch diamond mining and recovery in operation.

The South African interlude ended on 12 August when *Diamond* sailed north into the Indian Ocean to carry out her first Beira Patrol, a duty which fell to all frigates and destroyers as they passed on their way to and from the naval base at Singapore. Four days after leaving Simonstown *Diamond* relieved the guided missile destroyer *Devonshire* to begin her first five-week patrol along the coast of the Mozambique Channel, off what was then the Portuguese colonial port of Beira. As all those who were involved with the Beira Patrol will remember, the effect of long days slowly steaming along the Mozambique coastline under the blazing sun and usually just out of sight of land could have a detrimental effect on the morale of a ship's company and various ways of dispelling the monotony had to be found. There were inter-ship sports contests, which in *Diamond*'s case were played against *Carysfort* and *Tartar*, the prize being the much-coveted 'Beira Bucket'. There were angling and uckers contests, upper deck film shows and ships' concerts. On one occasion *Diamond* enjoyed the added interest of a passing American yacht, the *Invictus*, with a crew of five young people, including three attractive bikini-clad girls, which broke down some 15 miles off Beira. Fortunately, *Diamond* was able to go to the yacht's assistance and get her under way again. The help was obviously much appreciated by the *Invictus*' crew who hoisted a bikini top at the yardarm - which brought *Diamond*'s ship's company rushing on deck in record time.

*Diamond*'s first patrol ended on 23 September when she arrived at Mombasa's Kilindini Harbour for a 12-day break, but by 8 October she was once again off Beira, having relieved her sister *Dainty*. This time the inter-ship competitions were with *Leander* and *Manxman*, and on 9 November a belated 'Crossing the Line' ceremony was held. *Diamond*'s second patrol ended at 0500 on 17 November, when she was relieved by *Defender* and was then able to set course for Singapore. During her two long Beira Patrols *Diamond* had stopped only one ship, which turned out not to be a 'blockade runner', and she had exchanged signals with over 160 merchant vessels. Her passage to Singapore was made by way of Coëtivy Island, just south of the Seychelles, before setting course for Gan Lagoon to refuel from the resident RFA *Wave Victor*. She arrived alongside Singapore Naval Base during the forenoon of 28 November, having spent 114 of the 138 days out from the UK at sea. On 6 December, eight days after her arrival at Singapore, there was a final change of command when Commander A. Mancais RN took over from Commander Parry.

After her long period at sea *Diamond* was overdue for maintenance and remained alongside at Singapore for four weeks. On 27 December, however, together with *Aurora* (Flag FO2, FES) and *Grenville*, *Diamond* put to sea and set course for an official visit to Bangkok. Three days later she arrived in the Bight of Bangkok and began her passage upriver to the city's new harbour where, despite the disruption caused by torrential monsoon thunderstorms, she secured alongside for a four-day visit. For the ships' companies of all three ships it was a very happy place to see in the New Year.

On Friday 3 January 1969 *Diamond* and her two consorts left Bangkok bound for Hong Kong where, four days later, she secured alongside her sister *Diana* which had arrived the previous day and was undergoing maintenance. *Diamond*'s visit lasted nine days before she returned to Singapore to prepare for the annual 'FOTEX' exercises which began on 21 January off the island of Penang. During the course of the two-week series of manoeuvres

*Diamond* acted as planeguard for *Hermes*. Among other units taking part were the assault ship *Intrepid*, *Decoy*, *Cleopatra*, *Grenville*, *Aurora*, HMAS *Derwent* and the submarine *Onslaught*. During the latter stages of the exercises *Diamond* developed problems with her starboard plummer block which was overheating, and on her return to Singapore on 3 February was taken into the dockyard's floating dry dock to begin a 14-day maintenance period.

When *Diamond* sailed from Singapore on 27 February she was bound for Australia and the highlight of the commission, a five-day visit to Fremantle. Steaming by way of the Selat Strait *Diamond* arrived alongside H wharf in Fremantle Harbour on 6 March, and the ship's company enjoyed the tremendous hospitality of the people of both Fremantle and Perth. When she left the port on 11 March to make the return passage to Singapore there was general agreement on board that five days in Western Australia was not nearly long enough, but with a maintenance period scheduled to precede her long passage to the UK, it was all that could be spared. On her return to the waters around Singapore *Diamond* took part in three days of anti-submarine exercises with HMNZS *Blackpool*, before entering the naval base where the ship's company moved into the spacious shore accommodation at HMS *Terror*.

*Diamond*'s maintenance period lasted just four weeks, and on 15 April she sailed for Colombo at the start of her passage home. After spending a weekend in the Ceylonese port *Diamond* embarked the British High Commissioner to Ceylon, who was also the British Ambassador to the Seychelles and the Maldives, for the 24-hour passage to Malé, Seychelles, where he was able to present his credentials to the President of the islands before rejoining *Diamond* for the passage back to Gan and an RAF flight back to Colombo. After disembarking the High Commissioner at the entrance to Gan Lagoon the destroyer refuelled from *Wave Victor* before continuing her passage south to Port Louis, Mauritius, where she arrived during the forenoon of 28 April. The three-day visit was notable for the

successes of the ship's soccer team, but on 1 May she sailed to carry out her third Beira Patrol, where she relieved *London* and joined *Jaguar* and *Juno*. The patrol should, in fact, have been carried out by *Dainty*, but she had suffered a number of mechanical defects and had been delayed in Singapore Naval Base. Once again the patrol was dominated by inter-ship competitions for the 'Beira Bucket', and quizzes for the title 'Brain of Beira', which whiled away the long, hot days. This time *Diamond*'s stint lasted for only three weeks and at 0700 on 24 May, after having been relieved on station by *Dainty*, she set course for Simonstown, arriving alongside four days later.

*Diamond*'s final visit to South Africa lasted for just eight days, and on 5 June she set course into the Atlantic Ocean as she headed home. Pausing briefly to refuel at Freetown she continued her passage north to spend three days at Gibraltar. Finally, however, at 2130 on 25 June she secured to a buoy off Sheerness and next forenoon after Customs had been cleared she steamed upriver to Chatham to secure alongside. It was the end of the foreign leg of *Diamond*'s general service commission, and almost the end of the ship's operational service, for in September 1968 it had been announced that the Daring-class destroyers were to be withdrawn from service by the end of 1969. During the whole of July, while her ship's company took leave and the ship underwent maintenance, *Diamond* remained alongside at Chatham. It was 8 August before she put to sea to make a 12-hour passage to Portland for Navy Days. After leaving Portland the destroyer exercised briefly with the submarines *Andrew* and *Grampus* before steaming north to Middlesbrough as part of a nationwide 'Meet the Navy' recruiting drive. During one of the open days in the city a small girl fell into the water between the ship and the jetty, but fortunately one of the ship's divers, Able Seaman Knowler who was nearby, went straight into the narrow strip of water and quickly rescued the child who, apart from being very wet, was none the worse for her ordeal.

Leaving Middlesbrough during the forenoon of 21 August, *Diamond* steamed south to reach the Thames Estuary during the early hours of the next day, when she made a seven-hour passage upriver to secure to buoys off George Stairs, just downriver from Tower Bridge in the Pool of London, for her second 'Meet the Navy' visit. During the four-day stopover *Diamond* was opened to visitors each afternoon. When she left the Thames on 26 August it was to steam north to the Clyde where she carried out training exercises with the new nuclear-powered Polaris submarine *Revenge*. Three days later, after refuelling at Faslane, *Diamond* was at sea again and steaming south.

During September 1969 *Diamond* undertook the duties of guardship at Gibraltar, arriving alongside the South Mole on 5 September. In those days, with the Cold War at its height, one of the Navy's duties was to monitor Soviet naval movements through the Strait of Gibraltar. On 12 September, whilst on patrol, she took up station half a mile astern of a Soviet task force consisting of a Sverdlov-class cruiser, two destroyers and three frigates. The force was passing from the Atlantic Ocean to the Mediterranean and during the afternoon, shadowed by *Diamond*, it passed through the Strait. Later in the month, during the forenoon of 26 September, *Diamond* was once again shadowing a Soviet naval force as it steamed from the Mediterranean into the Atlantic Ocean. At 0100 the next morning, together with the Spanish Coastguard and the US Air Force, she was involved in the search for two seamen who had been lost overboard from the 15,000-ton Russian oil tanker MV *General Kravtsov*. At just after 1130 that forenoon the bodies of the two Russian seamen were recovered by *Diamond* just off Tarifa Island. *Diamond* then returned to Gibraltar where, at 1415, the two bodies were landed into the care of a port authority launch to be returned to *General Kravtsov*. Later in the day *Diamond* returned to the Strait to continue her patrol for a further 24 hours before returning to Gibraltar to refuel and then to set course for home.

*Diamond* arrived in Chatham Dockyard on 4 October, but there was only time for a short leave period for each watch before she sailed north ten days later to carry out planeguard duties for the air-

*During the 1970s* Diamond *became a familiar sight in Portsmouth Harbour, where she was laid up in Fareham Creek providing training facilities for the enginners of* HMS Sultan. *(World Ship Society)*

craft carrier *Hermes*. During the evening of 23 October the destroyer's divers recovered the aircrew dinghy from a ditched Gannet, the aircrew themselves having been picked up by the SAR helicopter. Two days later the destroyer began operating in the Clyde area with *Llandaff* and *Phoebe*, providing training for the submarine *Oracle*. This continued through to the end of November, interrupted by a short break at Portsmouth. In the first week of December *Diamond* was operating in the Irish Sea with the frigate *Cleopatra*, after which she made her final courtesy visit to Swansea for a weekend break. After leaving South Wales during the afternoon of 8 December the destroyer carried out three days of machinery and weapons trials before entering Portsmouth Harbour at 1550 on Thursday 11 December with her paying-off pennant flying and securing alongside South Railway Jetty. At 1557 'Finished with Main Engines' was rung off for the last time.

*Diamond* had returned to Portsmouth and not to Chatham for she had been chosen to take over the busy, but unremarkable, role of harbour training

ship for the marine engineering training school, HMS *Sultan*, replacing the destroyer *Crossbow*. On 16 December her ship's company moved into Portsmouth naval barracks, and at 0800 on 18 December 1969 *Diamond* was officially paid off into dockyard hands.

*Diamond*'s role as a harbour training ship lasted for ten years, and during the 1970s she became a familiar sight in Portsmouth Harbour's Fareham Creek. In the summer of 1980, however, she was relieved by the more modern County-class destroyer *Fife*, and in December that year she was placed on the disposal list. It was clear that there could only be one more sea passage left for *Diamond*, and on 9 November 1981, under the tow of the tugs *Dalmatian* and *Roysterer*, she slid quietly out of Portsmouth Harbour. The once proud destroyer had been sold to Medway Secondary Metals for demolition, and three days later she arrived at the company's Rainham yard. It was perhaps fitting that she was broken up on the Medway, only a few miles from Chatham Dockyard, which had been her base port for 17 years.

**HMS *Diamond*
Commanding Officers**

| Name: | Date Appointed: |
| --- | --- |
| Captain C. B. Alers-Hankey DSC RN | 12 October 1951 |
| Captain R. I. A. Sarrell DSO RN | 25 July 1953 |
| Captain T. L. Eddison DSC RN | 30 August 1954 |
| Captain M. G. Haworth DSC RN | 21 February 1956 |
| Captain J. A. C. Henley DSC RN | 27 August 1957 |
| Captain H. H. Dannreuther RN | 21 November 1960 |
| Captain J. D. Cartwright DSC RN | 3 January 1963 |
| Commander M. F. Parry RN | 31 July 1967 |
| Commander A. Mancais RN | 2 December 1968 |

**Battle Honours**

| | |
| --- | --- |
| Armada 1588 | Four Days' Battle 1666 |
| Kentish Knock 1652 | Orford Ness 1666 |
| Portland 1653 | Solebay 1672 |
| Gabbard 1653 | Schooneveld 1673 |
| Scheveningen 1653 | Texel 1673 |
| Lowestoft 1665 | Crimea 1854-55 |

# Part Three

# HMS DUCHESS

## October 1952 - April 1964

The third of the Daring-class ships to be commissioned was HMS *Duchess*, whose keel had been laid at John I. Thorneycroft's Woolston shipyard on Southampton Water on 2 July 1948. Although she was the last but one to be laid down she was completed quickly, and on Monday 9 April 1951, a wet day with south-westerly gales and torrential rain, she was launched by Lady Mountbatten. At the lunch which followed the ceremony Lord Mountbatten made an interesting comparison when he told the assembled guests that, when completed, the cost of *Duchess* would be almost exactly the same as that of the renowned battleship *Dreadnought* which had been launched some 42 years earlier. On 1 September 1952, some 17 months after her launch, *Duchess*' first commanding officer, Captain H. R. Law OBE DSC RN, was appointed to the ship. Seven weeks later, during the forenoon of 21 October the ship was

inspected by the Commodore Superintendent Contract Built Ships, and later that afternoon the main body of her ship's company arrived by rail from the Royal Naval Barracks, Portsmouth. Finally, at 1600 that day HMS *Duchess* was commissioned.

Two days after the commissioning ceremony *Duchess* slipped her moorings and, still under the Red Ensign, steamed down Southampton Water and through the Solent to begin her machinery trials in the Channel. These were concluded the same afternoon with a full-power trial and at 1615, just off the Nab Tower, the ship was formally accepted from the builder and the White Ensign was hoisted for the first time. An hour and a half later, at the end of her first foray to sea under the White Ensign, *Duchess* anchored in Southampton Water, off Netley. Over the days which followed the destroyer was put through a series of machinery trials, and

HMS Duchess *anchored at Spithead in June 1953, shortly before the Coronation Fleet Review.* *(Maritime Photo Library)*

these were followed by adjustments at Thorneycroft's shipyard. Finally, during the afternoon of Wednesday 5 November *Duchess* entered Portsmouth Dockyard for the first time, to secure alongside *Myngs* at South Slip Jetty.

*Duchess'* first commission would be served with the Home Fleet and, operating from Portland, it was to be some months before she left the waters of the south coast. Leaving Portsmouth on 5 January 1953 she made the short passage west to Weymouth Bay where she carried out daily training exercises with the aircraft carrier *Vengeance*, along with *Myngs*, *Verulam* and the submarine *Ambush*. During the afternoon of 22 January she secured to a buoy in Portland Harbour for what was to be a weekend break. Four days later, during the morning watch, with all leave expiring at 0700, the ship was being prepared for sea. The duty watchkeepers in A boiler room were flashing the oil-fired boilers, a procedure which involved lighting paraffin-soaked rags and holding them with metal rods in front of the fine spray of oil in the furnace until they in turn ignited. Suddenly, at 0500 there was a massive flashback of flame, almost like an explosion, from the furnace which shot out into the working area in front of the furnace, followed by a fierce oil fire which was fed by the hot spray of furnace fuel oil. Three of the boiler room personnel suffered severe burns, and Petty Officer Stoker Mechanic Wilfred Brooks was killed. As emergency parties fought to control and extinguish the blaze an MFV came alongside to evacuate the casualties. By 0600 the fire had been extinguished, but *Duchess* was unable to sail with the rest of the Portland Squadron, and it was 1330 before she was able to steam slowly out of harbour in order to pump out her flooded bilges. Three hours later she returned to harbour to secure alongside, and to begin the task of clearing up the disorder and mess left by the fire. Although *Duchess* was able to put to sea again on 27 January for a day of torpedo-firing practice, a further ten days of dockyard assistance was required to ensure that the ship was fully operational again.

During the first week of February *Duchess* was able to rejoin the fleet on training exercises out of Portland, which continued into the second week of the month, after which she returned to Portsmouth for six days. On 18 February, sailing via Portland, *Duchess* rendezvoused with the training carrier *Implacable* and set course for Gibraltar from where, during the first week of March, she joined other units of the Home Fleet, including *Vanguard*, *Indomitable*, *Theseus*, *Agincourt*, *Broadsword*, *Diamond* and *St Kitts*, for training exercises which were observed by the First Sea Lord, who also inspected *Duchess'* ship's company at Ceremonial Divisions in Gibraltar. After a four-day visit to Tangier, on 18 March *Duchess* once again joined Home Fleet units for the passage north and a return to base ports, arriving at Portsmouth on 25 March.

Following her return home *Duchess* underwent a six-week dockyard-assisted maintenance period, during which further work was carried out on A boiler room, and it was 7 May before she sailed for Portland. Once again *Duchess* began day-running training exercises, but on 28 May she joined her sister *Diamond* and the cruiser *Swiftsure* before sailing for the Thames Estuary and the start of the Coronation celebrations. The two destroyers secured to buoys at Gravesend where they were opened to visitors, and where *Duchess* received a visit from her sponsor, Lady Mountbatten. On Friday 4 June *Duchess* left Gravesend for the south coast of the Isle of Wight and the seaside resort of Shanklin where she spent a weekend at anchor. Despite the fact that she was well offshore, during her two-day visit she was opened to visitors and she proved a popular attraction for both local people and holidaymakers alike. On Tuesday 9 June, having left Shanklin at 0245, *Duchess* steamed round to Spithead where she took her place in Line D with *Defender*, *Diamond* and *Decoy* for the Coronation Fleet Review.

In the six days leading up to the Review there was a great deal of activity on board as virtually the whole of the ship's superstructure and hull was repainted. The Review took place on 15 June, and next day *Duchess*, together with *Agincourt* and *Swiftsure*, left Spithead for ports on the east coast.

Next day *Duchess* anchored in Bridlington Bay, off the small coastal resort of Hornsea, and from there she made the passage to South Shields, where she secured in the Tyne Dock. After spending six days on the River Tyne she again rendezvoused with *Agincourt* and *Swiftsure* to steam north for fleet exercises based on Invergordon. During this period *Duchess* acted as planeguard to *Eagle*, and underwent both her harbour and sea inspections. The exercises took the fleet through the Pentland Firth and into the Atlantic Ocean, and for *Duchess* ended on 15 July when she anchored off Douglas for a seven-day visit to the Isle of Man, before she made her way back to Portsmouth for leave and six weeks of maintenance.

*Duchess* sailed again on 1 September, and once again acted as planeguard to *Eagle* as the carrier prepared for a major exercise in northern waters. After rendezvousing with other units including *Vanguard*, *Swiftsure*, *Sheffield*, *Diamond*, *Battleaxe*, *Crossbow* and *Scorpion*, the force steamed north to begin 'Exercise Mariner.' This got under way on 22 September and took the fleet north to the Denmark Strait, where severe weather hampered *Eagle*'s flying programme. On 29 September *Swiftsure* and *Diamond* were withdrawn from the exercise following a collision at sea and on 3 October, to everyone's relief, the exercise ended at Greenock. Two days later, after ferrying the personnel of 812 Squadron to Loch Foyle, *Duchess* rejoined *Eagle* for flying training in the Atlantic. At 0745 on 6 October, shortly before she left the area for Invergordon, one of *Eagle*'s helicopters was approaching *Duchess* from astern in order to deliver and collect outgoing mail. Suddenly, however, without any warning the helicopter ditched into the sea just astern of the destroyer. Within minutes *Duchess* had stopped and launched her seaboat which quickly picked up an injured crewman, but there was no sign of the pilot who was lost when the helicopter sank. After a three-hour search of the area *Duchess* embarked *Eagle*'s surgeon before detaching to nearby Oban to land the injured rating and continue her passage to Invergordon. For ten days, between 14 and 24 October, *Duchess* contin-

ued to act as planeguard to *Eagle* in a nuclear fall-out exercise which took the fleet south to Portland for a five-day wash-up, at the end of which *Duchess* returned to Portsmouth for a refit which kept her out of service for almost three months.

During her refit *Duchess* spent two months high and dry in No 12 dry dock, and it was the first week of January 1954 before she was back alongside the sea wall. Including three days of machinery trials the refit ended on 25 January when the destroyer steamed to Portland to join other units of the Home Fleet for training exercises and the annual spring cruise. The fleet, under its new C-in-C, Admiral Sir Michael Denny, flying his flag in *Vanguard*, was led to sea during the morning of 5 February. Other units included *Eagle*, *Superb*, *Apollo*, *Diamond*, *Decoy*, *Venus* and *Corunna*. As a break from intensive exercises in the Western Mediterranean, *Duchess* accompanied *Diamond* and *Decoy* on a four-day visit to the French naval base at Oran. The training continued to mid-March, culminating in a joint Home/Mediterranean Fleet exercise which was controlled from *Vanguard*. On 23 March, after a three-day passage from Gibraltar, *Duchess* returned to Portsmouth for a four-week maintenance period and to give leave.

On 6 April 1954 there was a change of command when Captain Law was relieved by Captain D. G. Goodwin DSC RN, who, on 11 November 1940, as a Fleet Air Arm aircrewman, had taken part in the attack on the Italian Fleet at Taranto. On 29 April *Duchess* left Portsmouth to head south for Gibraltar, from where she was to take up her duty as escort to the royal yacht. The Queen and the Duke of Edinburgh were travelling back from Malta in the newly commissioned *Britannia* on the final stage of a Commonwealth Tour, and *Glasgow*, together with *Barfleur*, *Chequers* and *Saintes*, had provided the escort through the Mediterranean to Gibraltar. The royal yacht arrived in Gibraltar on 10 May, and, during a Joint Services Parade at RAF North Front, a contingent from *Duchess* marched past the Queen who took the salute. Next day, wearing the flag of Flag Officer, Flotillas, Home Fleet, Rear-Admiral J. W. Cuthbert, *Duchess* joined

Duchess *operating from Invergordon in May 1954.  (World Ship Society)*

the escort for the passage home.  At 1000 on 12 May, some 60 miles west-north-west of Lisbon, in a grey and misty drizzle, two Portuguese frigates, *Nuno Tristoa* and *Diogo Gomes*, and the destroyer *Dao*, steamed past in salute.  The ships finally arrived in the Thames Estuary on 13 May, and after detaching from the royal yacht *Duchess* steamed north to Rosyth and Invergordon. She then took part in a major Home Fleet training exercise, which also included *Vanguard*.  On 11 June the battleship fired one of the Navy's last 15-inch full-calibre broadsides and the occasion was photographed from on board *Duchess*.  The manoeuvres took the ships as far north as Scapa Flow, but on Saturday 19 June, together with her sister *Diamond*, which was flying the flag of the C-in-C Home Fleet, *Duchess* was detached for a three-week cruise into the Baltic. Calling at Oslo and then Copenhagen, the highlight of the cruise was a six-day spell alongside at Stockholm, after which *Duchess* left her sister to return via the Kiel Canal to Portsmouth.

The return home marked the end of *Duchess*' first commission, and on Tuesday 31 August 1954 she was recommissioned.  In those days the whole process of paying off and recommissioning a ship took place on the same day and the entries in *Duchess*' Official Log held at the National Archives

shows the sequence of events thus: -

0745 - Hands recommissioning fall in on the quarterdeck.
1030 - Men paying off fall in on the jetty.
1100 - Captain addressed ship's company.
1110 - Old ship's company march to RNB.
1310 - Men recommissioning stowing baggage.
1410 - New ship's company join from RNB. Muster on forecastle for Commissioning Service.

Eight days later, at 13.30 on Friday 10 September, *Duchess* left Portsmouth to rendezvous with *Diana* and *Diamond*, and to set course for Malta.  On 15 October, in company with *Centaur*, *Glasgow*, *Diamond*, *Decoy*, *Chevron*, *Charity*, *Comet* and *Constance*, as well as frigates and submarines, *Duchess* took part in what was described in *The Times* as a 'Parade of Naval Power', in the presence of the Emperor of Ethiopia who was embarked in *Gambia*.  He was given an extremely impressive display, which for *Duchess* included the firing of live anti-submarine Squid projectiles - well out of range of *Sanguine* and *Teredo* which were also taking part in the display, which ended with a high-speed steam past and a 21-gun salute.

During October and the first week of November *Duchess* carried out day-running training exercises in local waters off Malta, acting as planeguard to both *Centaur* and *Triumph*. In mid-November, on conclusion of the NATO exercise 'Novex 54', *Duchess* and *Jamaica* visited the Italian ports of Genoa, and Portoferraio on the island of Elba, where she anchored in the picturesque harbour, directly beneath the house in which the Emperor Napoleon had once been exiled. Returning to Grand Harbour on 20 November the destroyer spent the rest of the month on day-running exercises. On 10 December 1954, with other units of the Mediterranean Fleet, including *Albion* and *Centaur*, and with FO2 embarked, *Duchess* took part in 'Exercise Famous', which involved a ceremonial steam past of the dispatch vessel *Surprise* as Admiral Sir Guy Grantham took over as C-in-C Mediterranean from Admiral Lord Mountbatten. This was to be her final seagoing operational foray before the Christmas and New Year break.

On 4 January 1955, having embarked a Royal Marines Band, *Duchess* left Malta to rendezvous with *Jamaica* before setting course for Algiers where the C-in-C was making an official visit. This was followed by more day running from Grand Harbour, a visit to Palermo and a short maintenance period alongside the depot ship *Ranpura* in Lazzaretto Creek. On 17 February *Duchess* was at sea again and taking part in 'Exercise Febex', a convoy escort exercise with *Centaur* and the Dutch aircraft carrier *Karel Doorman*. This was closely followed by the Fleet Gunnery Trophy shoots. On 10 March *Duchess*, *Albion*, *Tyne* and *Apollo* took part in 'Exercise Sea Lance', another convoy exercise which also included the royal yacht *Britannia* with the Duke of Edinburgh embarked. The manoeuvres ended during the forenoon of 15 March when all units formed up astern of *Britannia* for a ceremonial entry into Grand Harbour, which had not seen so many men-of-war together for quite some time. That evening the floodlit fleet presented a spectacular scene and *Duchess*, secured on No 23 buoy at the head of the Darings in Dockyard Creek, looked very impressive. Four days later, at

1100 on 19 March, the Duke of Edinburgh visited *Duchess* to tour the ship and inspect the ship's company at Divisions. On 22 March, with other units of the fleet, including *Glasgow* and *Jamaica*, *Duchess* sailed from Grand Harbour to bid a ceremonial farewell to *Britannia* and the Duke of Edinburgh with a steam past. Two days later, after fleet manoeuvres, *Duchess* and other units set course for Naples where, at 0925 on 24 March, in thick fog, *Duchess* secured stern to on Molo Pascare. Less than an hour later a 9,644-ton American cargo ship, SS *Excambion*, owned by the American Export Line of New York, entered harbour and while manoeuvring to her berth in the thick fog she rammed *Duchess*' starboard bow. The force of the collision jolted the destroyer's stern back on to the jetty, buckling her starboard corner stern plates, and the forward progress of *Excambion* was not halted until her bows were under *Duchess*' starboard bow light. In the event she punched a hole in the destroyer's side from the stem to A frame on No 1 deck. There was also extensive but superficial damage to *Duchess*' superstructure. The merchantman suffered only minor damage to her stem.

Fortunately, there were no injuries in either ship and the damage to *Duchess* was well above the waterline. During the six days the destroyer was in Naples the ship's staff, together with shipwrights from *Jamaica* and *Tyne*, carried out some very effective temporary repairs. Steel plates were welded over the hole in the bows, guard rail stanchions were straightened and re-erected, and the starboard carley float support being beyond repair was completely cut away. By Sunday 27 March the damage was not nearly so obvious, but experts who had flown in from Malta decided that the ship should return immediately to the island's dockyard in order that permanent repairs could be made, which meant cutting short the cruise and cancelling a scheduled visit to Toulon. Despite the disruption to the itinerary the ship's company was still able to enjoy the Naples visit, particularly those who went sightseeing to Rome, Capri, Pompeii and Vesuvius. At 0715 on 30 March, however, *Duchess* left Naples to make a 24-hour passage back to Malta. One mem-

ber of the ship's company remembers that some nine hours out of Naples and within sight of Stromboli, on a gloriously sunny and calm day, the ship was stopped for 'Hands to Bathe'. However, he also recalls that although the day was pleasantly warm the sea temperature appeared to be just the opposite, and only the very hardy remained in the water until the end of the session. Continuing through the Strait of Messina the ship's company was treated to a spectacular view of the snow-capped peak of Mount Etna, before early next morning *Duchess* arrived in Grand Harbour and arrangements were made to move her into dry dock.

During the whole of April *Duchess* remained high and dry in Malta Dockyard's No 2 dry dock. It was 2 May when she put to sea again to carry out a day of trials before returning to Grand Harbour to pre-pare for FO2's inspection. During the evening of 22 May, with both the harbour and sea inspections completed, *Duchess* joined *Sheffield* (flag C-in-C Mediterranean), *Jamaica*, *Decoy*, *Diamond*, *Diana*, *Battleaxe*, *Scorpion* and RFA *Fort Duquesne*, for exercises and visits to ports in the Eastern Mediterranean. The first port on the agenda for the whole squadron was Istanbul, after which they dis-persed to a variety of destinations with *Sheffield*, *Duchess* and *Diana* making an important four-day visit to Alexandria. It was the first time for five years that a Royal Navy squadron had visited the Egyptian port, which had once been a stronghold of British power in the Mediterranean and the diplo-mats hoped that the Royal Navy, who are masters at healing old quarrels, would ease some of the diplo-matic tensions which surrounded the continued presence of British military bases in Egypt. As far as friendly relations with the Egyptian people were concerned the visit was judged to have been suc-cessful, but the violent incidents around the Suez Canal Zone bases continued unabated. From Alexandria *Duchess* steamed north to the waters around Cyprus, which was another of Britain's colonial problems in the Mediterranean area, and began a patrol of the island's coastline aimed at pre-venting guns and ammunition reaching the island's insurgents. During the patrol *Duchess* assisted

police launches to chase a small boat which was suspected of gun running, and although some very limited shore leave was granted, the dangers ashore were highlighted when a terrorist bomb exploded close to a British military base, injuring one serv-iceman. By 22 June, however, *Duchess* had returned to Grand Harbour. The summer cruise of 1955 marked the end of *Duchess*' foreign service leg of the commission and on Friday 24 June, in company with *Decoy*, *Diamond* and *Diana*, she left Malta to return home by way of Gibraltar and arrived at Portsmouth during the afternoon of 1 July, to begin a 13-week leave and maintenance period.

It wasn't until 28 September, after a day of trials, that *Duchess* steamed west to Portland and then on to the Clyde area where she carried out anti-subma-rine and torpedo-firing exercises. After a weekend break at Greenock and further exercises *Duchess* steamed round Scotland's north coast to the Rosyth area where, for six days in very heavy seas, she acted as planeguard to *Eagle* and took part in 'Exercise Phoenix I', designed to test the ability of carrier-borne aircraft to intercept high-level bombers. Also taking part were the light fleet car-riers *Albion*, *Bulwark* and *Centaur*. For *Duchess* the exercise ended at Rosyth on 29 October where she paid a brief call before making a popular seven-day visit to Hamburg. On 11 November, after leaving the River Elbe, *Duchess* returned to Portland where she remained until the end of November, with just a short break at Southampton. The first days of December saw *Duchess* at Cherbourg, and in late January 1956, with the aircraft carrier *Ocean*, she took part in 'Exercise Six Able', before making her final foreign visit to Ferrol in Portugal. On 2 February she returned to Portsmouth Dockyard and secured alongside the North West Wall. It was the end of the commission.

During the forenoon of Tuesday 21 February *Duchess*' old ship's company marched from their ship in Portsmouth Dockyard to the Royal Naval Barracks, and 15 minutes later the ship's new com-manding officer, Captain N. H. G. Austen DSO RN, joined the ship. An hour later the new ship's com-

pany marched from the barracks to the ship, which was recommissioned at noon.

*Duchess'* third commission began in earnest on Saturday 3 March 1956 when she left Portsmouth to join the Mediterranean Fleet at Malta. Steaming by way of Gibraltar she arrived in Grand Harbour on 12 March and immediately began a series of work-up exercises in local waters, which saw her day running until the second week of April. The destroyer's first major exercise, 'Medflex Dragon', came a week later and it involved some 60 warships from five NATO countries. The manoeuvres were led by the NATO Supreme Allied Commander, Europe, US General A. H. Gruenther in HMS *Surprise*. On board *Duchess* during the exercise was the Naval Correspondent of the Daily Telegraph who, one evening in the wardroom, was prevailed upon to get the ship a 'mention' in Peterborough's 'Day by Day' column of the newspaper. In particular he was told that the ship was looking for a Duchess's coronet which could be displayed as the ship's trophy. Soon afterwards the following duly appeared in the newspaper:

*Any Spare Coronets?*

'HMS *Duchess,* which has just joined the Mediterranean Fleet is anxious to hear from any Duchess with a coronet to spare. *Duchess* is one of our latest ships but she feels that her wardroom is incomplete without an emblem. *Faute de mieux* an imitation coronet will do – but not a tiara.'

Soon after the appeal Captain Austen received a postcard from the Duchess of Westminster, and within a short space of time her coronet had been presented to the ship and mounted in a trophy case in the destroyer's wardroom.

Returning, however, to the Mediterranean, 'Medflex Dragon' ended on 20 April with all 60 warships steaming in two lines past HMS *Surprise* as a salute to General Gruenther, who was retiring after a distinguished military career. *Duchess* followed up the exercise with a six-week maintenance period and it was the end of May before she put to sea again, this time to exercise with *Eagle*,

*In March 1956* Duchess *left Portsmouth for the Mediterranean.* (*Portsmouth Royal Naval Museum*)

*Manxman*, *Chevron* and *Diamond*, followed by visits to Istanbul and Golcuck. After leaving the Dardanelles on 12 June, *Duchess* steamed into the waters off Cyprus where she began another patrol of the coastline to intercept gun smugglers running between the Greek mainland and the island. The patrol lasted until mid-July when she returned to Grand Harbour, which is where she was on the evening of 26 July when, in the course of a three-hour speech to a vast crowd in Alexandria's Liberation Square, President Nasser of Egypt proclaimed the Egyptian Government's decision to nationalise the Suez Canal Company.

With Anthony Eden having taken the decision to invade Egypt in order to regain control of the Canal, and to topple Nasser from power, from mid-August onwards the Mediterranean Fleet began training in earnest. For most of this period *Duchess* acted as planeguard to *Eagle*, but she also carried out numerous bombardment exercises. This pattern continued into September, with convoy escort training included in the programme, and as a break from the intensive training routines there were short visits to Sicily and Toulon before, on 6 October, *Duchess* returned to Grand Harbour to begin a three-week maintenance period.

*Duchess* sailed from Grand Harbour at 0730 on Monday 29 October to rendezvous with the aircraft carrier group consisting of *Eagle*, *Albion* and *Bulwark*, and also other units, including the New Zealand cruiser *Royalist*, to set course for Port Said. It was not long, however, before *Royalist*, on the direct orders of the New Zealand Prime Minister, was withdrawn from the operation. Although she was quickly replaced by *Ceylon,* which meant operational efficiency was not affected, it was a clear indication of how isolated the British and French Governments were in the eyes of world opinion. During the eight days which elapsed between the sailing from Malta and the seaborne invasion of Port Said Britain and France went through an elaborate charade of acting as 'self-appointed peacemakers' between Egypt and Israel. In the meantime

the carrier group arrived in a position some 50 miles from the Egyptian coast in the early hours of 31 October. Next day the Fleet Air Arm attacks on Egyptian airfields began, and *Duchess* acted as planeguard escort to *Eagle*. At 0215 on 6 November, the morning that the seaborne invasion began, the destroyer anchored off the invasion beaches whilst the troops transferred from their transports to landing craft. At 0345 she weighed anchor and led in a section of the assault group as they approached the beaches, and afterwards kept up an anti-aircraft and anti-submarine patrol. By 0815, however, she was anchored just off Port Said where she remained for the rest of the day.

Over the days which followed *Duchess*, both before and after the ceasefire at midnight on 6/7 November, patrolled the waters off Port Said and she also acted as planeguard to all three aircraft carriers. During the afternoon of 9 November she left the Egyptian coast and returned to Malta, where she arrived two days later. On 17 November she returned to Port Said where she acted as planeguard to *Eagle* and *Albion*, but on 27 November, with the evacuation of British forces about to begin, *Duchess* was ordered to patrol the coast of Cyprus, a duty which continued through to mid-December when she returned to Port Said for the final stages of the withdrawal. Although most British troops had by that time been withdrawn and replaced by a United Nations force, the final evacuation was due to take place on 22 December and *Duchess* was required to cover the last troopships as they left the area. The destroyer arrived off Port Said during the forenoon of 16 December, and four days later she entered harbour to secure alongside the depot ship *Tyne*. On Friday 21 December, *Duchess* moved out of the inner harbour to an anchorage off the De Lesseps statue and next day, with all British troops having left Egypt, she should have sailed with the last troop convoy, but she was held back in the hope that a kidnapped British soldier might be released[1]. By 2000, however, with nothing having been heard, she weighed anchor and in company with *Jamaica*

---

[1] Second Lieutenant Moorehouse, West Yorkshire Regt, had been kidnapped on 10 December with the intention of being held for ransom. He had, however, suffocated when bound and gagged and locked in a tin trunk.

Duchess *at speed in May 1957.*                                    *(Ken Kelly)*

she sailed for Malta. The ill-considered and ill-fated Suez Campaign was over and *Duchess* had been the last Royal Navy ship to leave Port Said.

At 0740 on Christmas Day *Duchess* arrived alongside Grand Harbour's Boat House Wharf. She sailed again during the afternoon of New Year's Day 1957 to rendezvous with her sisters *Decoy* and *Diamond*, to make the passage home. Calling briefly at Gibraltar *Duchess* arrived back in Portsmouth during the afternoon of 9 January, where she was immediately taken in hand for a three-month dockyard-assisted maintenance period.

Although the last four months of the destroyer's commission were spent with the Home Fleet they would take her a long way from home waters. On 17 May, having carried out two weeks of trials, she joined *Diamond* and set course for the River Humber from where, the next day, the two destroyers took up the escort of the royal yacht *Britannia* carrying the Queen and Duke of Edinburgh on a State Visit to Denmark. On 25 May, having remained at Copenhagen during the visit, *Duchess* and *Diamond* escorted *Britannia* back to the Moray Firth where they took part in the Royal Review of the Home Fleet at Invergordon. At 1100 on Tuesday 28 May, during the course of the Review, the Queen visited *Duchess* for forty minutes to inspect representatives from *Diamond* and *Duchess* at Ceremonial Divisions. Two days later, following an impressive steam past, the two destroyers joined *Ark Royal* to set course for the United States and the International Naval Review at Hampton Roads,

*Duchess, dressed overall (foreground) and Diamond at the International Naval Review, Hampton Roads, Virginia, USA.* *(MoD/Crown Copyright)*

Virginia. Arriving at the US Naval Base, Norfolk, on 8 June *Duchess* secured alongside No.2 Pier, from where the ship's company enjoyed much lavish hospitality from the local people. The Review took place on 12 June and five days later *Duchess* sailed via Bermuda for home. After rendezvousing with *Ark Royal* the destroyer arrived in Liverpool on 28 June for a weekend visit to the city as part of the celebrations to mark the 750th Anniversary of the signing of King John's Charter, which led to the growth of the great city port from what had once been a small hamlet.

During the forenoon of 1 July, shortly before she left the Mersey, the ashes of a former ship's company member, EM1 Hawthorne who had died in June, were received on board and shortly afterwards the ship put to sea and stopped in the Irish Sea to con-

duct a funeral service. Next day the destroyer arrived back in Portsmouth and the last ten days of the commission saw her day running from Portsmouth, which included a visit to Brighton. Leaving the south coast resort during the forenoon of 24 July *Duchess* made a four-hour passage back to Portsmouth where she was paid off. It had been a busy commission for in addition to her role in the Suez Campaign she had taken part in the International Naval Review at Norfolk, Virginia, the 750th celebrations of the city of Liverpool, and many people had seen her star in a BBC Television documentary, 'The Royal Navy Now'.

At 0930 on 27 August *Duchess'* new commanding officer, Captain J. P. Scratchard DSC RN, joined the ship and relieved Captain Austen, then half an hour later the new ship's company marched

down to the ship from the Royal Naval Barracks. That same forenoon the recommissioning ceremony took place on the forecastle. A week later, on 3 September, *Duchess* put to sea to carry out a very short work-up before she rendezvoused with *Diamond* and left Portland for the Mediterranean, where she was to become the leader of the Fifth Destroyer Squadron.

Following her arrival in Sliema Creek on 16 September *Duchess* carried out a series of work-up exercises with her sister *Diana*, the submarine *Totem* and the cruisers *Birmingham* and *Tiger*. During October there were visits to Tripoli and to Civitavecchia, followed by a self-maintenance period in Grand Harbour. During what remained of 1957 *Duchess* made day running forays to sea, with Christmas and New Year being spent in Sliema Creek. On Wednesday 8 January 1958 *Duchess* left Malta to carry out a long, six and a half week Cyprus patrol, during which she intercepted and searched countless numbers of fishing boats and small merchant ships. On 31 January there was a weekend break in Beirut before she returned to the coast of Cyprus. This patrol ended during the forenoon of 21 February when, in severe weather, she set course for Malta. During the return passage there were problems with a leak in the ship's side, but was kept under control with pumps and upon her arrival in Lazzaretto Creek she secured alongside the heavy repair ship *Ranpura* for the problem to be rectified.

In early March *Duchess* and *Diamond* took part in 'Exercise Marjex' with *Eagle*, *Ark Royal*, *Sheffield* and *Kenya*. This was followed by visits to Taranto and to Ancona in the Adriatic, where *Duchess* carried out joint manoeuvres with the Italian Navy, concluding with a visit to Venice before returning to Malta. During April and May *Duchess* operated out of Malta, taking part in two major fleet exercises with *Ark Royal* and *Sheffield*. She had actually been scheduled to return home during May 1958, but her departure was delayed by unrest in Lebanon and during the latter half of May and the whole of June she remained off Cyprus as part of a naval force which included *Ark Royal*, *Eagle* and *Sheffield*.

Whilst at anchor off Famagusta some limited shore leave to the Golden Sands Rest Camp, which was a secure area for British service personnel, was granted, but by 4 July *Duchess* had returned to Malta. Next day, with her sisters *Decoy*, *Diamond* and *Diana*, she left for home, arriving alongside at Portsmouth during the afternoon of 11 July to begin an 11-week maintenance period.

The final three months of this commission were spent with the Home Fleet, and, after sailing on 10 September, she steamed north to Rosyth to take part in a major exercise in Scottish waters. This was followed by an Atlantic convoy escort exercise with *Birmingham*, *Diamond*, *Zest* and *Undine*, which was concluded at Portsmouth. On 3 October *Duchess* made a three-day visit to Southampton and the following weekend visited Cardiff before steaming up Channel to spend six days at Rotterdam. After leaving the Dutch port on 20 October *Duchess* joined *Birmingham*, *Decoy*, *Diana* and *Diamond* to head south for Gibraltar, from where she would operate until the last week of November. During this period, with *Diamond*, she made the passage up the River Guadalquivir to Seville, and with *Birmingham*, *Apollo* and the Portuguese destroyers *Dao* and *Tejo*, took part in 'Exercise Straitex' on the Atlantic side of the Strait of Gibraltar. On 24 November, with other units of the squadron, *Duchess* left Gibraltar to make the passage home, during which she took part in joint manoeuvres and exercises with French units, ending with a five-day visit to Brest. This was followed by two more days of exercises in the Clyde area with *Adamant* and the boats of the Third Submarine Squadron. Finally, however, on 9 December she anchored at Spithead and later that day steamed up harbour to secure alongside Portsmouth Dockyard's North Corner Jetty. It was the end of another commission, and ahead lay two years in Reserve.

During *Duchess*' two years in dockyard hands at Portsmouth the ship's after bank of torpedo tubes was removed and replaced by a deckhouse abaft the after funnel, which afforded a very limited space for additional messdeck accommodation. However,

although an improvised system of central messing was introduced and her sickbay and operations room were fitted with air-conditioning, by all accounts space for both officers and ratings remained limited. On 15 August 1960, with the ship's modernisation refit under way, *Duchess*' new commanding offer, Captain E. A. S. Bailey MBE DSC RN, was appointed to the ship, and four months later preparations were made to get the destroyer ready for sea once again.

HMS *Duchess* was recommissioned at 1415 on Tuesday 3 January 1961, at a ceremony which took place on the jetty alongside the ship as she lay at Portsmouth Dockyard's South-West Wall. Six days later, on 9 January, she put to sea to begin a series of trials which saw her day running until the third week of February, when she steamed to Portland to begin eight weeks of work-up exercises and manoeuvres, which were broken off in late March for maintenance and leave at Portsmouth. The exercises were resumed in mid-April and a week later *Duchess* successfully cleared FOST's harbour and sea inspections. Following her work-up *Duchess* remained in the Portland area carrying out anti-submarine training with *Diamond*, *Diana*,

*Falmouth*, *Wakeful* and the submarine *Tudor*. In mid-May she steamed north to Rosyth to undergo maintenance, before returning to Portsmouth. In early June she returned to northern waters for a training period off Scotland's east coast, which also included the Dutch aircraft carrier *Karel Doorman* and the submarine *Sea Scout*. These exercises ended in late June with visits to Aarhus and Sundsvall, and a southbound passage to Portsmouth by way of the Kiel Canal. During 18 days at her home port the destroyer underwent a period of maintenance and overseas leave was given; her next deployment would see her return to the Mediterranean Fleet at Malta.

On 24 July *Duchess* left Portsmouth to rendezvous with *Diamond* and *Diana* before setting course for Gibraltar and Malta, via Ajaccio, where she arrived during the forenoon of 7 August. The visit to the Corsican port was almost cut short when a report was received of a mutiny on a British merchant ship off Algiers. In the event, however, *Duchess*' assistance was not required and after calling at Rapollo she arrived in Grand Harbour on 18 August. After undergoing maintenance, including a period in dry dock, in mid-September *Duchess*

*Duchess' after 4.5-inch turret and her quarterdeck are shown to their best advantage in this photograph of the ship at anchor. (World Ship Society)*

sailed for the Eastern Mediterranean where, with *Diamond* and *Battleaxe*, she took part in a variety of training exercises, which were followed by a fleet regatta at Mudros. During October and November she operated from Malta with *Centaur*, *Lion*, *Tiger* and the submarine *Sea Devil* and, during the first week of December, visited Naples. The Italian break was followed by joint exercises with *Blake*, *Diana* and the Spanish destroyer *Jorge Juan*, before a Christmas and New Year break alongside *Ausonia* in Lazzaretto Creek.

The new year of 1962 got under way in earnest when, on 8 January, the destroyer sailed for training exercises with *Ark Royal* and *Tiptoe*, and later in the month there was a short visit to Genoa which was followed by more training in local waters off Malta. On 26 March, with *Diamond*, *Diana* and *Crossbow*, she left Malta bound for Gibraltar and home. The final leg of the passage was made in company with *Bermuda*, *Battleaxe*, *Diana* and *Dundas*, in the form of a convoy exercise. During the morning of 6 April, however, *Duchess* anchored off Spithead and six hours later, at 1130, she had secured along-side Portsmouth's South-West Wall, where families of the ship's company flocked aboard to greet their loved ones.

The second half of *Duchess*' general service commission was served with the Home Fleet. It began in early May with exercises in the Channel, Irish Sea and the Bristol Channel, with a visit to Milford Haven. Later in the month, in company with *Bermuda*, she steamed into the Baltic Sea to make official visits to Stockholm and Helsinki, returning to home waters in early June, with exercises in the North Sea. In mid-June, with *Centaur*, *Diamond*, *Diana*, *Battleaxe*, *Crossbow* and *Dundas*, she took part in 'Exercise Fairwind VII' in the North Sea, which was rounded off with a visit to Bergen. On 4 July she returned to Portsmouth to begin a three-month refit.

On 11 October 1962 she sailed to carry out a mini work-up at Portland, and in the second week of November joined *Hermes* to act as planeguard during exercises which included *Agincourt*, *Berwick*, *Lowestoft*, *Scarborough* and the cruiser *Belfast* on

her last fully operational commission. The manoeuvres ended with 'Exercise Smallex' off Ireland's south coast and in the Bristol Channel. On Friday 16 November, when flying from RNAS Brawdy to *Hermes*, one of the carrier's Whirlwind helicopters crashed into the sea off St David's Head, Pembrokeshire. Of five people on board all but one, the Government Minister Lord Windlesham, were picked up by rescue helicopters, although one later died on board *Hermes*. *Duchess* and other units were ordered to carry out a thorough search of the area, which they did for six days, but no trace of the helicopter or the missing minister was ever found. On 23 November *Duchess* returned to Portsmouth.

The final two weeks of *Duchess*' commission were spent in the North Sea, with a brief two-hour visit to Harwich and a five-day visit to Newcastle upon Tyne, where *Duchess* secured alongside Grain House Jetty, close to the city centre. Leaving the River Tyne during the morning of Monday 17 December, *Duchess* arrived off the Isle of Wight where she stopped for paintwork cleaning. Three hours later, at 1030, with her paying-off pennant flying and with the ship's company manning the upper decks, she steamed into Portsmouth Harbour to secure alongside Pitch House Jetty. Although she carried out the duty of Portsmouth Command's duty destroyer until 30 December, it was the end of her fifth commission.

At 1000 on 2 January 1963 *Duchess*' new commanding officer, Captain J. Bitmead DSO RN, arrived on board and two hours later the old ship's company left for leave or new drafts. At 1600 Captain Bitmead took command and Captain Bailey left the ship. Next day, at 0800, the new ship's company marched from the Royal Naval Barracks to the ship, and at 1430 that afternoon the recommissioning ceremony was held on the quarterdeck. Although nobody knew it at the time it was to be the ship's last commission with the Royal Navy.

Meanwhile, in the Far East, political events which would directly affect the future course of *Duchess*' career were taking place. Originally it had been

*Exercise FOTEX 63 in the South China Sea.* Duchess *is in the foreground with, in line abreast,* Otago, Quiberon, Albion, Cambrian, Salisbury, Vendetta *and* Plymouth. *In this photograph* Duchess *and* Plymouth *are just slotting into their positions.*                                                                                                          *(Author's Collection)*

planned that the first part of the general service commission would be served in the Mediterranean, but in December 1962 a rebellion occurred in the small oil-rich state of Brunei, a British Protectorate. Although it had been overcome it was quickly followed by the Confrontation with Indonesia, which was hostile to the British-backed plan for the formation of Malaysia[2]. During the years of Confrontation there were numerous armed Indonesian incursions by both regular army units and guerrilla forces into what had been British North Borneo and Sarawak. This deliberate policy of Confrontation, at a time when Britain had hoped to reduce its military commitment in South-East Asia, resulted in the need for a huge increase in men and equipment at the Singapore garrisons. In addi-

tion to its destroyers and frigates, the Indonesian Navy had acquired a powerful Soviet Sverdlov-class cruiser and with another such vessel on order, combined with intelligence reports that she might also acquire an aircraft carrier, it was clear that powerful naval forces would be required in the area in order to protect the new fledgling state of Malaysia. Thus it was Confrontation which caused *Duchess'* proposed deployment to the Mediterranean to be cancelled in favour of the Far East Fleet based at Singapore. On 7 March 1963, on completion of her work-up, she returned to Portsmouth to prepare for service in South-East Asia.

Having embarked stores and ammunition, and having undergone essential maintenance, on 8 April

---

[2] The new State of Malaysia was originally made up of North Borneo, Sarawak, Singapore and the Federation of Malaya.

1963 she left Portsmouth and sailing by way of Gibraltar and Malta arrived off Port Said 11 days later. By the evening of 20 April she was steaming south through the Red Sea and after three days in Aden harbour, which was more than enough for everyone, she put to sea to rendezvous and exercise with *Centaur*, *Aisne* and *Diana*, before escorting the carrier north to the Gulf of Suez. On 11 May, having seen *Centaur* safely into the Suez Canal for her passage home, she met the southbound *Ark Royal* and escorted her to Aden. On 13 May *Duchess* began her passage east to Singapore, sailing via Gan where she refuelled from the hulk *Wave Victor* and celebrated 'Crossing the Line'.

*Duchess* arrived at the Singapore Naval Base on Monday 12 June. After carrying out day-running exercises with other ships, on 25 June her ship's company moved into the spacious and airy shore accommodation of HMS *Terror*, while the destroyer herself was shifted into the King George VI dry dock. For all the officers and men the three-week break ashore must have felt like luxury after the cramped conditions aboard, and no doubt they made the most of the swimming pools, sports fields and other facilities. By mid-July, however, they were back on board, and on 16 July *Duchess* sailed to carry out machinery trials. Two days later, while steaming south of Singapore Island, *Duchess* sighted one of the Indonesian Navy's fast patrol boats about five miles away, which emphasised the need for vigilance in the waters around Singapore and on the west coast of the Malayan Peninsular. On 25 July, with *Ark Royal*, *Albion*, *Lion*, *Barrosa*, *Plymouth*, *Cambrian*, *Salisbury*, HMAS *Quiberon*, HMAS *Vendetta*, HMNZS *Otago* and the submarines *Anchorite* and *Amphion*, *Duchess* took part in the annual FOTEX (Flag Officer's Tactical Exercises) in the South China Sea, off Malaya's east coast. During the exercises and manoeuvres *Duchess* acted as escort for the commando carrier *Albion*. During the afternoon of 6 August units of the escort screen steamed in line abreast on *Albion*, making a very impressive sight. For most of the ships' companies the most popular period of such exercises were the weekends spent at anchor off the

island of Pulau Tioman which, with its idyllic beaches, provided a pleasant recreational setting. The exercises were concluded during the early hours of Friday 9 August when most units, including *Duchess*, returned to the naval base on Singapore Island's north coast.

On 13 August *Duchess* left Singapore to patrol the coast of North Borneo and Sarawak, calling at Jesselton (Kota Kinabalu), after which she returned briefly to Singapore before setting course for Hong Kong, where she arrived on 4 September. The destroyer's seven days alongside Hong Kong Dockyard's North Wall were interrupted on 5 September when she had to put to sea for 48 hours to ride out the tail-end of a typhoon. On 11 September she left the colony for the port of Sandakan on the northern coast of North Borneo, where she was acting as guardship on 16 September 1963, the day that the Federation of Malaysia came into being. Next day she left Sandakan to return to Singapore, carrying out routine manoeuvres with *Loch Fada*, *Cambrian*, *Vendetta* and *Otago* en route.

During October *Duchess* visited Manila before returning to patrol the northern coast of North Borneo, calling at Kuching where she embarked 77 officers and men of the Royal Malaya Regiment who were transferring to the minesweeper *Woolaston*. Returning to Singapore at the end of the month, it was 7 November before she sailed again, this time in company with *Barrosa* to the local exercise areas in the South China Sea. That evening she was ordered to Singapore's south coast where, off the Horseburgh Light, the 9,500-ton British merchantman *Woodburn* had run aground. At just after midnight the stranded vessel was located by searchlight, and at 0230 the tug *Nimble* passed tow ropes from *Duchess* to the *Woodburn*. Unfortunately, despite her best efforts, the destroyer was unable to free her, but she stood by her all day until 1740 when *Nimble* took over the salvage rôle. *Duchess* then returned to the South China Sea and anchored off Pulau Tioman where, for four days, the ship's company were able to enjoy swimming and banyan parties. Later in the month

*Duchess* made another visit to Hong Kong before returning to the Singapore exercise areas and 'Exercise Full Bore', during which she acted as planeguard to *Victorious*. The exercise continued well into December, but weekend breaks at Pulau Tioman provided some light relief. On 23 December *Duchess* returned to Singapore Naval Base to undergo a seven-week assisted maintenance period which was expected to take the destroyer through to June 1964, when she was scheduled to recommission at Singapore.

On Monday 10 February 1964, *Duchess* left the naval base to carry out post-refit trials, and next morning returned to Singapore where she embarked 140 troops of the 1/6th Gurkhas. She sailed for a fast passage to the mouth of the Sarawak River, where the men were transferred to the minesweeper *Fiskerton*. Meanwhile, during the evening of Monday 10 February, during exercises off New South Wales, the Australian Navy's aircraft carrier *Melbourne* collided with HMAS *Voyager*, one of their Daring-class destroyers which was acting as planeguard. The force of the collision cut the destroyer in two and she sank with the loss of 82 officers and men[3]. Initially this appalling accident did not affect *Duchess*' itinerary, and after leaving the Sarawak River during the afternoon of 12 February she set course towards Hong Kong for an 11-day break alongside the colony's dockyard.

Within days of the *Melbourne/Voyager* accident, however, both the British and American Governments had offered to replace the lost Australian destroyer, and the British Government considered it a matter of prestige that a Royal Navy vessel should be accepted. In a report dated 13 February 1964 the Admiralty decided that either *Defender* or *Duchess* should be offered and, as the former was just completing a long refit after which it was intended that she would be held in operational reserve, and the latter was already in the Far East, *Duchess* quickly emerged as the favourite. The official report states: 'The *Duchess* is planned to refit and recommission in Singapore in June 1964. If instead she were to be steamed to Australia and there taken over for a refit, there would be virtually no operational penalty for us. We should be saved the cost of refitting the ship in Singapore and the Australians might well be glad of the opportunity of including such modifications as they wish to suit her for service in the RAN.' The formal offer to the Australian Government for the loan of *Duchess* was made on 18 February and it was accepted seven days later when Sir Robert Menzies, the Prime Minister, announced the terms in the House of Representatives. Initially *Duchess* was to be loaned to the Australian Navy for a period of four years, with no charge for the ship herself. The RAN was, however, to accept responsibility for running costs, stores and refits, so that there would be no extra cost to the Royal Navy.

Meanwhile, on 27 February *Duchess* left Hong Kong to return to Singapore, and her final weeks with the Royal Navy were spent exercising with *Centaur*, *Barrosa*, *Lincoln* and the submarine *Alliance* in the South China Sea. On 9 March she returned to Singapore to undergo a final maintenance period prior to leaving for Australia. On 2 April the Flag Officer, Second-in-Command, Far East Station, Vice-Admiral J. P. Scratchard, made a final inspection of his old ship and later that week the first Royal Australian Navy officers joined her. At 0930 on 6 April, *Duchess* left Singapore Naval Base for Darwin, sailing via the Flores and Timor Seas, and arriving alongside Stokes Hill Wharf six days later. Next day she continued her passage to Sydney via Townsville, arriving alongside the former's prestigious Overseas Passenger Terminal beneath the Harbour Bridge, a berth usually reserved for the P&O passenger liners, at 1330 on 19 April. Half an hour later the handover ceremony took place in the ship's wardroom, with Mr L. H. Bury, the Minister for the Navy, Vice-Admiral Sir W. H. Harrington, the Chief of the Australian Naval Staff, the British High Commissioner and other dignitaries in attendance. Later in the month she steamed round to Williamstown Naval Yard at

[3] Readers interested in the *Melbourne/Voyager* accident should read *Where Fate Calls*, by Michael W. Hudson, published by Hodder & Stoughton, 1992.

Duchess, *seen here with* Crossbow, Diamond *and* Battleaxe. *(MoD/Crown Copyright)*

Melbourne, and in May 1964 the handover was completed.

In the event *Duchess* never returned to the Royal Navy, as in October 1967 the four-year loan was extended to 1972, and eventually she was acquired permanently by the Royal Australian Navy. During her service she spent a great deal of time in South-East Asia meeting and exercising regularly with Royal Navy units. In 1977 she was reduced to the role of training ship and finally, in June 1980, she was towed to Taiwan for demolition.

# HMS *Duchess*
## Commanding Officers

| Name: | Date Appointed: |
|---|---|
| Captain H. R. Law OBE DSC RN | 1 September 1952 |
| Captain D. G. Goodwin DSC RN | 6 April 1954 |
| Captain N. H. G. Austen DSO RN | 21 February 1956 |
| Captain J. P. Scratchard DSC RN | 27 August 1957 |
| Captain E. A. S. Bailey MBE DSC RN | 15 August 1960 |
| Captain J. Bitmead DSO RN | 2 January 1963 |

## Battle Honours

| Portland 1653 | Gabbard 1653 |
|---|---|
| Scheveningen 1653 | Barfleur 1692 |

# Part Four

# HMS DEFENDER

## December 1952 - May 1972

*Defender on the stocks shortly before launching from the shipyard of Alexander Stephen & Sons, Linthouse, Glasgow.*
*(University of Glasgow, UCS/16/22/7)*

The fourth ship of the Daring class to be completed was HMS *Defender* however, when the order went to the Clyde shipbuilders Alexander Stephen & Sons, the name *Dogstar* was originally chosen. At the end of the Second World War the cancellation of four of the proposed Darings led to the renamings. In June 1946, almost three years before work began, the name *Defender* was given to the Alexander Stephen contract. The first keel plates were laid on 22 March 1949 and 16 months later, on Thursday 28 July 1950, *Defender*

was launched by Lady Amy Bilsland, the wife of the Governor of the Bank of Scotland. The first key naval personnel were drafted to the ship in October 1951, and on 7 August 1952 *Defender*'s first commanding officer, Captain R. F. T. Stannard OBE RN, was appointed to the ship.

By the start of December 1952 the final fitting out of *Defender* had been completed and on 3 December the main body of the commissioning draft arrived at the shipyard to join the ship. Later that day *Defender* was commissioned, and two days

*On 27 July 1950* Defender *was launched into the waters of the River Clyde at Linthouse, Glasgow.*
*(University of Glasgow, UCS/16/22/8)*

later slipped her moorings and left Shieldhall Wharf to steam down the River Clyde. Two and a half hours later, off Greenock, a naval trials party was embarked and *Defender* got under way to be put through her paces in the Firth of Clyde. The trials ended with a series of runs at full power over the Skelmorlie measured mile and, at 1730, having concluded the initial trials satisfactorily, she stopped just off Cumbrae Island where she was officially accepted into naval service and the White Ensign was hoisted for the first time. That evening the ship anchored off Greenock and a tug came alongside to disembark shipyard workers and the trials party.

*Defender* remained in the Firth of Clyde until 14 December, when she set course for Chatham, arriving in the dockyard's No.3 basin during the afternoon of 16 December. On 23 January 1953, with the ship's company having taken seasonal leave, *Defender* steamed round to Spithead and Portland to continue her trials and to begin her work-up, remaining in the area until the first week of March. She returned to Chatham for essential maintenance. In late April she returned to Portland, and on 9 June anchored at Spithead for the Coronation Fleet Review. Seven days later, with the Review over, and in company with her sisters *Decoy*, *Diamond* and *Duchess*, she left Spithead and set course for Gibraltar on the first stage of her passage to the Far East, where she would arrive for the final weeks of the Korean War.

During the weekend of 28 and 29 June she made her southbound transit of the Suez Canal and after stopping at Aden for 24 hours, she steamed east by way of Trincomalee and arrived at the Singapore Naval Base on 16 July, where she officially joined the Far East Station. In mid-July 1953, although there were signs that the North Korean Government was becoming more amenable to a ceasefire, the Korean war still raged, and on 20 July *Defender* sailed for Hong Kong and the Japanese port of Sasebo, which was the Royal Navy's forward operating base. However, on 27 July, as *Defender* lay alongside the West Arm of Hong Kong Dockyard's Victoria Basin, the Korean War came to an abrupt end with the signing of a truce at Panmunjon. At the time it was not known if the truce would last, and three days later *Defender* sailed for Sasebo where she arrived on 2 August. With active operations over, *Defender* was ordered to join *Birmingham* and HMCS *Iroquois* to patrol off the island of Paengyong, just south of the 38th Parallel. *Defender* carried out several patrols in this area, on one occasion accompanying *Ocean*. These were some of the last patrols carried out by the Royal Navy in the Korean War, and on 1 October the

destroyer put in to the US Navy's Japanese base at Yokosuka. The visit was to prepare for joint RN/USN exercises in the waters off Okinawa which began three days later. During the eight days of exercises *Defender* operated with a US Navy Task Group, and when concluded she put into the US base at Buckner Bay, Okinawa, for what should have been a five-day visit.

At 1500 on 16 October, just as the first liberty men were waiting to go ashore, a signal was received ordering *Defender* to put to sea to patrol the Formosa Strait (Taiwan Strait) as it was thought that Communist Chinese forces were about to invade the Nationalist Chinese-held island. On board *Defender* all leave was immediately cancelled and that evening she sailed to begin the patrol, which lasted for five days and ended at Hong Kong on 21 October. *Defender* remained at Hong Kong until the second week of December when she undertook a week of day-running exercises. Her

Christmas break lasted just five days before, on 27 December, she sailed for more patrols of the Formosa Strait. In the third week of January 1954, with no Chinese invasion having materialised, she returned to Sasebo to join *Newcastle* for a final six-day patrol of Korea's west coast. Returning via Kure *Defender* returned to Hong Kong, from where on 14 February she sailed for Cap St Jacques (now Vung Tau) at the mouth of the Saigon River for six days of joint French, US and British exercises off the coast of what was still French Indo-China[1].

Also taking part were *Concord*, *Cossack*, *Morecambe Bay* and *Mounts Bay*, and on 21 February the combined fleet anchored in the Saigon River for the wash-up. Next day *Defender* and the other Royal Navy units sailed for Singapore.

Between 1948 and 1960 Britain was involved in a long-drawn-out insurgency campaign in Malaya which became known as the 'Emergency', against what were mainly Chinese Communist guerrillas.

*Defender in July 1953 as she sailed to join the Far East Fleet.*
*(Portsmouth Royal Naval Museum)*

---

[1] The decisive Battle of Dien Bien Phu in the Vietnamese War of Independence was about to begin.

As Malaya was populated chiefly by Muslim Malays the insurgents never had popular support in Malaya, and fortunately for Britain the campaign was nowhere near the scale of resistance to French colonial rule, and later the American occupation of Indo-China/Vietnam, but for over ten years the Malayan Emergency proved to be a drain on manpower and financial resources, and it was only finally overcome after Britain promised Independence to Malaya. In early 1954 British forces had begun a series of operations designed to eliminate guerrilla forces in different areas of the Malay Peninsular. One such operation was opened in the eastern part of the State of Johore. On Monday 8 March *Defender* was ordered to play her part in the operation, and so at 0800 she left the naval base to steam down the Johore Strait as usual. However, after passing the island of Pulau Ubin, instead of turning into the Strait of Singapore and out into the open sea, she turned north into the Johore River, before steaming slowly for nine miles up an uncharted stretch of the river as far as Telok Sengat where she anchored. From this position her main 4.5-inch guns fired over 100 rounds at designated insurgent targets in the jungle, some nine

miles away. By 1600 she had manoeuvred back downriver and returned to the naval base, after what has been described as a 'unique feat of navigation'. Later in March *Defender* made a series of goodwill visits to ports on the Malay Peninsular. Starting at Georgetown, Penang, she moved down the coast to Port Swettenham (Port Kelang) and Malacca, before moving round to the east coast and north to Kuala Trengganu, and for some relaxation, the offshore islands of Pulau Redang and Tioman - ideal locations for bathing and banyan parties. By the end of April *Defender* was back at Singapore and preparing to steam back to Japanese and Korean waters for major exercises with the US Navy's Seventh Fleet. In company with *Birmingham*, *Newfoundland*, *Charity*, *Consort* and *Contest*, *Defender* left Singapore on 6 May to steam to Yokosuka, via Hong Kong and Kure. The exercises began on 31 May and included a beach landing off Okinawa as well as a night action in the Tsushima Strait. *Defender*'s part in the manoeuvres ended in mid-June at Hong Kong where she prepared for FO2's harbour and sea inspections. On 20 July the destroyer went into dry dock in Hong Kong at the start of a two-month refit, during which time

Defender *at Hong Kong in January 1954.*                    *(Author's Collection)*

the ship's company moved into shore accommodation in the dockyard and in the nearby China Fleet Club. During this period the ship received a high-level VIP visit from the First Lord of the Admiralty and government ministers who inspected the forward seamen's messdecks. Then on 29 September, with the ship's company back on board, the destroyer began two days of post-refit trials. Finally, on Saturday 2 October she left the Far East Station to begin her passage home via the Pacific and Australia.

*Defender*'s passage into the Pacific, in the form of a convoy escort exercise, was made in company with *Birmingham*, *Cockade*, *Comus*, *Concord*, and the Australian units *Quadrant*, *Tobruk*, *Hawkesbury* and *Anzac*. On 12 October they arrived in the old wartime anchorage of Seeadler Harbour, Manus, and for eight days they carried out a series of training exercises. On 20 October, with *Tobruk*, *Defender* left Seeadler Harbour and set course for Sydney where she secured alongside a berth at Garden Island seven days later. *Defender*'s stay in Sydney was limited to just three days after which she moved on to Melbourne and Fremantle, leaving the latter on 18 November to make a nine-day passage across the Indian Ocean to Colombo. Pausing just long enough to embark fuel and stores she steamed west to Aden, and by 2245 on 8 December had cleared Port Said and set course for Malta. After leaving Grand Harbour during the forenoon of 13 December *Defender* made a fast, non-stop passage to Chatham, where she arrived at 1000 on 20 December, just in time for Christmas.

Although she had completed 18 months' foreign service her first commission was not yet over, and on 2 February 1955 she left Chatham to carry out a short work-up at Portland before sailing back to Gibraltar and the Mediterranean, where she joined a force which included *Albion*, *Centaur*, *Apollo*, *Glasgow*, *Battleaxe*, *Barfleur*, *Daring* and *Delight*, for 'Exercise Sea Lance'. This major exercise involved an amphibious landing of Royal Marines and a simulated nuclear explosion. For relaxation *Defender* then spent six days at Calvi on the island of Corsica. The exercise ended at Malta on 15 March and seven days later, with the rest of the fleet, she left Grand Harbour to act as escort to the royal yacht *Britannia* on her passage to Gibraltar. This was the last operational duty of the commission and on 27 March, with *Delight*, she left Gibraltar bound for Chatham, arriving off Sheerness on the last day of the month. Next morning she moved up the Medway and by 0815 she was secured alongside in Chatham Dockyard where she paid off into dockyard hands to undergo a two and a half month refit.

On Monday 13 June *Defender*'s new commanding officer, Captain M. L. Hardie DSC RN, joined the ship and at 0900 the next day he officially took command. Just over an hour later the new ship's company marched from the barracks to the ship, and at noon *Defender* was recommissioned. On 20 June, she moved to a buoy off Sheerness, and three days later, having embarked a Royal Marines Band for the passage to Malta, she sailed back to the Mediterranean.

*Defender* arrived in Grand Harbour on 4 July and for the first seven weeks of the deployment she was day running from Malta. During this period she carried out in-flight trials with helicopters embarking and disembarking personnel and stores to and from her quarterdeck. For the Royal Navy this was a new way to perform transfers between ships, or between ship and shore, and the trials carried out by *Defender* would illustrate the versatility of helicopters and their suitability for carrying out naval operations; by the late 1950s planners were looking to build flight decks on future frigates and destroyers, something which today is taken for granted. On 27 August *Defender* landed her Royal Marines Band at Messina, before returning to Maltese waters to carry out exercises with *Sheffield* (flag C-in-C Mediterranean), *Delight* and *Surprise*. The exercises ended on 1 September when the squadron put into Venice for a seven-day courtesy visit. For *Defender* this was followed by a visit to Ancona and exercises with the French Navy off Toulon. At the end of September, in company with *Delight*, she called at Cagliari and Naples and, in early October, she underwent FO2's harbour and sea inspections.

Later in the month she carried out exercises with *Birmingham* and on 19 October, following her return to Grand Harbour, began a 12-week refit during which the ship's company moved to shore accommodation at Ricasoli Barracks, some distance from No.4 dry dock, which is where *Defender* spent most of the refit.

On 12 January 1956, with everyone back on board, *Defender* was once again ready for sea, and that afternoon sailed for a series of post-refit trials and training exercises with *Birmingham* and the submarine *Sea Devil*. In February , with the withdrawal of British troops from the Suez Canal Zone well under way, (under the terms of the 1954 Anglo/Egyptian Agreement this had to be completed by 10 June 1956) *Defender* put into Port Said to act as guardship and to cover the arrivals and departures of troop transports. On 18 February she left Port Said to steam north to Britain's main colonial trouble spot in the Mediterranean, the island of Cyprus, where she began her first patrol of the coastline in the continuous operation to prevent arms and ammunition being smuggled in from Greece. Later in the month she returned briefly to Port Said to cover the embarkation of troops and the departure of another troop transport, before returning once again to the coast of Cyprus for another patrol. On 13 March she returned to Grand Harbour, and two days later she sailed for home, arriving in Chatham on 26 March.

*Defender* remained alongside at Chatham throughout April, while the ship's company took their seasonal leave, and in early May she sailed from the Medway to rendezvous with *Delight* and to make a short visit to the French naval base at Brest, before steaming north by way of Scotland's west coast to Invergordon. The two ships arrived in the Moray Firth on 12 May where they were joined by other units of the Sixth Destroyer Squadron, including *Battleaxe*, *Comet*, *Contest* and *Scorpion*. There then followed two weeks of squadron training exercises, and a visit from the First Sea Lord, Admiral of the Fleet Lord Mountbatten. For *Defender* and *Delight* the exercises concluded with a weekend visit to Hartlepool, following which the

destroyers left Tees Bay during the forenoon of 4 June. An hour later they rendezvoused in the North Sea with the Canadian destroyer HMCS *St Laurent* and the royal yacht *Britannia*, the latter having sailed from Teesport with the Queen and Duke of Edinburgh for a three-day State Visit to Sweden. As they steamed north, low grey clouds gave way to gales and squalls of heavy rain and the four ships ploughed their way through an angry Baltic Sea to arrive in Stockholm during the forenoon of 8 June, where they were escorted into harbour by Swedish destroyers. The royal visit coincided with the city's hosting of the 16th Olympic Equestrian Games, and once the State duties were over the royal visitors stayed on in a private capacity to watch some of the equestrian events, flying back to London on 18 June, which meant that *Britannia* did not require the destroyer escort for her return passage. *Defender* and *Delight* left Stockholm on Monday 18 June and steamed to the German naval base at Kiel before going their separate ways on 25 June, with *Delight* returning to Devonport via the Kiel Canal and *Defender* making the short passage to Copenhagen where she joined the depot ship *Tyne*, which was flying the flag of the C-in-C Home Fleet who, during the visit, inspected *Defender*'s messdecks. From Copenhagen the destroyer steamed into the North Sea to carry out a convoy exercise with *Glasgow*, before heading south to Dover where she arrived alongside the Prince of Wales Pier during the forenoon of 13 July.

*Defender* had been chosen to carry King Faisal of Iraq across the Channel at the start of his two-day State Visit to London. Faisal's dynasty had been created by the British authorities under the ill-fated Mandate of the inter-war years but, in the event, his hold on Iraq would last only two more years before he and his family would be murdered in a bloody nationalist coup. Crossing the Strait of Dover on 15 July, *Defender* anchored off Ostend and the following morning moved into harbour and alongside where, at 0800, King Faisal and his entourage, together with the Duke of Gloucester, embarked. As soon as they were safely on board *Defender* set sail and, at 1230, with HM Ships *Carron*,

*Cavendish* and *Vigilant* as escorts, and as a fly-past of RAF Shackleton aircraft roared overhead, *Defender* entered Dover Harbour where the VIP guests boarded a train to London's Victoria Station. *Defender* then returned to Chatham, disembarking her Royal Marines Band at Margate en route, and by the afternoon of 27 July had begun a nine-week dockyard-assisted maintenance period. The day before, however, while *Defender* had been de-ammunitioning, President Nasser of Egypt proclaimed his Government's nationalisation of the Suez Canal Company. It was a display of Arab nationalism which the British Government would not easily come to terms with.

During the whole of August and for most of September, as *Defender* lay in No 9 dry dock at Chatham, the political negotiations over the future ownership of the Suez Canal dragged on, seemingly endlessly. At the same time, however, military preparations for an invasion of Egypt were taking shape, and when *Defender* sailed on 29 September she steamed north to Invergordon to begin a two and a half week period of intensive training in the North Sea. This ended on Friday 19 October with a five-day visit to Hamburg, and when she left Germany she was bound for Gibraltar and Malta. After a fast passage south, at 0130 on 29 October *Defender* paused off Gibraltar for just long enough to embark an extra diving team consisting of two officers and 19 ratings, and their equipment, before resuming her passage to Malta. She arrived in Grand Harbour at 0620 on Wednesday 31 October, and after a hectic few hours spent refuelling, storing and ammunitioning, she sailed at 1530 the same afternoon to join the Anglo-French invasion force bound for Port Said. During the brief Suez campaign *Defender* acted as planeguard to *Albion* and *Bulwark* as they carried out intensive flying operations. On 17 November, however, with the invasion having been stopped and a United Nations force about to take over temporarily until the Egyptian authorities once again took control of Port Said and

Defender *at Hamburg on 19 October 1956.*

*(Ken Kelly)*

the Suez Canal, all that remained, for the second time within the space of six months, was for British troops to be withdrawn from Egypt. By that time *Defender* was at anchor outside Port Said Harbour and conditions were relaxed enough for 'Hands to Bathe' to be piped during the afternoon watches. On 18 November, having disembarked her extra divers to *Tyne*, *Defender* sailed for Malta. It was the end of her participation in the Suez campaign.

She arrived in Grand Harbour on 24 November, and, nine days later, there was a change of command when Captain P. G. Sharp DSC RN relieved Captain Hardie. During the following eight weeks *Defender* operated from Malta, mainly day running and carrying out anti-submarine training with *Tudor*. In January 1957 she again acted as plane-guard to *Albion*, but at the end of the month, in company with *Jamaica*, she visited Naples and Taranto. On 6 February, after leaving the Italian naval base, the destroyer made the passage to Cyprus to take her turn on the patrol which was still attempting to enforce an arms blockade of the island. For almost seven weeks *Defender* plied the coast of Cyprus, and on a daily basis stopped and searched numerous small boats, fishing vessels and merchant ships. On occasions she would anchor off Dhekalia, but shore leave was confined to organised sports parties at nearby British bases. Refuelling was usually carried out at Dhekalia, whilst alongside the anchored RFA *Wave Knight*. On 27 March *Defender* left Cyprus to make a visit to Palermo, before returning to Malta to secure alongside Grand Harbour's Canteen Wharf to begin a three-month refit.

On 11 July *Defender* left Grand Harbour to carry out her post-refit trials, and at the end of the month she carried out training exercises with *Kenya* and *Tudor*. These exercises continued into August, with some relaxation coming in the form of the Fleet Regatta at Augusta. On 27 August, in company with *Dainty*, *Defender* made an eight-day visit to Naples and on leaving the Italian city she set course for home, calling at Marseilles and Gibraltar en route. At the time an outbreak of 'Asian' influenza was sweeping across Europe, and large numbers of

*Defender*'s ship's company fell victim to the illness. So serious was the outbreak that at 1200 on 31 August both *Defender* and *Dainty* were ordered to cut short their visit to Marseilles and proceed to Gibraltar. Two days later they secured to buoys in Gibraltar Harbour, and were immediately placed in quarantine. For 19 days the outbreak of flu delayed the return home, and the sickbay saw a steady stream of personnel being admitted to the Military Hospital in Gibraltar. One unfortunate rating in *Dainty* died from the disease, but finally, during the forenoon of 21 September, the quarantine restrictions were lifted and five days after that the two destroyers sailed for their home ports. *Defender* arrived in Chatham on 1 October, where the ship's company was able to take some belated leave.

Although *Defender*'s second commission was almost over there remained one final duty for the ship, and on 31 October she left Chatham to rendezvous with *Daring*, *Dainty* and *Delight* to take part in the NATO exercise code-named 'Sharpsquall', which took place in the North Sea and the North Atlantic. In addition to the three Darings, also taking part were *Eagle*, *Albion*, *Bulwark*, *Gambia*, *Sheffield*, *Apollo*, *Hardy*, *Salisbury*, *Scarborough*, *Torquay* and the submarine *Springer*, all commanded by the C-in-C Home Fleet, Admiral Sir John Eccles, in *Maidstone*. The manoeuvres took the fleet round the north of Scotland and into the Atlantic, and *Defender* made short visits to Rosyth, Portree on the Isle of Skye, and Londonderry. On 6 December, after steaming at full speed down the Irish Sea, *Defender* made her way up Channel to arrive off Sheerness two days later, where she was de-ammunitioned. Next day she steamed up the Medway and into Chatham Dockyard where she secured alongside *Delight*. In February 1958 the ship's company was reduced to a refit complement, and it would be early 1959 before she sailed again.

During her ten months in dockyard hands some modernisation work was carried out on *Defender* which, like that of her sisters, provided for a limited amount of additional accommodation. On 30 December 1958 the destroyer's new commanding

*On 5 May 1959* Defender *arrived at Lazzaretto Creek, Malta, whre she joined the Mediterranean Fleet.* (Author's Collection)

officer, Captain G. H. Carew-Hunt RN, was appointed to the ship, and in early 1959 the main body of the ship's company joined from the Royal Naval Barracks. On Thursday 15 January *Defender* left Chatham to undergo 24 hours of trials, and by the evening of the next day she was back alongside at Chatham Dockyard. Four days later, at 1415 on 20 January, the recommissioning service was held at the barracks, and final preparations were made to get the ship ready for sea and active operational service once again.

*Defender* left Chatham on 27 January to begin her trials in the North Sea, and in early February she steamed round to Portland to undergo her work-up. This lasted for just over a month until 12 March when the destroyer secured alongside at Portsmouth. Four days later she steamed north to the Firth of Clyde from where, with *Exmouth*, *Paladin* and *Pellew*, she took part in anti-submarine training. At the end of March *Defender* returned to Chatham to give leave, but by mid-April she was back at Portland. At the end of the month, however, she sailed for the Mediterranean, calling briefly at Gibraltar and arriving at Malta's Lazzaretto

Creek on 5 May, to secure alongside *Ausonia*. During the remainder of the month *Defender* operated in local waters off Malta, but at the end of May she returned to the coast of Cyprus to begin a patrol of the island's coastline. This time, however, the political situation was very different from that which had existed during her 1957 patrol, for in February 1959 Britain had finally agreed to grant Independence to Cyprus. The Greek-Cypriot leader Archbishop Makarios had returned to the island from exile to a rapturous welcome from the Greek population, and his return brought the long-running insurgency to an end. However, the Royal Navy would continue the arms blockade until the end of 1959 and *Defender* would be one of the last ships to be employed in that rôle. Since conditions were now more relaxed than they had been previously, while at anchor off Limassol shore leave was granted to the ship's company.

On 13 June, in company with *Birmingham*, the destroyer left Limassol to return to Grand Harbour, where she rendezvoused with *Armada* to embark the First Sea Lord by light jackstay and make a ceremonial entry into Sliema Creek, where the VIP

visitor disembarked. Four days later *Defender* took part in the NATO exercise 'Whitebait', which also involved *Birmingham* and units of the First and Third Destroyer Squadrons, together with Italian and US Navy units. The exercise ended in late June, and in early July *Defender*, *Birmingham*, *Dainty*, *Delight* and *Blackpool* set course for the Dardanelles and a four-day visit to Istanbul. During August and September there were visits to Port Vendres in the south of France, close to the Spanish border, Sardinia, Mudros, Salonika and Venice. In mid-September she took part in training exercises with *Belfast*, and in October visited Tunis. November saw her carry out her final 17-day patrol off Cyprus, and this ended with a visit to Naples before taking part in exercises off Malta, with *Tiger*, *Eastbourne*, *Battleaxe* and *Zest*. On 11 December *Defender* secured alongside Grand Harbour's Boiler House Wharf to begin a nine and a half-week

assisted maintenance period.

On 17 February 1960 *Defender* put to sea again, and her final weeks on the Mediterranean Station were spent mainly in local waters around Malta, with a short visit to the Libyan port of Tripoli. However, during this period she began to experience problems with her port main engine, and when she left Malta on 14 March to return to Chatham her port shaft was left trailing and she made the passage to Gibraltar on one engine. After six days of repairs at Gibraltar, on 24 March she left for Chatham, arriving off the Great Nore Lightship during the evening of 27 March. Next day she made the short passage to the Medway and upriver to Chatham Dockyard.

*Defender* remained at Chatham undergoing repairs and maintenance for two months, and when she sailed again on 8 June it was to set course for Invergordon. Throughout the remainder of the

*Defender* keeping station as an aircraft carrier takes on more fuel.
*(Syd Goodman Collection)*

month she acted as planeguard to *Centaur* during manoeuvres which included 'Exercise Fairwind V', an air defence exercise in northern waters. Following this she visited Bergen, before steaming north to Icelandic waters and fishery protection duties. For almost two years Britain and Iceland had been locked in a dispute over the limits of the latter's territorial waters, and on occasions Icelandic gunboats had fired at British trawlers in an effort to drive them from their newly claimed 12-mile limit. During *Defender*'s patrol there were no such incidents, and the destroyer acted as 'nursemaid' to the British trawlers in the area. On one occasion a sick crew member from the trawler *Weland* was hauled across to *Defender* on a liferaft for treatment in the destroyer's sickbay. On 30 July the destroyer's first Icelandic patrol ended and she set course for Chatham, arriving two days later to give seasonal leave.

On 30 August *Defender* left Chatham to rendezvous with *Hermes*, to whom she acted as planeguard during training exercises off Scotland's east coast as the carrier prepared for 'Exercise Swordthrust', described as a 'supreme test of the country's air defence organisation'. Also taking part were *Ark Royal, Gambia, Daring, Saintes, Tyne* and the submarine *Trenchant*. During the course of the manoeuvres *Defender* stayed close to *Hermes* as the fleet steamed north into the Arctic. On 29 September, however, *Defender* was detached to steam south for Rosyth. After five days in the Firth of Forth she returned to Icelandic waters to carry out her second Icelandic patrol where, once again, she played 'nursemaid' to the fishing fleet, making regular liferaft transfers of mail and occasionally transferring sick men from the trawlers for treatment in her sickbay. In turn the trawlers kept *Defender* supplied with fresh fish, while fuel, mail and stores were delivered by RFA *Wave Ruler*. There were sighs of relief, however, when at 0800 on 21 October *Daring* relieved *Defender* of her patrol duties and the latter steamed south for Portsmouth, arriving alongside Fountain Lake Jetty three days later.

*Defender*'s third commission was coming to an end, but before she was laid up in Reserve she accompanied *Gambia* on visits to Aberdeen, Hamburg and Rotterdam. These were followed by fleet manoeuvres in the South-Western Approaches with *Gambia, Daring, Blackpool* and *Zest*, and a final four-day visit to the French naval base at Brest. On Saturday 3 December the destroyer left Brest and set course for Sheerness, where she arrived the next evening to carry out the process of de-ammunitioning. On 6 December she steamed upriver to Chatham and on 13 December Captain Carew-Hunt left the ship. At 1045 next day the ship's company moved ashore to the Royal Naval Barracks, and that afternoon *Defender* was paid off into 'care and maintenance'. It would be three long years before she put to sea again.

For over three years *Defender* lay in Reserve at Chatham, and at one stage there were rumours that if she left the base it would only be under tow to the scrapyard. In the event these were to prove unfounded and in late 1963 she was taken in hand by the dockyard to undergo a refit. Some consideration was given to fitting her with Seacat anti-aircraft missiles, but this plan was dropped and very little in the way of modernisation work was carried out. With the commissioning of the first four County-class destroyers, *Devonshire, Hampshire, Kent* and *London*, it was apparent that the Darings had been downgraded from their original classification as 'Daring-class' ships, something between a destroyer and a light cruiser, and were now classified as destroyers, with their commanding officers no longer substantive Captains. It was a clear indication that their rôle in the fleet was downgraded. On 9 December 1963 *Defender*'s new CO, Commander J. R. Alston, was appointed to the ship, and in early January 1964 a steaming crew joined from the Royal Naval Barracks. Finally, on 13 January 1964, after her long lay-up, the ship was brought to immediate notice for steam.

At 1700 on 23 January *Defender* left Chatham Dockyard to undergo four days of machinery trials in the North Sea, but less than 24 hours later a serious leak in A engine room's main superheated steam pipe caused an emergency shut down of all

machinery and the evacuation of the engine room itself. The ship was immediately sent to anchor and after four hours the engineers were able to isolate the offending pipe, which meant the ship could limp back to Sheerness for repairs. On 26 January she resumed her trials and, after successfully steaming at full power for most of a forenoon, returned to Chatham Dockyard where the temporary ship's company moved back to barracks and the ship herself returned to dockyard hands.

It was 1 May 1964 before naval personnel moved back on board again to prepare the ship for sea service, but *Defender* remained firmly alongside until 10 July, when she left Chatham to carry out two months of trials and work-up. During July she operated from Portsmouth, but in August she steamed west to Portland and Devonport. In mid-August she left Plymouth Sound for Gibraltar to take part in 'Exercise Rockhaul', before returning to Chatham by way of Lisbon. On 28 August *Defender* arrived off Sheerness where she embarked families of the ship's company for the final passage up the River Medway to Chatham Dockyard where she was laid up again.

On 12 January 1965 *Defender* was shifted and secured alongside *Diamond*, which had just completed a two-year commission, and two days later *Diamond*'s ship's company marched to the Royal Naval Barracks where they recommissioned *Defender* under the command of Commander J. R. S. Gerard-Pearse RN, who had been appointed a week earlier. At 1130 that day the Ensign and Jack were lowered in *Diamond* and hoisted in *Defender*. All that remained was for the ship's company to move their kit and equipment from *Diamond* to *Defender*.

Although she had recommissioned, *Defender* remained at Chatham Dockyard undergoing essential refit work and it was 9 April 1964 before the Admiral Superintendent carried out his final inspection of the ship. The destroyer then sailed on 20 April to carry out a long series of trials, and to undergo her work-up at Portland. During her two months at the Dorset base it seemed the long lay-up had taken its toll, for she spent almost two weeks

undergoing machinery repairs. Finally, however, in early July she steamed north to the Firth of Clyde where, with *Dundas* and *Opossum*, she carried out anti-submarine exercises. On 23 August, having given leave at Chatham, *Defender* held a 'Families Day', with relatives and friends embarking at Folly Point to make the eight-hour passage to Portsmouth where they were disembarked. Next day, at 1400, the destroyer sailed via Gibraltar to Malta and the Mediterranean Station.

Arriving off Malta in early September *Defender* joined the aircraft carrier *Eagle* and acted as her planeguard during flying operations off the island. In mid-August, together with *Eagle*, *Dainty*, *Londonderry* and *Lowestoft*, she took part in the NATO exercise 'Emerald Green', but *Defender* continued to suffer major mechanical breakdowns and three times during the space of 24 hours she was brought to a stop by power failures. The final part of the exercise, which took place during the last week of September, involved convoy escort duties after which *Defender* returned to Grand Harbour to undergo dockyard repairs to her main propulsion machinery. In October the destroyer carried out anti-submarine exercises with *Rhyl*, *Naiad* and the French destroyer *Casabianca*, which ended with a five-day visit to Naples. In November and December *Defender* visited Livorno, Piraeus and Beirut, before returning to Grand Harbour where she spent Christmas and New Year.

In early January 1965 *Defender* visited the Greek island of Milos, before beginning several weeks of day running from Grand Harbour. In early March she left Malta to return home by way of Gibraltar, and once at Chatham Dockyard spent three weeks undergoing dockyard-assisted maintenance. It was mid-April when *Defender* sailed again, and after ammunitioning at Portsmouth she rendezvoused with *Dainty* to carry out joint training exercises with units of the Federal German Navy, after which she visited Kiel and Oslo. Leaving Norway on 3 May *Defender* steamed south to Portsmouth where she spent another 18 days undergoing essential engine repairs. On 23 May, in company with *Tiger*, *Dainty*, *Lowestoft* and *Rhyl*, *Defender* left

Portsmouth to carry out exercises in the North Sea, but within 24 hours of leaving harbour the destroyer's engines were again causing trouble and she returned to Chatham for yet more repairs. Finally, during the evening of 28 May *Defender* was able to leave the Medway and steam north to Rosyth to join her sister *Dainty*, and at 1600 on Monday 30 May the two destroyers left the Firth of Forth carrying with them six veterans of the Battle of Jutland - the one and only major encounter between the British and German battlefleets during the four long years of the Great War. Next day, off the Jutland Peninsular, *Defender* and *Dainty* rendezvoused with the Federal German Navy frigates *Karlsruhe* and *Braunschweig*, to conduct a joint ceremony to mark the 50th anniversary of the Battle of Jutland, and to pay tribute to the 9,000 dead of the two navies.

Off the Danish coast *Defender*, *Dainty*, *Karlsruhe* and *Braunschweig* followed roughly the same course as was taken 50 years earlier, on that grey misty evening off the Skagerrak when the two battlefleets met briefly and indecisively, before conducting a short and simple ceremony marked by the placing of wreaths. A signal from the German frigates summed up the mood of those on all four warships: 'It is much more pleasant that we meet today as friends and allies in NATO.' At 1740, with the ceremony over, *Defender* and *Dainty* detached, with the latter making for Newhaven while *Defender* set course for Great Yarmouth where she arrived during the forenoon of 1 June, suffering once again from engine trouble. During the three days off the East Anglian resort, leave to the engine room department was restricted as repairs were made to the main engines, and after returning to Portsmouth the destroyer spent two weeks day running and carrying out high-speed manoeuvres with *Brave Borderer*. Later in the month, with *Dainty*, she steamed north to the Firth of Clyde for anti-submarine exercises with *Thermopylae* and *Opossum*, which ended with a three-day visit to Stonehaven as *Defender* made her way to Rosyth for the annual Home Fleet Assembly.

On 11 July, with *Tiger*, *Lowestoft*, *Rhyl*, *Torquay* and *Wakeful*, *Defender* was involved in joint manoeuvres which took the ships round Scotland's north coast, pausing briefly to bombard the ranges at Cape Wrath, before they split up and went their separate ways. *Defender* paid a 24-hour visit to North Shields before crossing the North Sea to Copenhagen. During the afternoon of 22 July *Defender* arrived off Sheerness to embark families and friends, before steaming up harbour to secure alongside Chatham Dockyard's No.3 basin to begin a five-week maintenance period and to give leave to the ship's company.

The final leg of *Defender*'s commission was to be spent in the Caribbean, and on 30 August she left Chatham, calling at Devonport and Ponta Delgada, and arriving at Bermuda's Ireland Island naval base on 9 September. This first visit to Bermuda was short and on 14 September, after 24 hours alongside a prominent 'flag-showing' berth at Hamilton, she left for the Bahamas and her first patrol of the outlying islands or Cays, and particularly Lobos Cay some 40 miles off the coast of Cuba which was being used as a staging post by unscrupulous 'people smugglers' who were making large sums of money 'assisting' refugees to leave Cuba, often to leave them stranded on the small islands. These long patrols under the hot Caribbean sun were generally tedious duties broken only by short refuelling stops at Freeport, Nassau or the US naval base at Florida's Key West. On one occasion *Defender* refuelled at the US naval base of Guantanamo Bay in Cuba, but no leave was granted and the first break came in the third week of October when the destroyer secured alongside No 1 Pier at Chaguaramas on Trinidad, where maintenance could be carried out.

*Defender* left Trinidad on 2 November to begin a further tour of Caribbean islands, calling at Curacao, Dominica - where she took part in an internal security exercise with a company of Royal Marines - Antigua, San Juan, Montserrat and Bridgetown, Barbados, where she arrived on Sunday 27 November for the island's Independence celebrations. Together with Royal Marines from *Zest*, *Defender*'s Detachment provided a Guard of

Honour for the ceremony which took place on Bridgetown's Savannah, a grass stadium which was usually used for horse racing. Although Barbados had been self-governing since the late 1950s, at midnight on 30 November the island gained full independence. During the forenoon of 1 December the Duke and Duchess of Kent, who had represented the Queen at the ceremony, visited *Defender*. At 1415 the ship sailed for Bermuda where she was scheduled to spend Christmas and arrived alongside the island's naval base during the forenoon of 4 December. Eighteen days later, on 22 December, she moved round the island to a prestigious cruise ship berth at Hamilton where she was due to spend the Christmas holiday, but in the early hours of the next day she was ordered to sea and to proceed with all dispatch to the island of St Vincent, where there was political unrest. Leaving Bermuda at 0800 *Defender* steamed south, but as the situation on St Vincent stabilised she was ordered to the US naval base at San Juan, Puerto Rico, where she arrived at 0730 on Christmas Day. For three days *Defender* remained at four hours' notice for steam, but as the situation on St Vincent remained calm, on 28 December she resumed her original schedule and sailed for the US port of Savannah, which was the highlight of the deployment.

At 0930 on Saturday 31 December *Defender* secured alongside Savannah's Ocean Terminal at the foot of Fahm Street, an ideal spot for liberty men coming and going to and from the city. At midday, with all the official calls over, buses arrived at the ship to take ship's company members to the riverfront near the 'Ships of the Sea' museum where an 'Oyster Roast' had been organised by the city authorities while the Mayor of Savannah and senior civic officials were entertained to lunch on board *Defender*. That afternoon all manner of clubs and organisations, including the nearby Hunter Air Force Base, opened their doors to the destroyer's officers and men. Even the under-age junior ratings were not forgotten as the city's 'Coat of Arms Teenage Club' awarded them honorary membership. It was said that all on board, apart from the duty watchkeepers, saw in the new year of 1966 in style. During the afternoon of New Year's Day the ship was opened to the public, and next day the ship's company gave a party for 40 orphans and underprivileged children from the city. On the final day of the visit the ship's company enjoyed an afternoon barbecue organised by the city's authorities and when *Defender* sailed at 0900 on 4 January 1966 all on board agreed that four days was by no means long enough for a visit to Savannah.

From the southern shores of the USA *Defender* steamed to Freeport and Nassau, where landing parties from the ship were able to assist those from *Zest* who were helping to maintain electricity services during a strike. On 14 January *Defender* began her second Bahamas Patrol, and six days later she rescued one Cuban refugee from the island of Anguilla Cay and landed him at Key West. On 31 January the patrol ended when the destroyer left Nassau to return to Hamilton, Bermuda, where she spent a last weekend before sailing for home.

*Defender* left Bermuda on 6 February to set course for Ponta Delgada, where she refuelled, and during the evening of 14 February she anchored off Spithead. Next forenoon, with her upper decks manned and flying her paying-off pennant, she steamed up harbour to secure alongside Portsmouth's South Railway Jetty. Two days later, however, she sailed for Chatham where she secured alongside the dockyard's No 3 basin. Three days later, on 20 February, the ship's company moved ashore to the Royal Naval Barracks and at 1200 *Defender* was paid off and taken over by the dockyard to undergo a four-month refit.

On the same afternoon that *Defender* paid off, the ship's new commanding officer, Commander G. M. F. Vallings RN, was appointed, but it was 30 June 1967 before the refit was completed and the final inspection took place. On Saturday 1 July *Defender* was recommissioned for the last time, with the ceremony taking place on a warm summer's day, which made for a pleasant family occasion. During the days which followed, the new ship's company prepared the vessel for sea, and on 19 July she began her post-refit trials which continued until the third week of September, during which time it was

said that *Defender* locked in and out of Chatham Dockyard so frequently that she was nearly awarded the 'key of the dockyard'. On 18 August she paid a three-day operational visit to Cherbourg and during the last weekend of that month she took part in Navy Days at Chatham. Two days later, after embarking a Fishery Protection Officer, she put to sea bound for Portland and en route stopped the trawler *Jesus Maria Joseph* so that the Ministry official could inspect the vessel. Shortly afterwards she disembarked her government passenger at Margate, after which she continued her passage to begin three weeks of weapons trials off the south coast, which ended at Portsmouth on 20 September.

At 1315 on 21 September *Defender* left Portsmouth to head north for a four-day visit to Newcastle upon Tyne. However, the visit quickly fell behind schedule after she was ordered to search for, and assist, the Portsmouth-based MFV *Aberdovey*, which was lying disabled off the mouth of the River Somme on the French coast. *Defender* located *Aberdovey* at 0700 on 22 September at anchor and with her propeller fouled by wires. The destroyer's divers spent more than an hour cutting away the offending obstruction only to find that the vessel's engines wouldn't start, and it took another two and a half hours to make repairs and get her under way back to Portsmouth. *Defender* herself finally arrived in the River Tyne a day late, but the four days in the city provided a pleasant break before the trials and tribulations of the ship's work-up at Portland, which began on 28 September. At 0815 on 13 October, two weeks into the work-up whilst at anchor in Portland Harbour, the Dutch destroyer *Holland*, which was drifting without power, collided with *Defender* punching a two-foot hole in her bow, just six feet above the waterline. The necessary repairs took 24 hours to complete after which the destroyer was able to continue with her work-up. In late November she returned to Chatham to give leave prior to a deployment on the Far East Station.

During the afternoon of 4 January 1968 *Defender* left Chatham to begin the passage east, arriving at Gibraltar on 9 January to spend two weeks as the

colony's guardship. On 22 January she continued her passage, and with the Suez Canal closed she sailed via Freetown and the Cape of Good Hope. Six days after leaving Gibraltar there was a brief refuelling stop at Freetown, and two days later the crossing of the equator was celebrated in style. During the forenoon of 6 February *Defender* arrived at Simonstown, but for the ship's company there were only three days to enjoy this welcome break before she sailed into the Indian Ocean to take her turn on the Beira Patrol, the United Nations' oil blockade of the Mozambique port which in November 1965 followed Rhodesia's (Zimbabwe) illegal Unilateral Declaration of Independence.

*Defender*'s first patrol was short, and after relieving *Ajax* she operated with the frigate *Tartar*, but on 17 February she was ordered north to the Gulf of Aden where she joined *Bulwark* and *Eskimo*, which were patrolling off Aden. The former Crown Colony had been granted independence in November 1967, and given the continued political turmoil the ships were there to evacuate the sizeable British community at the Little Aden oil refinery should it become necessary. Fortunately the political turmoil did not seriously affect this important oil installation and intervention was not required. After joining *Bulwark* on 25 February *Defender* acted as planeguard for 24 hours before being ordered to Gan and on to the Cocos Islands to rendezvous with *Eagle*. On the last day of February, having steamed some 9,000 miles since the first day of the month, *Defender* spent two and a half hours alongside the fuelling hulk *Wave Victor* in Gan Lagoon before continuing her Indian Ocean passage. On Monday 4 March, within sight of the Cocos Islands, *Defender* rendezvoused with *Eagle*, which was returning to Singapore after visiting Australia, and provided the carrier's escort for the five-day passage to the naval base. For two days the carrier carried out some intensive flying operations before both units steamed through the Sunda Strait, within sight of Krakatoa, arriving alongside the naval base during the forenoon of 9 March.

On 6 April, following a four-week maintenance

Defender *dressed overall and anchored at Spithead in the mid-1960s.*
*(Maritime Photo Library)*

period at Singapore, *Defender* accompanied *Eagle* to the Subic Bay area to carry out planeguard duties during exercises with US Navy units. However, shortly after arriving off the Philippines, both ships were ordered back to Singapore, and arrived off Raffles Light in the early hours of 13 April, where they were then ordered to proceed at speed to the Gulf of Aden to join Task Force 317, which included *Albion*, off the Trucial Oman coast. Once again political unrest in the newly independent territory of Aden, a military coup and threat to nationalise the British Petroleum oil refinery at Little Aden, indicated that it might, once more, be necessary to evacuate British nationals. In the event, however, the turmoil subsided and no military intervention was necessary. So on 22 April *Defender* set course for the return to Singapore, where she refuelled before continuing east to Hong Kong. She arrived in the colony on 3 May and spent nine weeks undergoing maintenance alongside the dockyard's North Arm.

On 4 July, in company with *Puma*, *Defender* sailed for Bangkok, but trouble with the engine room lubrication pumps necessitated a return to Singapore and it was 15 July before she secured

alongside Bangkok's new port terminal for a three-day visit. This was followed by major exercises in the South China Sea, where she joined *Glamorgan*, *Euryalus*, HMNZS *Otago*, HMAS *Vendetta* and the submarines *Cachalot* and *Rorqual*. There was a period of light relief when the fleet anchored off Pulau Tioman and on 8 August, with the exercises over, *Defender* returned to the naval base at Singapore. On 31 August 1968 there was a final change of command when Commander M. J. F. Rawlinson RN took over from Commander Vallings.

*Defender*'s last exercises with the Far East Fleet began on 16 September 1968 when, in company with the newly arrived *Hermes*, she joined *Glamorgan*, *Diamond*, *Diana*, *Euryalus*, *Grenville*, *Puma*, *Parramata*, *Vendetta* and RFA *Olna* for exercises in the South China Sea, during which *Defender* acted as planeguard escort to *Hermes*. On 22 September the force set course for the Balabac Strait, steaming across the Sulu Sea and into the Celebes Sea where they rendezvoused with an amphibious force which included *Albion*, *Intrepid*, *Triumph*, *Caprice* and RFA *Tidespring*. The whole task force then made its way into the Bismarck Sea

where, at midnight on 30 September, off the Admiralty Islands, 'Exercise Coral Sands' began. With opposition provided by a US Navy force and the Australian carrier *Sydney*, which was in the role of commando carrier, the exercise involved a major amphibious landing on Townshend Island, after which *Defender*, *Puma* and RFA *Tarbatness* visited the town of Newcastle, north of Sydney. The nine-day visit was memorable for the generous hospitality and the visits to Hunter Valley wine country offered by the ex-servicemen's clubs. A few members of the ship's company were able to visit relatives in Sydney, Melbourne or Brisbane, before *Defender* steamed north to Townsville and then returned to Singapore, the passage being made inside the Great Barrier Reef. On 4 November she arrived at the naval base and three days later she began her passage home.

After leaving Singapore *Defender* made the long Indian Ocean passage to Gan where, on 12 November, she refuelled from the hulk *Wave Victor* and then from Addu Atoll steamed south to take over the Beira Patrol. Once again, however, her stint was short and on 23 November, just five days after having taken over, she was relieved by *Danae* and set course for Simonstown. During the passage she rendezvoused with her sister *Decoy* which was on her way out to the Far East, and on 26 November she secured alongside Simonstown Dockyard. After only a short stay of 72 hours *Defender* was at sea again and steaming north for home. She made a refuelling stop at Gibraltar and arrived at Spithead during the morning of 17 December, steaming up harbour during the forenoon. Next day she made the final leg of her passage, and during the afternoon of 19 December she secured alongside Chatham's No.2 basin for Christmas.

During January 1969 *Defender* underwent her final dry docking and maintenance period, and on 19 February she left Chatham for the Mediterranean, calling at Portsmouth and Gibraltar en route. Arriving at Malta on 2 March the destroyer pitched straight into a series of day-running, gunnery training exercises off the island and on 11

*In autumn 1969* Defender *paid her last visit to Portsmouth. Here she is shown flying her paying-off pennant as she steams past Southsea seafront on her way up harbour.*
*(Maritime Photo Library)*

*On 3 September* Defender *approaches Pitch House Jetty for her final visit to Portsmouth.*
*(Maritime Photo Library)*

March, having concluded ten hours at sea, *Defender* returned to Grand Harbour's Canteen Wharf where, as normal, shore leave was granted. However, six hours later, at just after midnight on 12 March, a distress call was received from the 9,148-ton Pakistani-registered cargo vessel MV *Chenab*, some 70 miles north-east of Malta, whose 9,000hp Sulzer diesel engine was completely immobilised. As many liberty men as possible were recalled from shore, and by 0125 *Defender* had passed the break-water on her way to rescue the crippled vessel, which she reached at 0450. At sunrise a boarding party led by the First Lieutenant crossed to *Chenab*, and at just after 1000 the destroyer had the merchantman in tow, but the first tow rope parted and it was 1140 before a second line was passed and the tow was resumed. For over 18 hours, at speeds of between three and ten knots, *Defender* towed *Chenab* to Malta, arriving off Grand Harbour at 0630 on 13 March, where the merchantman was taken over by tugs. For the rest of the day *Defender* carried out weapons training, before returning to Grand Harbour at 1820. Two days later the destroy-

er sailed for the Turkish port of Marmaris where she took part in a NATO exercise involving Greek, Italian, Turkish and US Navy units. At just after midnight, with the NATO fleet anchored off Marmaris, ship's divers were engaged in 'Operation Awkward' (a diving operation aimed at frequent searches of a ship's hull for explosive devices) when one of the Turkish divers was reported missing and a full-scale search was launched. At 0200 the following morning *Defender*'s diving team recovered the body of the missing Turkish diver and returned it to the submarine rescue ship *Kurtaran*. The unfortunate event preceded the main exercises, which took place in the eastern Mediterranean and the Aegean Sea and which, for *Defender*, concluded on 26 March at Izmir.

On 2 April *Defender* left Malta for the last time to make the two-day passage to Gibraltar where she carried out guardship duties for three weeks. In the late 1960s one of these duties was to shadow units of the Soviet Fleet as they passed through to the Atlantic, or eastbound into the Mediterranean. During her stint *Defender* spent two days following

a powerful force consisting of the cruiser *Sverdlov*, a Kashin-class destroyer and a nuclear-powered submarine. On a second occasion, with the submarine *Otter*, she shadowed a force of Kashin-class destroyers and three submarines which passed from the Atlantic to the Mediterranean. *Defender*'s final encounter with the Soviet Navy came on 20 April when she kept watch over *Sverdlov* and an accompanying destroyer which had anchored off the coast of Morocco. On 24 April *Defender* left Gibraltar and four days later she secured alongside Chatham Dockyard's No.3 basin.

*Defender*'s last four months of operational service began on 19 May when, with *Hampshire*, *Kent* and *Andromeda*, she sailed for the Baltic and courtesy visits to Stockholm, Gothenburg and Copenhagen, returning to Portsmouth by way of the Kiel Canal. On 25 June she left Fountain Lake Jetty to set course for Aberystwyth and Swansea, where she represented the Royal Navy for the Investiture of the Prince of Wales. Unfortunately, heavy seas disrupted shore leave at Aberystwyth, but on 1 July she began a pleasant six-day visit to Swansea where she was able to secure alongside King's Dock. By 7 July she had returned to Chatham to prepare for her final weeks of operational service.

On 4 August *Defender* left Chatham and, steaming by way of Portland and Devonport returned to Gibraltar for another brief period of duty as the colony's guardship. On 22 August she made her last foreign visit with a weekend in Tangier, and for the rest of the month she joined the minesweepers of the 10th Mine Countermeasures Squadron, manned entirely by Reservists, for 'Exercise Rockhaul', during which time she flew the flag of Rear-Admiral B. C. G. Place VC, Admiral Commanding Reserves. On the last day of August *Defender* left Gibraltar to return, via Portsmouth, to Chatham where she arrived alongside the Dockyard's No 3 basin at 0830 on 5 September. Later that day her ship's company moved into the Royal Naval Barracks and on 23 September *Defender* was paid off for the last time.

For over two years *Defender* lay in Reserve at Chatham, but in early 1972 she was towed to the Firth of Forth where she was used to monitor the effects of underwater explosions on her hull. In May that year, with the experiments completed, she was sold to J. A. White & Co Ltd, and made the short journey to Inverkeithing where she was broken up.

## HMS *Defender*
## Commanding Officers

| Name: | Date Appointed: |
| --- | --- |
| Captain R. F. T. Stannard OBE RN | 7 August 1952 |
| Captain J. C. C. Henley RN | 2 February 1954 |
| Captain M. L. Hardie DSC RN | 14 June 1955 |
| Captain P. G. Sharp DSC RN | 19 November 1956 |
| Captain G. H. Carew-Hunt RN | 30 December 1958 |
| Commander J. R. Alston RN | 9 December 1963 |
| Commander J. R. S. Gerard-Pearse RN | 7 January 1965 |
| Commander B. J. Straker OBE RN | 19 May 1966 |
| Commander G. M. F. Vallings RN | 20 February 1967 |
| Commander M. J. F. Rawlinson RN | 26 August 1968 |

## Battle Honours

| | |
| --- | --- |
| Heligoland 1914 | Matapan 1941 |
| Dogger Bank 1916 | Malta Convoys 1941 |
| Jutland 1916 | Greece 1941 |
| Calabria 1940 | Crete 1941 |
| Spartivento 1940 | Libya 1941 |

# Part Five

# HMS DAINTY

## February 1953 - February 1971

Dainty *shown here in the River Medina at East Cowes, Isle of Wight, shortly after her launch by Lady Emilie Lang.*
*(T. Ferrers-Walker)*

Two of the eight Daring-class destroyers were built by south coast shipbuilders, and although *Dainty* did not enter service until early 1953 her keel was laid at the Cowes shipyard of J. S. White & Co on 17 December 1945. In the immediate post-war years, with building materials in short supply and with priority being given to merchant tonnage, warship construction was affected by shortages, delays and cancellations. Thus it was almost five years after her first keel plates were laid that *Dainty* was ready for launching. The ceremony took place on Wednesday 16 August 1950 when the wife of the Secretary to the Admiralty, Lady Emilie Lang, sent the destroyer down the stocks at East Cowes and into the River Medina.

Although she had taken to the water and freed up the slipway, the task of fitting out was slow, and it was December 1952 before the ship, at a cost of £1,450,000, neared completion. On 18 December 1952 her first commanding officer, Captain H. J. F. Lane OBE RN, was appointed. However, *Dainty*'s first commission would only consist of a series of short trials before she was laid up in Reserve. Fred Hall, an 18-year-old Electrical Mechanic, remembers joining *Dainty* in early 1953:

'*Dainty* was my first ship and I formed part of the main commissioning draft. We left RNB Chatham in the early hours of a cold winter morning to board a special train from Gillingham to Portsmouth and Southsea Station and on arrival we marched to RNB

Portsmouth where we were given a meal, before forming up on the parade ground in departmental divisions. Then, preceded by a Royal Marines Band, we marched down Queen Street and into the dockyard where we were embarked in waiting ferries which took us directly to J. S. White's shipyard at East Cowes where we finally joined the ship and settled into the new messdecks.'

*Dainty* left White's shipyard at 1115 on Thursday 26 February 1953, to carry out a series of initial machinery trials in the Channel, south of the Isle of Wight, and at 1630 that day she was accepted into Naval service and the White Ensign was hoisted. Two hours later, with her first working day at sea over, she anchored in Cowes Roads. Over the following days *Dainty* carried out a series of day-running trials returning each evening to Cowes Roads, but on 7 March she made the short passage to Portsmouth Dockyard which, for the next seven days, was be her base. On 14 March Lady Lang, *Dainty*'s sponsor, visited the ship and next day the destroyer sailed for Portland to continue her trials.

During the early evening of 19 March *Dainty* left the Portland area bound for the River Thames where she was to have joined *Myngs*, *Orwell* and *Sluys*, as escort to the Yugoslavian Navy's training ship *Galeb*, which was carrying President Tito back home after a State Visit to London. In the event fog delayed her passage up Channel and *Dainty* joined the escort off Dover and steamed to Gibraltar in company with *Sluys* and *Galeb*, with *Myngs* and *Orwell* being detached when south of Plymouth. Arriving in Gibraltar on 25 March *Dainty* and *Sluys* were relieved by *St James* and *Solebay*, but for the ship's company there was time for a run ashore in Gibraltar before they both sailed for home, arriving in Portsmouth Harbour on the last day of March.

The whole of April was spent alongside at Portsmouth while the ship's company took seasonal leave, and it was 2 May when *Dainty* slipped

Dainty *at sea early in her career.* (T. Ferrers-Walker)

from her berth alongside *Vanguard* and left Portsmouth for further trials. For 14 days the destroyer tested her guns, torpedo firing equipment, main propulsion machinery and radar before, at 1345 on Saturday 16 April, she steamed back into J. S. White's East Cowes shipyard. Five days later she was paid off into the hands of her builder and the White Ensign was lowered. The main body of the ship's company returned to Chatham Barracks, while the ship had defects to be remedied before she was towed to Portsmouth Harbour to join the Reserve Fleet.

By late 1955 *Dainty* had been towed up to Barrow-in-Furness where a number of Reserve Fleet frigates and destroyers had been cocooned and laid up in Vickers Armstrong's shipyard. In January 1956 the ship was subjected to a test mobilisation when, at short notice, she was brought out of Reserve and into an operational state in the shortest possible time. Code-named 'Exercise Sleeping Beauty', the aims of the exercise were to bring *Dainty* forward from de-humidified Operational Reserve and have her made ready to proceed to a working-up base in no more than 28 days. She was also required to prepare for a shake down period and to carry out as many sea trials as practicable whilst on passage to the work-up base. It was appreciated, however, that the exercise was not totally realistic in that only *Dainty* was being brought out of Reserve and that she would be manned entirely by regular naval personnel, while under wartime conditions most of her ship's company would be newly called-up Reservists.

The exercise began on 27 January 1956, with the appointment of Captain I. W. T. Beloe RN to take command of the ship. He was soon joined by key officers and ratings, as well as a small workforce from Vickers Armstrong, the company which had been maintaining the ship, to begin the task of removing the sealed cocoons covering the vital equipment. A few days later, on 9 February, the main body of the ship's company arrived in Barrow by special trains from Portsmouth. One member of *Dainty*'s temporary complement was LSBA Bill Stanton, who recounts his experiences during that bitterly cold February of 1956:

'On arrival at RNB Portsmouth I joined the main body of the men who had been detailed to join *Dainty*, to be informed that our joining the ship and getting her ready for operational service was all part of a war mobilisation exercise. During the evening of 8 February, on a bitterly cold night, we were taken in trucks to Portsmouth Railway Station and on arrival there was almost a wartime atmosphere on the platform. The WVS were out in force and handing out tea and biscuits, and when the train pulled into the station it was a "special" just for us. We made a very uncomfortable overnight journey to Barrow-in-Furness, arriving at dawn on a thoroughly unpleasant, bitterly cold day, with sleet and snow sweeping over the docks. Once off the train we were mustered outside the station and marched to the docks, coming to a halt outside a small local café close to the ship. Having mustered virtually the whole ship's company of 200 outside the café, we were then sent inside in batches of 30 for a very basic breakfast and a steaming mug of hot tea. Meanwhile, outside the café, while one batch of men was eating, the rest of us stood at ease in the appalling weather, getting soaked to the skin and waiting patiently for the whole process to be completed. Needless to say there was a great relief when we continued our march to the ship to carry out our joining routine and find our messdecks. As a Leading Sick Berth Attendant I was in a very cramped forward mess, which accommodated 17 of us. Everyone slung a hammock, which was complicated by the fact that there weren't enough slinging hooks and at least two members of the mess had to search the ship looking for a spare berth.'

Over the weeks that followed the ship's company worked hard in difficult conditions, with the ship's divers having to break the ice in the harbour before

*With the inevitable dghajsas in the foreground,* Dainty *enters Malta's Grand Harbour.*
*(World Ship Society)*

they could remove the underwater sealing cocoons, and for a short time the snow-shrouded *Dainty* depended upon a single portable generator for her electrical supply. Bill Stanton remembers receiving the sickbay medical supplies on board, where,

> '...being the sole medical representative on board I had to sort through them and stow them away. I remember being very impressed with a green canvas roll containing stainless steel surgical instruments for emergency operations, but I hoped I would never have to use the saw, hammer and chisel. As for anaesthetic, all I had were ampules of ether which had to be put on a gauze pad, broken, and then placed over an unfortunate patient's mouth and nose. Thank goodness I was never called upon to use them.'

Finally, however, on Wednesday 29 February, *Dainty* was manoeuvred through the Barrow locks and out into the Walney Channel and Morecambe Bay to start her sea trials. It had taken 32 days to

bring the ship out of Reserve and to sea, which was four more days than scheduled. During March *Dainty* carried out trials in some extremely inclement weather, and tested her guns and equipment. Bill Stanton remembers that when the after 4.5-inch guns were fired the sickbay located beneath them shook violently and the cupboards rattled so much he thought they would fall off the bulkhead, but apart from asbestos lagging falling into sick cots, everything remained intact. During the trials *Dainty* put into Barrow on a number of occasions, but on 7 April she left for the last time for six days of gunnery and squid firings. Finally, on 15 April, after a full-power trial, she steamed into Portsmouth Dockyard where she was paid off into dockyard hands, and once again placed in Reserve.

In the summer of 1956, as the Suez Crisis slowly built up, *Dainty* was brought out of Reserve to undergo a refit prior to being commissioned for her first fully operational deployment. On 2 August 1956 Captain D. C. E. F. Gibson DSC RN was appointed as her commanding officer. During the

autumn of that year the ship was moved to Devonport, and on Tuesday 4 December 1956 she was commissioned. Seven days later she began her trials and these continued into the second week of January 1957 when, after a four-hour full-power trial, they were successfully concluded. On 11 January, in company with *Ark Royal*, the destroyer left Devonport and set course for Malta. During the passage she acted as planeguard escort to the carrier, and after a brief pause at Gibraltar arrived in Grand Harbour on 19 January where, in the aftermath of the Suez Crisis, the last units of the invasion fleet were making their way home.

*Dainty*'s first weeks on the Mediterranean Station were spent in company with *Agincourt*, *Alamein*, *Carysfort* and the submarine *Tudor*, working up in the local exercise areas. During this period she was day running and each evening she would return to a berth in Marsaxlokk Bay, Grand Harbour or Sliema Creek. For her ship's company the bars and music halls of Strait Street, more popularly known as 'The

Gut', became familiar during runs ashore, as did the Barracca Lift and the ever-faithful dghajjas waiting alongside Customs House Steps to return liberty men safely to their ship. It was March before there was any change of routine for *Dainty*, and on 5 March, with *Jamaica*, *Cavendish* and *Carysfort*, she left Malta to visit Leghorn (Livorno), and the French resort of St Raphael. By the end of March, however, she was back at Malta's Lazaretto Creek to undergo a period of self maintenance before beginning her first Cyprus Patrol.

On 16 April, together with *Carysfort*, *Dainty* left Malta to carry out anti-submarine training with *Tally Ho*, but at the end of the day's exercises, instead of returning to Malta, she set course for Cyprus where she was to carry out her first patrol of the island's coastline in order to help prevent the smuggling of arms and ammunition to EOKA guerrillas. Arriving at Dhekalia on 19 April, the destroyer refuelled from RFA *Blue Ranger* before starting her first patrol. Every day she intercepted,

*Dainty ships a heavy sea while refuelling fom RFA Wave Master in February 1957, in the Bay of Biscay.* (Ken Kelly)

boarded and searched numerous fishing boats and small merchantmen, and she even located and rescued the crew of a small Army launch which had broken down off the coast. On 25 April, however, violent earthquakes in the eastern Mediterranean caused the destroyer to alter her schedule. The earthquakes caused considerable damage in southwest Anatolia, and particularly in the Turkish port of Fethiye where a severe 45-second tremor wrecked 80 per cent of the buildings, killing and injuring a great many of the 5,000 inhabitants. Next day, when the extent of the damage became apparent, *Dainty* was ordered into Famagusta to embark tons of blankets, tents, medical stores and a team of naval and military doctors, before setting course for Fethiye. After a fast overnight passage, at 1025 on Sunday 28 April, a beautiful sunny day, *Dainty* steamed into Fethiye Harbour. Set against a backdrop of picturesque high mountains the town looked calm and peaceful, but as the destroyer approached her anchorage her ship's company could see that many buildings had been destroyed or severely damaged. *Dainty* anchored some 500 yards from the shore, and over the next 30 hours all the relief stores and supplies were off-loaded into lighters and ferried ashore. In addition a 40-strong landing party assisted with the construction of tents and the distribution of stores in the town. Next day, with Turkish Army units having taken over the relief duties, *Dainty* weighed anchor and returned to her patrol off the coast of Cyprus. Throughout the month of May the destroyer continued to intercept and search suspicious ships round the coast. On 25 May she played host to the Governor of Cyprus, Field Marshal Sir John Harding, who wished to see for himself the work the Royal Navy was doing on the patrol.

*Dainty*'s patrol ended during the evening of 3 June when she and *Carysfort* rendezvoused with *Birmingham* (flag C-in-C Mediterranean), *Kenya*, *Comet*, *Contest* and *Surprise*, for an official visit to Istanbul. The squadron anchored off the city during the forenoon of 5 June and remained for seven days before *Kenya* and *Dainty* weighed anchor to steam north out of the Bosphorus and into the Black Sea.

It was the first time since the signing of the Montreux Convention in 1948 that warships belonging to a power other than a Black Sea country had entered the sea. In the event *Kenya* visited Samsun and *Dainty* the port of Zonguldak. The fact that the entry into the Black Sea by Royal Navy warships irritated the Soviet authorities was made evident a few days later, when under the same Convention, a Soviet cruiser and two destroyers made the passage from the Black Sea into the Mediterranean to visit Albanian ports, which was intended as a counter-demonstration on the part of the Soviet authorities.

*Dainty*'s visit to Zonguldak ended on 17 June when she set course for Malta and a three-week maintenance period. It was mid-July before she put to sea again and for the remaining weeks spent in the Mediterranean she operated mainly in local waters around Malta. For seven days, with *Birmingham*, *Kenya*, *Armada*, and *St Kitts*, as well as US Navy units, she took part in 'Exercise Combine'. In early August, with *Cumberland* and *Tally Ho*, she carried out more anti-submarine training, and this was followed by Mediterranean Fleet exercises, when she joined *Daring* and *Defender* for convoy escort training. The exercises ended at Augusta, after which the three Darings visited Naples which, for *Dainty* and *Defender*, would mark the start of their passage home. At the end of August they arrived in Marseilles, and left for Gibraltar on 5 September. Soon after leaving the French port, however, a virulent and highly infectious form of influenza broke out on board which spread rapidly and on arrival in Gibraltar on 7 September the ship was placed under strict quarantine regulations. With over 100 cases of the illness on board *Dainty* and *Defender* it was apparent that their return to the UK would be delayed, and a number of men from both *Dainty* and *Defender* were admitted to the military hospital at Gibraltar. On 9 September, one of *Dainty*'s ship's company, 19-year-old Able Seaman Mason, died from pneumonia which was a direct result of the influenza. It was 20 September before the quarantine restrictions were lifted, and three days later *Dainty* and

*A good starboard view of* Dainty *under way.*                    (*Portsmouth Royal Naval Museum*)

*Defender* were able to put to sea to participate belatedly part in 'Exercise Strikeback'. With more than 35,000 personnel, 12,000 of them British, 100 ships and 700 aircraft, at that time it was NATO's greatest fleet exercise and the area covered ranged from the Arctic Circle to points near the equator. The primary object of the exercise was to improve the combat readiness of the forces by testing air and anti-submarine procedures as well as under way replenishments and communications. The exercise was commanded by the US Navy's Vice-Admiral R. B. Pirie, flying his flag in USS *Forrestal*, with the British carrier force consisting of *Eagle*, *Ark Royal* and *Bulwark*. Both *Dainty* and *Defender* were employed in an anti-submarine role, and their late arrival meant they were limited to just three days. During the afternoon of 26 September, after refuelling at Gibraltar, both ships made a fast passage home, with *Dainty* arriving at Portsmouth during the afternoon of 30 September.

The final deployment of *Dainty*'s first commission began on Wednesday 15 January 1958, when she left Portsmouth for Portland where units of the Home Fleet, including *Maidstone*, *Bulwark*, *Bermuda*, *Ceylon*, *Camperdown*, *Daring*, *Defender* and *Delight*, had assembled for a cruise to Caribbean waters and joint exercises with the United States and Canadian Navies. The force left Portland on 17 January and by the end of the month, having crossed the Atlantic, had dispersed for their various 'Flag-Showing' visits round the West Indian islands. *Dainty* visited the Dutch island of Aruba where she secured alongside in Orangestadt, and from the Lesser Antilles steamed north-west to the Windward Group and Pointre-a-Pitre on the French island of Guadeloupe, before making an overnight passage to Castries on the island of St Lucia. On 15 February the fleet reassembled in Admiralty Bay off the Grenadine island of Bequia for several days of inter-ship regattas, sporting fix-

tures and recreational leave; *Dainty* also held Admiral's Ceremonial Divisions. During the second half of the cruise *Dainty* visited Antigua and the islands of St Kitts and Nevis. On 1 March she left her anchorage of Basseterre, St Kitts, and steamed north for Bermuda, arriving alongside the Ireland Island naval base two days later where, once again, the fleet had reassembled.

After the warm and pleasant weather and the runs ashore in the Caribbean, the final part of the deployment was to consist largely of a series of major exercises in the Western Atlantic, involving both US and Canadian Navy ships, which began on 10 March. For a time *Dainty* acted as planeguard escort for both *Bulwark* and HMCS *Bonaventure*, and embarked the First Sea Lord onto the quarterdeck by a helicopter transfer. Staying on board for just an hour the VIP visitor left the ship by the same method to return to *Bulwark*. On 14 March the whole force made a ceremonial entry into Halifax, Nova Scotia. Four days later they sailed to carry out the final phase of the exercise and to make the return transatlantic crossing. *Dainty* arrived in home waters on 30 March, and after a pause off the Isle of Man she was detached from the main force to return to Portsmouth, where she arrived alongside on 2 April. It was the end of the destroyer's first full commission, and ahead lay a nine-month refit in Portsmouth Dockyard.

In the new year of 1959, after a nine-month lay-up and refit period, *Dainty*'s new commanding officer, Captain John Wells DSC RN, one of the Navy's foremost gunnery specialists, was appointed to the ship. A few days later, at 1000 on Tuesday 20 January, the new ship's company marched from the Royal Naval Barracks into Portsmouth Dockyard to join the ship. That afternoon, in front of the C-in-C Portsmouth, Admiral Sir Guy Grantham, the assembled officers and men and their families, *Dainty* was recommissioned for service on the Mediterranean Station.

Ten days after the ceremony *Dainty* began her post-refit sea trials, which continued throughout February, and in early March started her work-up at Portland. This gruelling routine lasted for three weeks before there was a break for seasonal leave, after which it was resumed in mid-April and finally ended at the end of that month. On 29 April, together with *Delight*, the destroyer joined the aircraft carrier *Eagle* which, with the Queen embarked, spent a day at sea before returning to Devonport for a modernisation refit. On 30 April *Dainty* held a Families Day at sea and eight days later left Portsmouth bound for the Mediterranean. From a damp and foggy Channel *Dainty* steamed through a calm Bay of Biscay into bright Mediterranean sunshine, and after a brief 24-hour stop at Gibraltar steamed east to Sicilian waters off Augusta to take part in the NATO exercise 'Medusa'. There she operated with the Greek frigates *Niki* and *Panthir* (both ex-US Navy vessels) and the submarine *Tally Ho*. On 18 May, after leaving Augusta, *Dainty* passed and saluted King Paul of the Hellenes as he sailed for a State Visit to Italy, and next day the destroyer arrived in Sliema Creek. After only ten days at Malta *Dainty* became the centre of attention for the press when, at 1255 on 28 May, a blisteringly hot day, she led the destroyers *Armada* and *Camperdown* and the minesweepers *Crofton* and *Puncheston*, to sea as they escorted HMS *Surprise* with the outgoing Governor of Malta, Sir Robert Laycock, embarked for the passage to Nice, from where he would proceed by train to London. Next day the destroyer left Malta and set course for Cyprus where, although Independence had been promised and the bloody insurgency was at an end, the Navy was continuing its patrols of the coast. By this time, however, conditions were more relaxed than they had been during the previous commission, and the long periods at sea were broken by swimming parties to Golden Sands beach at Famagusta, a sailing regatta at Kyrenia and camping expeditions to Medfoba. *Dainty* also provided a contingent for the Queen's Birthday Parade in Nicosia. When she left Cypriot waters on 6 July the destroyer was given a spectacular send-off with members of the Parachute Regiment making a sky-diving water jump and landing very close to the ship.

After leaving the coast of Cyprus and rendezvousing with *Armada* and *Delight*, *Dainty* set

course for Istanbul and another visit to the city, but by mid-July 1959 she was back at Malta and undergoing maintenance. Following this period at Malta, in early September *Dainty* joined the newly recommissioned cruiser *Belfast* for her work-up from Malta, before the cruiser continued her passage out to the Far East Station. In mid-September *Dainty* began a series of visits to Mediterranean ports, the first of which was Trieste, where she secured stern to at the city's Central Square and despite heavy rain which marked the visit, she became the centre of attention. From Trieste she steamed to Venice where she was again allotted a prestigious berth, close to St Mark's Square. *Dainty*'s third port of call was the Sicilian port of Trapani, where 2,800 of the islanders took the opportunity to visit the ship. *Dainty*'s football team had some success ashore when they managed a win over the crack Italian Army team of the 60th Calabria Infantry Regiment. By 3 October she was back in Malta and a week later she was at sea again and off Cartagena taking part in 'Exercise Spanex', a series of Anglo-Spanish anti-submarine exercises which also involved *Birmingham*, *Daring* and *Finisterre*. A visit to Palma, Majorca, was included which, in those days before the introduction of package holiday tours, was considered by most of the ship's company to have been the best run ashore of the commission.

After returning to Malta to remedy an engine defect, at the end of October *Dainty* carried out weapons training with *Delight*, and on 11 November underwent an Admiral's inspection. On 19 November, together with *Daring* and *Delight* (Second Destroyer Squadron), *Battleaxe* and *Crossbow*, and the submarine *Token*, she sailed for exercises with units of the Italian Fleet based at Taranto. It was her third series of NATO anti-submarine exercises, and these were punctuated by visits to the Italian naval base at Taranto. Leaving on 30 November *Dainty* steamed close inshore off the island of Stromboli which, to the appreciation of the many keen photographers on board, gave off a few

*28 July 1960 and the destroyers* Dainty *and* Battleaxe *steam past guests embarked in the aircraft carrier* Centaur *during 'Shop Window' demonstrations.*　　　　　　　　　　　　　　　　　　　　*(Ken Kelly)*

puffs of smoke. For two days *Dainty*, *Delight*, *Defender*, *Battleaxe* and *Crossbow* exercised with the aircraft carrier *Victorious* before, during the forenoon of 3 December, *Dainty* secured stern to in Naples Harbour for a six-day pre-Christmas visit. Despite some wet and windy weather members of the ship's company visited Pompeii and Herculaneum and some even got as far afield as Rome. Leaving Naples on 9 December *Dainty* rendezvoused with the cruiser *Tiger* and exercised with her before returning to Malta's Sliema Creek, where she spent Christmas and New Year.

*Dainty* spent seven weeks in Malta undergoing a dockyard-assisted maintenance period, which included two weeks high and dry in No.3 Graving Dock. It was 1 February 1960 before she put to sea again to spend two weeks day running on post-refit trials. Finally, in mid-February she returned to Cyprus where many old friendships were renewed, among them the Second Battalion Parachute Regiment, which was affiliated to the ship. At the end of February she went alongside at Famagusta, a feat of seamanship which demanded a high standard of ship handling, as at that time she was the biggest warship to have manoeuvred alongside. In early March she left the Cyprus patrol and returned to Malta where she rendezvoused with the aircraft carrier *Albion* for exercises. On 14 March, in company with *Delight* and other units of the Second Destroyer Squadron *Dainty* left Malta and set course for home. During the return passage she visited Algiers where, despite the complicated war of independence which was raging, warm hospitality was extended to the ship's company. In return a children's party was held on board and 100 youngsters arrived to be entertained by 'pirates', with an enormous tea in the wardroom. On 22 March the destroyer arrived in Gibraltar, and three days later she steamed into a rough and stormy Atlantic Ocean to take part in a NATO exercise.

Some three days into the exercise, which involved 30 warships, during the early hours of 28 March when *Dainty* was in the Bay of Biscay, a signal was received to the effect that the two-year-old daughter of one of the ship's officers was dangerously ill in a Portsmouth hospital. Permission was quickly given for *Dainty* to leave the exercise, and that forenoon she was detached to make for Penzance at her best speed, where it was intended to land the officer. In the event, however, heavy seas made the landing impossible, and eventually he was transferred to a launch in Plymouth Sound, from where he made the journey to Portsmouth. *Dainty* herself arrived off Spithead during the morning of 1 April, and a few hours later she was alongside South Slip Jetty, where she was welcomed by a large gathering of wives and families, a Royal Marines Band and even a NAAFI tea stall. *Dainty*'s homecoming had a happy ending with the eventual full recovery of the little girl whose illness had precipitated the destroyer's dash to Plymouth.

Although she was back at her home base the commission was far from over and on 28 April, with the ship's company having taken their foreign service leave, the destroyer sailed north for a five-day visit to Liverpool. This was followed in mid-May by a fishery protection patrol off Iceland, and by 22 May she was in stormy Arctic waters off the island's north coast. As well as playing nursemaid to the British trawlers in the area, during the evening of 29 May *Dainty* went to the assistance of an Icelandic trawler which had 'caught' a drifting Second World War mine in one of its nets. After rendering the device harmless the destroyer continued her patrol, which took her as far east as the North Cape, but by 11 June she had returned to Portsmouth. After a week's break at her home port *Dainty* sailed north again, this time to take part in exercises with *Centaur*, *Bermuda*, *Battleaxe* and *Delight* off Scotland's east coast. In early July there were visits to Bergen and Karlskrona, followed by seven days of day running 'Shopwindow' displays in the Channel, during which the destroyer acted as planeguard to *Centaur*. During the last week of July, in company with *Truncheon*, *Dainty* carried out exercises in the Clyde areas. In the first week of August she was guardship in Cowes Roads for the annual Cowes Week regattas. On 5 August she returned to Portsmouth's South Railway Jetty to undergo ten days of maintenance and to prepare for her second

*Shown here in August 1964,* Dainty *is day running from Portsmouth. She looks to be in pristine condition and showing little sign of having been laid up in reserve for three and a half years.* *(Maritime Photo Library)*

Arctic fishery protection patrol.

At 2300 on Friday 26 August, *Dainty*'s mooring ropes were being singled up as she prepared to depart for Icelandic waters when, down below in B engine room, five telemotor leads which controlled the port rudder were found to have been cut through; in addition several steel nuts and bolts were found in the gearbox of the port main engine. So serious was the damage that sailing had to be postponed indefinitely, the Police were informed and a full-scale investigation into what was clearly an act of deliberate sabotage began. Meanwhile, at Devonport, HMS *Delight* was ordered to take *Dainty*'s place on the fishery protection patrol. On board *Dainty* it was not long before four engine room ratings were arrested and charged with causing malicious damage to the ship, but four days later, at 0800 on 5 September, *Dainty* was able to head north. In the event, however, she was not able to make the Icelandic Patrol, for on 8 September she put into Rosyth Dockyard for further repair work to her gearbox. As for the four ratings who caused the damage, each was sentenced to two

years' imprisonment and dismissed with disgrace from the Royal Navy. It was 26 September before *Dainty* was fully seaworthy once again and on 2 October, after acting as planeguard to *Ark Royal*, she returned to Portsmouth for further dockyard repairs.

On 16 October *Dainty* left Portsmouth to make a four-day visit to the Irish port of Cobh, before sailing north to Icelandic waters to carry out her second fishery protection patrol. During the first week of November, however, she was back in the North Sea and carrying out training exercises with *Gambia*, *Defender* and *Delight*, which ended on 14 November with a five-day visit to Hamburg. During the afternoon of 19 November, when *Gambia* led the three destroyers to sea again, *Dainty* was flying her paying-off pennant and two days later, at 1050 on 21 November, she secured alongside Portsmouth's Fountain Lake Jetty. As soon as gangways were in place families and friends swarmed aboard, and *Dainty* was put on 'extended notice' for steam. In early December 1960 the remaining members of her ship's compa-

ny moved to the Royal Navy Barracks and *Dainty* was paid off. It would be over three years before she put to sea again.

*Dainty* lay in Reserve at Portsmouth until April 1964 when she raised steam again to carry out three days of engine trials. On 13 April she went back into dockyard hands to undergo a two-month refit. She was now under the command of Commander T. M. B. Firth RN, and at 1330 on 20 July she was recommissioned at Portsmouth Dockyard. It was, however, to be a very short commission. On 29 July she began a series of engine trials, during which she was day running from Portsmouth. On

15 August, after a night at a buoy off Cowes, the Daily Express International Offshore Powerboat Race was officially started by *Dainty*'s saluting gun. Once the participants were under way she escorted them through the Solent and along the Channel coast as far as Tor Bay where she anchored for the night before returning to Portsmouth. During the rest of August and into the first week of September *Dainty* continued her day-running trials, with a weekend alongside Southampton Docks. During the last week of September she spent three days at Portland, and in October visited Devonport and Oslo. During the afternoon of 16 October she

*A fine aerial view of* Dainty *at speed and in line ahead.* (MoD/Crown Copyright)

returned to Portsmouth and once again paid off into Reserve. This time, however, she would be laid up for only five months.

During December 1964 and the first week of January 1965 *Dainty* was high and dry in Portsmouth Dockyard's No.15 dry dock as she underwent a refit, but the rest of the winter was spent alongside No.3 basin. By mid-March 1965, with the Indonesian Confrontation making great demands on the ships and men of the Royal Navy, moves were afoot to make her ready for sea again. On 15 March her new commanding officer, Commander P. Maslen MVO RN, was appointed, and two days later he was joined by the ship's company who moved on board from the Royal Naval Barracks. On 23 March *Dainty* was moved out of the basin and alongside the sea wall at Fountain Lake Jetty.

At 1130 on Friday 9 April 1965, some 15 years after her launch, *Dainty* was commissioned for the third time, but in fact it would be only her second fully operational commission in the 12 years since her completion. The ceremony was attended by the C-in-C, Portsmouth, Admiral Sir Varyl Begg, and during the two weeks which followed *Dainty*'s ship's company prepared their vessel for sea. At 1100 on 24 April she left Portsmouth to carry out trials in the Channel, and these continued throughout May and into the first week of June. Clearly the long periods laid up had led to some deterioration of her machinery and on one day of the trials B boiler room had to be evacuated after a major superheated steam leak, and on another occasion the ship had to be anchored quickly after her steering gear jammed. In the second week of June, however, *Dainty* began a very busy seven-week work-up period at Portland, during which she operated with *Berwick*, *Londonderry*, *Naiad*, *Rhyl*, *Salisbury* and the submarine *Otter*. The work-up finally ended during the forenoon of 29 July when she returned to Portsmouth to undergo maintenance and to give leave.

At 1200 on 31 August *Dainty*, in company with *Londonderry*, left Portsmouth bound for Gibraltar. Originally the destroyer was scheduled to spend just a weekend at Gibraltar, but after leaving for Malta on 6 September she suffered another major steering gear failure and was forced to return for two days of repairs. *Dainty* finally left Gibraltar on 11 September and set course for the Sicilian Strait where she rendezvoused with a NATO fleet, including USS *Forrestal*, INS *Impetuoso* and *Canopo* and the Greek destroyers *Aspis* and *Thyella*. In addition to *Dainty* the Royal Navy's contribution to the exercise included *Defender*, *Lowestoft* and *Rhyl*, and visits to Augusta and Rhodes were included. The NATO manoeuvres ended in Malta on 29 September, but four days later *Dainty* was off the Libyan coast fending off 'attacks' by Italian MTBs. In mid-October there was a visit to Bari, after which *Dainty* returned to Grand Harbour for three weeks of maintenance.

On 8 November 1965 *Dainty* left Malta to steam westward to Gibraltar, where there was a 24-hour pause before she continued on into the Atlantic Ocean. After a brief call at Funchal on 12 November, the destroyer steamed into severe southwesterly gales and mountainous seas as she set course for Bermuda and a deployment in the Caribbean. On 20 November she arrived at Bermuda's Ireland Island naval base, where there was a seven-day break for maintenance before she steamed on to Puerto Rico where, at 0830 on 29 November, she relieved *Whirlwind* as the Bahamas guardship. Later that day she left for her first patrol off the Cay Sal Bank between Cuba and Florida, which actually forms part of the Bahamas group. In the mid-1960s the remote island of Cay Sal was being used as a half-way staging post by dubious groups involved in 'people trafficking' and it was also suspected that politically motivated groups were using the route to infiltrate into the Bahamas and Florida, and for these reasons the Royal Navy kept up a patrol off the Bahamas Banks. During *Dainty*'s four-week patrol she practised the landing of security platoons on Anguilla Cay, and on 21 December rescued a group of Cuban refugees from the island of Lobos Cay, transferring them later in the day to the US Coastguard gunboat *Androscoggin*. Refuelling stops were made at

*Dainty* manoeuvres past an oil tanker in the Kiel Canal during her visit of April 1966 to Kiel and the Baltic.
(T. Ferrers Walker)

Nassau, Freeport or the US naval base at Key West, and these often involved an overnight stop which gave the opportunity for a run ashore. During the forenoon of Christmas Eve the destroyer put into Freeport for a three-day Christmas break, followed by two days alongside at Key West before she headed back to Freeport for the New Year festivities. This marked the end of *Dainty*'s Bahamas patrol and after leaving Freeport on New Year's Day, she set course for Bermuda to begin a two-week maintenance period at Ireland Island.

On 18 January 1966, having been relieved as the Bahamas guardship by *Rothesay*, *Dainty* steamed to Fort Lauderdale for an enjoyable five-day visit, which was followed by a 'flag-showing' cruise to Montego Bay, Kingston, Jamaica, and St Maarten in the Dutch Antilles - known in the 1960s as the

'Beach Island' of the Caribbean. On 9 February she paid a 28-hour visit to Barbados and at 0040 on the morning of 11 February she rendezvoused with the royal yacht *Britannia* off the island of Tobago. This marked the start of a two-week period as escort to the royal yacht as the Queen visited most of the islands of the Leeward and Windward groups which were British possessions, starting with Grenada later that day. The royal tour took in St Vincent, Barbados, St Lucia, Antigua, Dominica, Montserrat, St Kitts, Nevis and the British Virgin Islands. Each visit rarely lasted longer than 36 hours and, with full ceremonial entries into each port, the ship's laundry was kept busy providing immaculately pressed, spotlessly clean, white No 7 suits for every occasion. Finally, during the evening of 23 February, *Dainty* took her leave of

the royal yacht and returned to Bermuda. This time the destroyer's visit to the naval base was limited to just three days and on 1 March she left for home. During the return passage *Dainty* made a short refuelling stop at Ponta Delgada, before arriving back at Spithead during the evening of 10 March. Next forenoon, having received Customs clearance, *Dainty* weighed anchor and made a full ceremonial entry into Portsmouth Harbour, arriving alongside at 1130. Ten minutes later the first long leave party left the ship.

During the four weeks *Dainty* spent alongside in Portsmouth Dockyard her ship's company took leave and the ship herself underwent essential maintenance. On 11 April there was a change of command when Commander F. E. B. Brown RN relieved Commander Maslen, and next day *Dainty* sailed for three days of exercises off Portland before returning briefly to Portsmouth and sailing for the North Sea and anti-submarine exercises with *Defender* and units of the Federal German Navy. These ended on 23 April with a visit to Kiel. From the German naval base *Dainty* steamed into the Baltic for a five-day visit to Oslo, before returning to Portsmouth for a three-week maintenance period. It was clear that by the late 1960s the Daring-class destroyers, and particularly *Dainty*, were requiring more frequent and longer maintenance periods in order to keep the main propulsion machinery, which dated from the 1940s, running.

On 23 May, together with the cruiser *Tiger* and other units of the 23rd Escort Squadron, including *Defender*, *Lowestoft* and *Rhyl*, *Dainty* steamed north for naval gunfire support exercises on the Cape Wrath ranges, after which they steamed south to Rosyth for Navy Days in the dockyard. At 1600 on Monday 30 May, after embarking a group of Jutland veterans, including Rear-Admiral A. D. Nicholl, *Dainty* sailed to rendezvous with *Defender* to carry out a joint commemoration ceremony, with units of the Federal German Navy, to mark the 50th anniversary of the Battle of Jutland. Next day in a position Long 56°42'N/Lat 05°40'E, some 160 miles west of the Danish Jylland (Jutland) Peninsular, the two destroyers rendezvoused with the Federal German Navy's destroyers *Braunschweig* and *Karlsruhe*, to steam in formation across the battle area taking roughly the same course as was taken by the battlecruisers in 1916. On board the British and German ships the embarked veterans held simple ceremonies which were marked by the laying of wreaths on the sea. After the ceremony *Dainty* sailed south for a five-day visit to Newhaven, before returning to Portsmouth.

*Dainty* spent the first weeks of June day running with *Tiger* and other units of the 23rd Escort Squadron, and in the second half of the month operated from the Clyde carrying out anti-submarine weapons training with *Opportune* and *Thermopylae*. These continued during the first week of July and for *Dainty* they ended at Falmouth on 8 July, when she arrived at the port to take on the role of guardship to competitors in the Tall Ships Race, which were making the 800-mile voyage between Falmouth and the Skaw at the northern tip of Denmark. Ashore in Falmouth crowds of holidaymakers and sightseers had lined the shore below Pendennis Castle and the sailing ships were surrounded by a vast fleet of dinghies, motor boats, catamarans, small cruisers and excursion vessels. At just after midday on 9 July, after embarking official guests and press representatives, *Dainty* slipped her moorings and steamed out into Falmouth Bay to await the start of the race, which was scheduled for 1430. As soon as they were on their way *Dainty* landed her passengers and accompanied the sailing ships on their passage up Channel and through the North Sea. Next day, at 1500, with the sailing fleet still off the south coast, a young sailor from the Swedish schooner *Gladen* was taken ill and transferred by dinghy to the destroyer, from where he was taken off by helicopter and evacuated to hospital ashore. The race ended during the forenoon of 15 July and with her duties over, *Dainty* paid a five-day, goodwill visit to Copenhagen before returning to Portsmouth to give leave.

On 31 August 1966, having completed a five-week maintenance and docking period, *Dainty* left Portsmouth to rendezvous with *Defender* and *Rhyl*

and to set course for the Mediterranean. After arriving in Sliema Creek on 8 September the destroyer's first weeks on station were spent in local waters, and at the end of October she carried out self maintenance in Gibraltar before returning to the eastern Mediterranean for visits to Istanbul and Marmaris. This was followed by a short visit to the ancient Arabian port of Haifa, and a return to Malta on 19 December in time for Christmas. The new year of 1967 brought more training exercises in local waters off Malta, but on 7 March *Dainty* left Grand Harbour to return home. The last leg of the passage was made with her sister *Diana*, and she arrived alongside Fountain Lake Jetty during the forenoon of 16 March to pay off. It was the end of *Dainty*'s third full commission.

For six months *Dainty* lay alongside at Portsmouth undergoing her final long refit, and on Monday 1 May, Commander M. J. Rivett-Carnac RN relieved Commander Brown as the ship's commanding officer. Finally, on 25 September 1967, after five months in the non-tidal basin or dry dock, *Dainty* was shifted to the sea wall at North Corner Jetty. At 1100 on Tuesday 3 October, in the presence of Vice-Admiral D. C. E. F. Gibson, Flag Officer Naval Air Command, who had commanded *Dainty* between August 1956 and April 1958, the ship was recommissioned for her final General Service Commission.

Two weeks after the recommissioning ceremony *Dainty* left Portsmouth Dockyard to carry out her post-refit trials, but on the second day she was kept alongside for over 48 hours as the engineers struggled to rectify problems with the turbo-generators. It was the first of many problems with her machinery which would dog the ship throughout the commission, as the years took their toll on her now elderly propulsion machinery. During October and November *Dainty* ran her trials from Portsmouth, and on 31 October she escorted the old Cunard passenger liner *Queen Mary* through the Solent and into the Channel as she began a 39-day voyage, via Cape Horn, to retirement at Long Beach, California. On 8 January 1968, after spending Christmas and New Year at Portsmouth, *Dainty* sailed for Portland

to begin her work-up. That afternoon during anti-submarine weapons training, fire broke out in B boiler room, and the resulting loss of power left the destroyer dead in the water for almost an hour. Fortunately, the personnel on duty were able to quickly extinguish the blaze, and for the next three months *Dainty* operated a gruelling routine as the ship's company worked up to full operational efficiency. During this period she operated with *Diamond* and *Jaguar* and the German destroyer *Bayern*, and on 20 March, having successfully completed her Operational Readiness Inspection, she returned to Portsmouth.

*Dainty*'s last operational deployment began on 22 April when she left Portsmouth for Gibraltar where she spent eight weeks as guardship at the colony and underwent more repairs after a main steam leak. During this period there was a brief visit to Tangiers, and the Minister of Defence, Denis Healey, paid a short visit to the ship. The long periods spent alongside provided an excellent opportunity for the engineers to carry out maintenance on the elderly machinery, which was becoming very temperamental. The guardship duties ended on 17 June when *Dainty* left Gibraltar to steam north for Kiel and seven days in company with *Galatea*, as they represented the Royal Navy at the annual 'Kieler Woche'. Warships from eight nations attended the event which, as always, provided a pleasant interlude for the ships' companies. However, on board *Dainty* there was little relaxation for some members of the ship's company, for during the evening of 22 June a hole was found in the ship's side, four feet below the waterline at the starboard side of B boiler room. For most of the night the ship's divers were down carrying out temporary repairs. Seven days later *Dainty* made her way south through the Kiel Canal and back to Portsmouth where, on 1 July, she embarked families at Spithead before steaming up harbour and into D lock dry dock for permanent repairs to her hull.

On Wednesday 1 August there was a final change of command when Commander R. W. Moland RN took over from Commander Rivett-Carnac and next day, with her repairs complete, *Dainty* was refloat-

ed. Originally the destroyer had been due to sail to the Far East Station on 8 August, but machinery problems in B boiler room first delayed and then cancelled the sailing, giving the ship's company an extra five more runs ashore in Portsmouth. It was on Tuesday 13 August that *Dainty* sailed for a short exercise period off Portland, before setting course for Gibraltar and the Far East. However, during the evening of 14 August, whilst off Cape Finisterre, she was suddenly diverted to the Caribbean via Ponta Delgada. Political unrest in Antigua, which was still a Crown Colony, meant that *Dainty* had been ordered to make for and stand by off the island in case military intervention became necessary. With the Soviet suppression of the uprising in Czechoslovakia grabbing the news headlines, the political situation in Antigua was largely ignored by the world's press. In effect a new Constitution for the island, which gave internal self-government, had come into force, but falling short of full independence it had met with some opposition. In the

event, however, the troubles subsided without any serious disturbances, and after anchoring off St John's Harbour on 23 August, the ship's company was able to enjoy a pleasant time ashore. On 3 September *Dainty* steamed to the neighbouring island of Grenada, and ten days later she was released to continue her passage to the Far East via Simonstown.

Before leaving the Caribbean *Dainty* refuelled at Trinidad, and on 9 September King Neptune was welcomed aboard for the Crossing the Line ceremony, with Commander Moland providing his first 'victim', before the ship settled down for the ten-day transatlantic crossing. During the passage various training exercises were organised, and during the morning of 12 September *Dainty* rendezvoused with RFA *Wave Chief* to carry out two days of replenishment. Finally, at 0920 on 21 September the destroyer arrived alongside Simonstown Dockyard's West Jetty for what would be an all too brief visit to the Cape. Such was the hospitality,

Dainty *at sea in 1967 shortly after recommissioning.*

*(World Ship Society)*

with a flood of invitations received on board, that the four-day stopover was far too short to accept them all, and on 25 September the ship left Simonstown for the Beira Patrol. The passage north into the Indian Ocean was not without incident, and less than 24 hours after leaving harbour *Dainty*'s speed was reduced by a defective forced draught fan in A boiler room. On 28 September there were further mechanical problems when a turbo-generator in A boiler failed and had to be shut down. Fortunately, the next day *Dainty* was able to relieve *Leander* on the patrol.

*Dainty*'s first Beira Patrol was carried out in company with *Carysfort* and although it lasted only nine days, this was long enough to compete for the 'Beira Bucket', which had been instigated by *Dainty*'s PTI and which subsequently became a much coveted trophy, during a relaxed afternoon of fun and games between the two ships' companies. On 8 October *Dainty* was relieved by *Diamond*, and was able to set course for Kilindini Harbour, Mombasa, for more much needed maintenance.

The two-week period at Mombasa gave the opportunity for some members of the ship's company to spend a few days' station leave at Silver Sands rest camp, while others enjoyed a 'safari' in the Tsavo Game Reserve. For those staying in Mombasa town there was always the pleasure of an icy-cold Tusker lager and a slap-up meal at The Copper Kettle in Kilindini Road.

During the last week of October *Dainty* sailed to relieve *Diamond* and to carry out her second Beira Patrol, but soon after leaving harbour she developed engine trouble and had to return to Mombasa for repairs. It was 8 November before she put to sea again, this time bound for Singapore via Gan. Once again, however, the passage was plagued by machinery problems, this time the cause of the trouble being an overheating plummer block (a large bearing upon which the propeller shaft rests). On 13 November, whilst the ship was secured to a buoy in Gan Lagoon, the engineers carried out an oil change on the offending bearing, and seven days later she arrived alongside Singapore Dockyard. During the six weeks that *Dainty* lay alongside the

dockyard a great deal of maintenance work was carried out on her main propulsion machinery, but as Lieutenant Mike Critchley, one of the ship's officers, has commented,

'*Dainty* really was well past her useful days in the fleet'.

On 30 December 1968, with the Christmas festivities over, *Dainty* sailed for training exercises in the South China Sea. On New Year's Day she left the Pulau Tioman area for Penang where she anchored off Georgetown. Two days later she began 11 days of anti-submarine training with *Onslaught* and *Forth*, before returning to the naval base at Singapore. This time, however, it was to be only the briefest of visits, for next day *Dainty* sailed for Hong Kong, where many members of the ship's company became acquainted with the bars and clubs of Wanchai for the first time. A group of volunteers from the ship 'adopted' a small village school at Fan Lau on the island of Lantau, just west of Hong Kong island, and during the ship's stay they repainted the building and built a swing and see-saw for the children. On 3 February *Dainty* left Hong Kong for exercises in the Subic Bay area, but these were cut short by more machinery problems and the destroyer returned to Hong Kong for repairs.

By this time *Dainty*'s programme with the Far East Fleet was well behind schedule, and a much anticipated visit to Japan had to be cancelled as the engine room department struggled to keep the ship running. Finally, however, on 20 February *Dainty* was able to sail for Kota Kinabalu (formerly Jesselton) on the island of Borneo. Once again the passage was not without incident, and during the evening of 21 February an overheated port steering motor sent black smoke billowing through the after part of the ship. Fortunately, fire parties dealt quickly and efficiently with the problem, and three days later *Dainty* secured alongside at Kota Kinabalu, with the minesweepers *Houghton* and *Sheraton* berthed alongside her. With the Indonesian Confrontation having ended in August

Dainty *laid up at Portsmouth in the 1970s with the LST* Anzio *astern.*
*(Author's Collection)*

1966, the Royal Navy was engaged in 'flag-showing' visits to the more remote and vulnerable areas of Malaysia, and during *Dainty*'s visit the C-in-C, Far East Station, used the destroyer to host an official reception for local dignitaries.

*Dainty* left Borneo on 25 February and steamed into the South China Sea to rendezvous with her sister ship HMAS *Duchess*, to carry out training exercises in the Gulf of Thailand, only 100 miles from the Vietnamese coast, before steaming further north to the Bangkok River, where she moored to buoys four miles south of the city itself. After four days of sampling the delights of Bangkok, long before it became a package holiday destination, it was back to the Singapore exercise area for *Dainty*'s ship's company, and to the annual FOTEX exercises in the South China Sea, which also coincided with 'D2's' harbour and sea inspections. On 28 March *Dainty* left Singapore for Hong Kong, arriving alongside the North Wall during the forenoon of 31 March. The ship's second stay in Hong Kong had not been scheduled to last for three weeks, but once again machinery breakdowns kept the ship firmly alongside, and when she did return to Singapore she spent a short spell in the floating dry dock. By the second week of May the ship was once again ready for sea, and at 1530 on Monday 12 May, with her paying-off pennant flying, she left Singapore for her passage home.

On 17 May *Dainty* arrived in Gan to refuel from the hulk *Wave Victor* and four days later there was some light relief when she anchored off Farquhar Island for the day and both watches were able to enjoy a few hours on the beautiful sandy beaches. At 0700 on 24 May she relieved *Diamond* on the Beira Patrol, which then set course for home. This time *Dainty*'s partner on the patrol was the frigate *Leander* which, on 27 May, won the 'Beira Bucket'. During June *Dainty* operated on the patrol in conjunction with *Juno*, but on 3 July she completed her 48th, and last, day on the patrol and at midnight, having been relieved by *Decoy*, set course for Simonstown, arriving alongside the South African dockyard during the afternoon of 7 July. *Dainty*'s visit to the naval base lasted just three days longer than her first brief stopover, but now everyone on board was looking forward to the return home and there were few tears when, at 1030 on 14 July, the destroyer left Simonstown for the long, 16-day passage home.

During the forenoon of 24 July, when she was west of Senegal, *Dainty* rendezvoused with the homeward-bound commando carrier *Albion*, which had left Durban ten days earlier, and the two warships remained in company for the rest of the passage. On the forenoon of Tuesday 29 July *Dainty* was in the Bay of Biscay and fast approaching Ushant when, at 1110, there was another total steam failure and the destroyer was left without any power. With the ship's final major breakdown being blamed on contaminated fuel oil, the engineers struggled for an hour to relight the boilers and raise steam; at 1240 there was sufficient to get under way again and at 0715 the next morning *Dainty* anchored at Spithead. Three hours later, with the ship's company manning her decks and the paying-off pennant flying, she steamed up harbour to secure alongside Portsmouth Dockyard's South Slip Jetty. *Dainty*'s operational career was over, and for the hard-pressed engine room department it was not a moment too soon. They had done extremely well to keep the ship steaming to and from the Far East.

During the three weeks which followed her arrival home *Dainty* was de-ammunitioned, and on 15 August she was towed into No.3 basin and secured alongside the frigate *Wakeful*. On 22 August most of her remaining ship's company left the ship for long leave and new drafts and at 1200 the Ensign was lowered and the ship officially paid off. At 1330 the remaining members of the ship's company moved into the Royal Naval Barracks, and the ship's log was signed off for the last time by Lieutenant Roger Hicks. During the last commission, despite the many machinery problems, she

*Dainty lunder tow as she makes her way to the shipbreaker's at Cairnryan.*　　　　　　　　*(Tim Meredith)*

*Almost the end for Dainty as she succumbs to the shipbreaker's at Cairnryan. Her after 4.5-inch turret still stands intact as the ship is reduced to scrap metal.* (Richard Holme/Shipbreaking Queenborough Ltd)

had steamed some 70,000 miles, while her total mileage since leaving the builder's yard was recorded at over 250,000.

For 17 months *Dainty* was laid up at Portsmouth before being sold to Shipbreaking (Queenborough) Ltd, a company which had, until then, specialised in breaking up tugs and barges at Glasson Dock, near Lancaster. In February 1971 she arrived under tow at Cairnryan, and by the end of the year had ceased to exist. There is, however, one item from the ship which has survived - the ship's bell - which now hangs in the square at Adamstown on Pitcairn Island. Its job there is to announce the arrival of visiting ships to the island, and the launching of the longboats to meet them.

**HMS *Dainty***
**Commanding Officers**

| Name: | Date Appointed: |
| --- | --- |
| Captain H. J. F. Lane OBE RN | 18 December 1952 |
| Captain J. W. T. Beloe RN | 27 January 1956 |
| Captain D. C. E. F. Gibson DSC RN | 2 August 1956 |
| Captain J. G. Wells DSC RN | 10 January 1959 |
| Commander T. M. B. Firth RN | 31 March 1964 |
| Commander P. Maslen MVO RN | 15 March 1965 |
| Commander F. E. B. Brown RN | 11 April 1966 |
| Commander M. J. Rivett-Carnac RN | 1 May 1967 |
| Commander R. W. Moland RN | 1 August 1968 |

**Battle Honours**

Atlantic 1940          Calabria 1940
Mediterranean 1940-41          Libya 1940-41
Malta Convoys 1941

# Part Six

# HMS DECOY

## April 1953 - March 1970

*Decoy in the Firth of Forth during her acceptance trials. She had not been formally handed over to the Royal Navy and still wears the Red Ensign.* *(Author's Collection)*

On 22 September 1946, at a small ceremony in the Scotstoun shipyard of A. Yarrow & Co Ltd on the River Clyde, the first keel plates were laid for the fourth of the new Daring-class destroyers. It would be, however, over six years before the ship was completed. In the immediate post-war years, although the country had been on the winning side in the Second World War, Britain was virtually bankrupt and in order to retrieve the shattered economy all the resources that were available for shipbuilding had to be given over to rebuilding the much depleted merchant fleet. So the new destroyer, like her sisters, remained on the stocks as construction proceeded at a very slow pace. It was some two and a half years after the keel plates were laid that the ship was ready for launching, but only so that the slipway could be freed up for other contracts. The launch date was Tuesday 29 March 1949 and Mrs J. Dugdale, the wife of the Parliamentary and Financial Secretary to the Admiralty, named her *Decoy* and sent her down the slipway into the River Clyde. Although she was the first of the Daring-class destroyers to be launched, she would be the last but one to be commissioned. In April 1950 the first naval officer and a handful of key personnel made the journey to the Clyde to stand by the ship, but it would be another three years before she was ready for service. In the autumn of 1952 she ran her Contractor's Sea Trials in the Clyde area, which were not successful as the

ship suffered some damage to her main engines, and she returned to the shipyard for repairs and modifications.

On 7 April 1953 *Decoy*'s first commanding officer, Captain R. H. Maurice DSO DSC RN, was appointed to the ship and 13 days later the Captain Contract Built Ships inspected *Decoy*, which was now lying in a basin at Dalmuir and, having satisfied himself that the ship was indeed ready for service, he signed Admiralty Form D448. One hour later, at 1300 on 20 April, Captain Maurice led the advance party of 12 officers and 68 ratings on board; next day they were joined by a further steaming party of 138 ratings and at 0945 HMS *Decoy* was commissioned.

With the ship ready for sea, on 22 April she slipped her moorings and, assisted by tugs, she steamed downriver to carry out a full day on initial machinery trials before anchoring off Greenock. Three days later she carried out another day of trials before steaming back upriver to Dalmuir Basin where, at 1200 on 28 April, Captain Maurice provisionally accepted the ship from the builders. Such

was the interest in those days that the BBC broadcast the radio programme '*A Fighting Ship is Born*' from the destroyer.

For two weeks after her acceptance *Decoy* lay in Dalmuir Basin as stores and equipment were embarked. On 10 May when she was opened to the public she proved a popular attraction for local people. Three days later she began a seven-day series of machinery trials in the Clyde area after which she steamed south to arrive at her base port of Devonport on 21 May. *Decoy*'s first operational duty came 14 days later when she steamed up Channel to take her place in D Line at Spithead for the Coronation Review of the Fleet. At 1650 on 15 June, the day of the Review, as the ship's company manned and cheered ship, HMS *Surprise*, which was acting as royal yacht, steamed past *Decoy* and that evening the historic day ended with a fireworks display. Next day, after the departure of *Surprise*, *Decoy* left Spithead for Portland where she carried out five weeks of trials before returning to Devonport in late July to give leave and to take part in Navy Days at the base.

*An early port side view of* Decoy *in June 1953.*          *(Portsmouth Royal Naval Museum)*

On 1 September *Decoy* sailed to rendezvous with her sisters *Diamond* and *Duchess* and the battleship *Vanguard*, to rehearse for a major exercise, codenamed 'Mariner', which was due to start later in the month. Next day, however, came tragedy as *Decoy* suffered her first fatality when, at 2130, Able Seaman T. S. Brockbank was lost overboard. *Decoy* was in the North Sea at the time, some 65 miles east of Skegness and steaming north for Invergordon. Despite a four-hour search no trace of the missing man was found. Six days later, having joined *Swiftsure* and the submarine *Trespasser*, the destroyer began ten days of rehearsals before taking a long weekend break at Invergordon. 'Exercise Mariner' itself began on Tuesday 22 September when, at 1600, steaming in line ahead, *Vanguard* led *Decoy*, *Diamond*, *Duchess*, *Battleaxe*, *Scorpion*, *Sheffield* and *Eagle* to sea and north to Arctic waters. For seven days in heavy seas and bitterly cold weather conditions, the fleet practised convoy escort duties and anti-submarine exercises. During the evening of 29 September, however, when they were west of Iceland, *Diamond* was in collision with the cruiser *Swiftsure*, causing severe damage to both ships, but fortunately no serious casualties. Shortly after the accident *Decoy* stood by *Swiftsure* in case the cruiser required assistance in extinguishing a fierce blaze which had broken out. At 0200 on 30 September, when the cruiser was under way again, *Decoy* took station a mile ahead of her and led the damaged vessel to Hvalfjord in Iceland where they arrived that afternoon. Two days later, during the afternoon of 2 October, with both *Diamond* and *Swiftsure* having undergone temporary repairs, *Decoy* escorted both ships out of Hvalfjord and as far south as the Thames Estuary, before returning north to Rosyth for a 14-day maintenance period. During November she sailed south to complete her trials and work-up at Portland, before returning to Devonport on 1 December to give leave and to undergo a docking period.

On 29 January 1954, after a fast passage from Plymouth Sound, *Decoy* returned to Portland to join the newly repaired *Diamond* along with *Duchess*, *Barrosa*, *Crossbow*, the cruiser *Superb*, *Apollo* and

*Vanguard* which was flying the flag of the new C-in-C Home Fleet, Admiral Sir Michael Denny. On 5 February *Vanguard* led the fleet to sea for the Home Fleet's spring cruise, setting course for Gibraltar and the warmer waters of the Western Mediterranean. At Gibraltar *Decoy* hoisted the flag of Rear-Admiral J. L. Cuthbert, the Flag Officer, Flotillas, Home Fleet, and soon afterwards the fleet began its programme of training exercises and courtesy visits. During this period the fleet was joined by *Eagle*, and at the end of February *Decoy* joined the carrier for a visit to the French North African naval base at Oran. In the second week of March the Home Fleet was joined by units of the Mediterranean Fleet, including the cruisers *Bermuda* and *Gambia*, as well as the training carriers *Implacable* and *Indefatigable*, for a week of intensive exercises. On 28 March the Home Fleet units, including *Decoy*, set course for home and arrived at Devonport on 1 April.

On 7 May, with her ship's company having completed their seasonal leave, *Decoy* left Plymouth Sound to make a visit to Brixham before rejoining *Vanguard* and other units of the Home Fleet, including her sister *Diana*, to provide the escort for the brand new royal yacht *Britannia* as she brought the Queen home from her Commonwealth tour. Altogether some 15 units of the Home Fleet took part: *Vanguard*, *Decoy*, *Diana*, *Jamaica*, *Apollo*, *Agincourt*, *Barrosa*, *Aisne*, *Corunna*, *Venus*, *Virago*, *Verulum*, *Vigilant*, *Orwell* and *Obdurate*, a formidable force of ships. Having left Tor Bay at just before midnight on 13 May, they rendezvoused with *Britannia* at 0900 the next day some nine miles south-south-east of Plymouth where, after firing a royal salute, they took over the escort from *Glasgow*, *Barfleur* and *Saintes*. The fleet made an impressive sight as it steamed up Channel passing within four miles of Start Point, then just two and a half miles off Berry Head and four miles south of Portland Bill. At 1700, off Anvil Point, Dorset, the ships of the Home Fleet steamed past *Britannia* and cheered ship before detaching to their bases, leaving *Jamaica* and *Decoy* to continue the escort up Channel to the Thames Estuary. After leaving the

Decoy *in May 1954 during service with the Home Fleet.* (Maritime Photo Library)

royal yacht, *Decoy* continued on to Invergordon where, with other units, she remained until the first week of June. She made a weekend visit to the picturesque French port of Lorient on the Bay of Biscay, before returning to Devonport at the end of her first commission. By 22 June *Decoy* had paid off and was beginning a two-month refit period.

On Monday 16 August 1954 *Decoy*'s new commanding officer, Captain M. N. Tufnell DSC RN, joined the ship, and on 7 September most of the ship's company left for new drafts, leaving just a small 'care and maintenance' party. Next day, at 1000, the new ship's company joined and at 1500 that afternoon the Recommissioning Ceremony was held on the forecastle. *Decoy*'s first commission had been served with the Home Fleet, but the first leg of her second commission would be spent in the Mediterranean, based at Malta. Nine days after commissioning she left Devonport bound for Gibraltar and Malta, arriving in Grand Harbour on 25 September where she joined her sisters *Diana*, *Diamond* and *Duchess*, and for the first two weeks of the deployment the three destroyers worked up in the local exercise areas off Malta. On 8 October *Decoy* formed part of the squadron which provided a gunnery display for Emperor Haille Sellasie of Ethiopia, who was embarked in the cruiser *Gambia*,

and this concluded with a ceremonial steam past and salute. Throughout the rest of the month *Decoy* continued to carry out training exercises in local waters, and on 1 November she embarked the C-in-C Mediterranean Fleet, Admiral Lord Louis Mountbatten, for a demonstration of firepower off Grand Harbour. In mid-November she visited Portoferraio, Elba, and at the end of the month she arrived in Port Said where, after an agreement to provide for the phased withdrawal of British troops from the Suez Canal Zone over a period of 20 months, there was finally an end to the insurgency which had fought against the British presence. *Decoy*'s visit was to act as guardship at Port Said, and throughout the visit, with the security situation having improved, shore leave was granted to the ship's company until 2330 each evening. In mid-December the Band of the Grenadier Guards visited the ship and gave an impressive display of Beating Retreat on the jetty alongside the ship. Two days later *Decoy* steamed south into the Suez Canal to Port Suez, where shore leave was granted, but only until 2130. After four days at the southern end of the Suez Canal *Decoy* steamed north to anchor off Fayid, close to the British base areas, where the ship's company was able to enjoy the Christmas festivities. Finally, on the last day of

December, *Decoy* left Port Said for the return passage to Malta.

After arriving in Grand Harbour on 3 January 1955 there was an overnight break for the ship's company before *Decoy* was back at sea again, this time accompanying the cruiser *Jamaica* (flag FO2) and her sister *Duchess* for a six-day official visit to Algiers. This was followed by three months of exercises off Malta, ending with a visit to Naples, and in April the ship underwent a maintenance period in Grand Harbour. On 22 May, with 40 RAF personnel as passengers, *Decoy* left Grand Harbour to join *Sheffield* and *Jamaica*, (flying the flags of C-in-C and FO2, Mediterranean respectively), her sisters *Diamond*, *Duchess* and *Diana*, *Battleaxe*, *Scorpion* and RFA *Fort Duquesne*, for exercises in the Eastern Mediterranean, which were followed by visits to various ports in the area. From 26 to 30 May the fleet visited Istanbul, and on leaving the Turkish city, while other units dispersed for further goodwill visits, *Decoy* returned to Grand Harbour to prepare for her passage home to Devonport.

On 24 June, carrying five additional passengers in the form of an Army Brigadier and four students, *Decoy* left Malta and after a 36-hour stop at Gibraltar arrived in Plymouth Sound during the evening of 30 June. Next forenoon she steamed up harbour to Devonport Dockyard, where she would spend the next two months undergoing maintenance. At the end of July she took part in Plymouth Navy Days when, over three days, she attracted some 14,000 visitors. On the last day of August, with *Glasgow*, the destroyer sailed north for Invergordon for a series of day-running exercises followed by the NATO exercise code-named 'Sea Enterprise'. This involved an impressive force of aircraft carriers, with *Eagle*, *Albion*, *Centaur* and *Bulwark*, as well as the Canadian carrier *Magnificent* taking part. In addition to *Decoy* and her sister *Diana*, the cruiser *Glasgow* and eight other destroyers including *Agincourt*, *Charity* and *Chieftain* were present. The exercises ended at Trondheim on 28 September, after which *Decoy* and *Diana* made a four-day visit to Copenhagen.

The short visit to Denmark preceded what was to be one of the most important official exchange visits of naval warships in the 1950s, which had been arranged between the Foreign Secretary, Anthony Eden, and the Soviet Foreign Minister, Marshall Bulganin, at the 'Four Power' diplomatic conference held in Geneva in July that year. The arrangement provided for a simultaneous exchange of visits by naval squadrons, with *Triumph*, wearing the flag of the C-in-C, Home Fleet, Admiral Sir Michael Denny, *Apollo*, *Decoy*, *Diana*, *Chevron* and *Chieftain* visiting Leningrad (St Petersburg). At the same time a Soviet squadron under the command of Admiral Gdovka, C-in-C, Baltic Fleet, flying his flag in the cruiser *Sverdlov*, and accompanied by the cruiser *Alexandr Suvorov* and four destroyers, would visit Portsmouth.

At 0945 on 10 October *Decoy* and *Diana* left Copenhagen to rendezvous with *Triumph* and the other members of the squadron. Two days later, at 1400, they arrived off the mouth of the Neva River at Leningrad, where they were met by the Soviet destroyer *Odaryonny*. After passing the Soviet Baltic Fleet Naval Base at Kronstadt the squadron was escorted by tugs into the canal which gives access to the river then, watched by large crowds, they steamed into the heart of the great city to secure to buoys close to the Schmidt Bridge. One member of *Decoy*'s ship's company describes the reception:

'The crowds, many of whom had never seen a British warship before, were there in thousands, cheering and shouting, and before long singing. Many of the ship's company swapped songs, with the crowd and sailors singing alternately, much to the delight and enjoyment of the crowds. It was different from what we had expected, and it came as a pleasant surprise. Each day during the whole of our stay the crowds gathered in the early morning to watch the ships, and did not disperse until very late at night.'

The squadron's stay in Leningrad was well organised with a busy schedule of entertainment laid on

each day, including coach tours of the city and visits to museums. One of the highlights of the visit was a much-publicised football match between a squadron team, who had never played together before, and a Soviet naval team at the Kirov Stadium in front of a crowd of 80,000. Although the squadron team were beaten by 4 - 0 it was by no means a walkover. At the end of the match the Royal Marines Band received a thunderous ovation from the huge crowd. No restrictions were placed on the movements of the ships' companies, and those who visited the Red Army and Soviet Navy Clubs were well looked after.

Originally it had been planned that the squadron would leave during the evening of Sunday 16 October, but with gale force winds blowing it was considered too dangerous to attempt the passage of the winding River Neva, and sailing was delayed until the following afternoon. Although strong winds were still blowing, at 1330 the four destroyers slipped their moorings and, watched by large crowds on Vasil 'yevskiyo Island, began their slow passage downriver to the open sea. Led by *Chevron*, the destroyers passed Kronstadt at 1700 and soon afterwards anchored to await the arrival of *Triumph* and *Apollo*. Next morning at 0700 the squadron weighed anchor and set course for Rosyth, where they arrived on Trafalgar Day. Two days later, with her sisters *Diamond* and *Duchess*, *Decoy* took part in 'Exercise Phoenix I', and on 4 November she made a six-day visit to Middlesbrough before making her way, via Portsmouth and Dartmouth, to Devonport, where she arrived on 21 November. It was the end of her second commission.

Following her arrival in Devonport in November *Decoy* underwent a 16-week refit, with Christmas and New Year being spent in No.2 dry dock. On 10 February 1956 Captain P. J. Hill-Norton RN relieved Captain Tufnell as the destroyer's new commanding officer, and on 21 February the main body of the new ship's company marched from the Royal Naval Barracks to join the ship which, by this time, was lying in No 4 basin at Devonport Dockyard. That afternoon the recommissioning ceremony was held on the forecastle, but it was to be another two weeks before the destroyer put to sea again.

On 12 March *Decoy* sailed for five days of post-refit trials before leaving Portland for Gibraltar,

*Decoy at anchor off Portland, with the guns of A and B turrets at maximum elevation.*
*(T. Ferrers-Walker)*

Malta and the Mediterranean Fleet. Following her arrival she spent the first month carrying out a work-up in the local exercise areas around Malta and in the first week of May, with *Daring*, she sailed for Port Said to spend five days as guardship at the port. This was followed by a 12-day patrol off Cyprus where she intercepted and searched fishing boats and small merchantmen which were suspected of 'gun-running' arms and ammunition to the EOKA insurgents on the troubled island. On 22 May she left the area to return to Port Said, before steaming south through the Suez Canal to pay a four-day courtesy visit to Aqaba. On 31 May she headed north again to stop briefly at Port Said, before carrying out her second Cyprus patrol then returning to Grand Harbour after an absence of six weeks.

When, on 26 July, just six weeks after the final troop withdrawal from the Suez Canal Zone, President Nasser of Egypt nationalised the Suez Canal Company, *Decoy* was in Grand Harbour undergoing a four-week maintenance period, so she missed the first two weeks of exercises in preparation for the reoccupation of the former military base area in Egypt. When she did sail, on 13 August, it was straight into intensive training exercises as planeguard escort to the aircraft carriers *Eagle* and *Bulwark*, as well as convoy escort and naval gunfire support exercises. Throughout the second half of August and into September *Decoy* kept up a relentless schedule of training, with only short periods of relaxation in Sliema Creek. On 18 September, together with *Jamaica*, *Decoy* was steaming from an area east of Crete to the coast of Libya, and two days later she was heading back to Grand Harbour. At 1345 on Thursday 20 September, when she was some 200 miles south-east of Malta, one of the practice torpedo warheads on the after torpedo mounting exploded. Fortunately, there were no casualties, but there was some structural damage, and *Decoy* secured alongside Grand Harbour's Somerset Wharf the next morning for an unscheduled 18-day stopover while repairs were carried out. On Tuesday 9 October, with her repairs completed, *Decoy* sailed to continue her pre-invasion training

exercises, and this time she acted as planeguard to *Albion*. During the two weeks which followed she paid a short visit to the Italian port of Civitavecchia, before returning to Sliema Creek on 25 October. Next day, in company with *Alamein*, she sailed for Cyprus and anchored off Limassol at 0230 on 29 October. Less than 24 hours later, at 0013 on 30 October, *Decoy* weighed anchor and put to sea to join the Suez invasion convoy and by 2000 that evening she was some 200 miles north of Port Said. By 0015 on Wednesday 31 October *Decoy* was just a few miles from Port Said, and that afternoon she joined her sisters *Diamond* and *Duchess* as part of the escort screen to the carrier group, *Eagle*, *Albion* and *Bulwark*, which would commence air operations against Egyptian airfields in the early hours of the following morning. For three days during the air operations *Decoy* acted as support ship to *Bulwark*, and at 0645 on 2 November, while acting as planeguard to the carrier, she headed the search for the pilot of a Seahawk which had ditched on landing. Unfortunately, although wreckage and the pilot's official logs were recovered, there was no trace of the pilot himself. During the afternoon of 5 November *Decoy* joined the invasion convoy for the final stages of its passage, and between 0405 and 0443 on 6 November she opened fire with her main armament to bombard the beaches of Port Said in support of the landing by 42 Commando, Royal Marines. By early afternoon, with the troops established ashore, she had anchored off Port Said harbour where she remained for the rest of the short, ill-fated campaign. At midnight on 6/7 November, with the British and French Governments having agreed to ceasefire demands by the United Nations, the invasion was at an end.

During the forenoon of 9 November *Decoy* weighed anchor and set course for Malta, passing en route through the US Sixth Fleet's carrier force, which included USS *Coral Sea* and USS *Antietem* which, often in a hostile manner, had been shadowing and monitoring the joint Anglo-French invasion fleets. At 1710 on 11 November *Decoy* arrived alongside Grand Harbour's Hamilton Wharf, where she began a 17-day maintenance period. At the end

of November, with the final stages of the Anglo-French evacuation of Port Said about to get under way, *Decoy* returned to Port Said to patrol the harbour entrance, and during the evening of 22 December formed part of the escort for the last troop convoy which left Port Said. Four days later she secured to No.7 buoy back in Sliema Creek, to celebrate a rather belated Christmas, and at 1545 on 1 January 1957 she sailed from Malta to join her sisters *Diamond* and *Duchess* for the passage home. Steaming by way of Gibraltar she arrived in Plymouth Sound during the late evening of 8 January and next forenoon steamed up harbour into the Dockyard to end the foreign service leg of the commission.

On 19 February 1957, with the ship's company having taken a late Christmas leave period, *Decoy* left Devonport to make a short visit to the French port of Nantes on the Loire River, before returning to Portland to carry out a six-day training programme. During March the destroyer carried out a series of day-running exercises from Londonderry with *Chaplet* and *Chieftain*, before moving to the Clyde area for anti-submarine training. On 30 March she returned to Devonport for a three-month refit, returning to sea in mid-July for a training period at Portland. On 26 July she left Portland for the last foreign visits of the commission, making a four-day call at Amsterdam and a five-day visit to Gothenburg, arriving back at Devonport on 9 August at the end of the commission.

At 0850 on Tuesday 27 August *Decoy*'s new commanding officer, Captain F. P. Baker DSC RN, was appointed to the ship, and five hours later he was joined by the new ship's company. No sooner had the men stowed their kit than the ship was recommissioned, and preparations were made for the C-in-C Plymouth's inspection before further service with the Mediterranean Fleet. With the former having been passed with flying colours, on 4 September *Decoy* left Plymouth Sound in company with *Diana* to steam east for Portland where they were to carry out a short work-up before leaving for the Mediterranean. At 1807 that evening, however, as she steamed into the eastern entrance to Portland

Harbour, *Decoy* suffered a steering gear breakdown. Despite the fact that her starboard anchor was quickly dropped, the destroyer drifted and grounded with her port side to the outer breakwater, and her bows east abreast the east beacon. Fortunately, as it happened, the tug *Restive* was in the harbour with a film unit aboard who had just spent a day at sea shooting scenes portraying wartime maritime rescues, and the tug was able to come to *Decoy*'s aid within minutes. Once lines were secured, she was able to hold the destroyer off the breakwater, and at 2015 two more tugs arrived on the scene; working under floodlights which had been set up on the breakwater, they were able to pull *Decoy* clear and tow her to the Outer Coaling Pier, where the ship's divers began a survey of the hull.

Fortunately, the ship was not making water and during the forenoon of 6 September was towed out of harbour by two tugs, but once into the open waters of Lyme Bay the tugs were slipped and, escorted by *Diana*, she was able to proceed slowly under her own power. She passed Berry Head at 2330 the same evening and arrived alongside No.7 wharf at Devonport Dockyard during the afternoon of 7 September. Soon afterwards she was moved into No.9 dry dock.

It was Saturday 21 September before *Decoy* was ready for sea again and that forenoon she moved out into Cawsand Bay anchorage, before sailing for Gibraltar the next day. On 30 September she arrived in Malta's Sliema Creek, and during most of October she continued the work-up which had been interrupted at Portland, which meant day running with nights at anchor in Marsaxlokk Bay. The work-up ended on 24 October, after which *Decoy* underwent a two-week maintenance period before sailing to Cyprus to undertake a four-week patrol of the island's coast. During the patrol countless fishing boats were intercepted, stopped and searched, and the patrol ended on 5 December when *Decoy* left her anchorage at Famagusta to pay a weekend visit to Beirut. By mid-December the destroyer was back at Malta where, apart from excursions in local waters, she remained for Christmas and New Year.

Decoy *lying at anchor.*                                    (*T. Ferrers-Walker*)

On 11 January *Decoy* left Sliema Creek bound for seven days in Monaco where, at that time, she was the largest vessel to secure alongside the city state's Quai des Etats-Unis (United States Quay). On her departure LSA F. J. Goodey remembers,

'What seemed to the whole population of the principality had lined the harbour to see us off'.

*Decoy* then rendezvoused with *Agincourt* and *Barrosa* for exercises, which were followed by a short visit to La Spezia. By the end of January *Decoy* was back at Malta undergoing a refit and dry docking. During this period, at 1230 on Sunday 2 March, while the destroyer was secured to No.22 buoy in Grand Harbour, a serious flashback occurred in A boiler room, followed by a fire. Fortunately, there were no casualties and the fire was extinguished before any serious damage was done. Six weeks later, during the afternoon of 15 April, while *Decoy* was still at her buoy, the tank landing ship *Striker*, which was berthing at the east

dockyard, collided with her. Once again damage was minimal and next day, with the refit over, *Decoy* left harbour to carry out exercises with *Ark Royal*, *Sheffield* and *Diana*.

During the first week of May *Decoy* underwent FO2's harbour and sea inspections, and these were followed in mid-May by a second Cyprus patrol which lasted for six weeks, broken only by a fleeting return to Malta to land a senior Army officer and a detachment of Royal Marines from Akrotiri. During the second half of the patrol *Decoy* acted as planeguard to both *Eagle* and *Ark Royal* as all vessels stood by off the Cypriot coast in case intervention was ordered to deal with political disturbances in Lebanon and Jordan. In the event no intervention was necessary and on 4 July she returned to Malta. *Decoy*'s deployment in the Mediterranean was coming to an end and during the forenoon of 5 July, together with *Diamond*, *Diana* and *Duchess*, the three other ships of the Fifth Destroyer Squadron, she left Malta for Gibraltar and home, arriving in Plymouth Sound during the morning of Friday 11 July. Late in the forenoon she led *Diana* up harbour

and both ships secured alongside the dockyard's No.1 wharf.

Following her arrival at Devonport *Decoy* began a nine-week maintenance period, which included 17 days in dry dock, and it was 16 September before she put to sea again to head north for a brief visit to Belfast and onward to Arctic waters. In late August 1958 Iceland had unilaterally declared a 12-mile fishing limit around its coastline, which Britain did not recognise, and with the British fishing fleet still trawling just off Iceland's three-mile limit the Royal Navy had to protect the trawlers from the small, but highly mobile and aggressive Icelandic Coastguard patrol ships, commonly referred to as 'gunboats', which were intent on cutting the trawlers' warps. LSA Goodey's memories of this period are the boatloads of fresh fish which were delivered daily to *Decoy* by one or more of the trawlers. The fishery protection patrol lasted for just over two weeks, and on 6 October she left Icelandic waters and steamed south to make a five-day visit to Pembroke Dock followed by a six-day visit to Rotterdam.

After leaving Dutch waters on 24 October, *Decoy* rendezvoused with *Diamond*, *Diana* and *Duchess*, as well as the submarine depot ship *Adamant*, and set course for Gibraltar. On 3 November, flying the flag of the Second Sea Lord, Vice-Admiral D. E. Holland-Martin, *Decoy* left Gibraltar for a four-day visit to Tangier after which, with other units of the Home Fleet, including *Birmingham* and *Apollo*, and units of the Portuguese Navy, she took part in exercises in the Western Mediterranean and the Atlantic as the fleet slowly made its way home. The final training exercise involved the destroyers taking on duties of convoy escort ships, with *Decoy*, *Diana* and *Duchess* providing a screen for *Adamant*. For *Decoy* and *Diana* the exercises and the operational duties of the commission ended on 9 December, when the two destroyers returned to Devonport Dockyard.

By the end of the year most of *Decoy*'s ship's company had been drafted away from the ship, and in March 1959 she was taken in hand by Devonport Dockyard for a modernisation refit, at which time she would become the only Daring-class destroyer to be fitted with the Seacat guided missile system during her Royal Navy service.

During *Decoy*'s long period laid up and in refit in Devonport Dockyard she underwent a thorough overhaul and some reconstruction to fit her out for her role as a Seacat anti-aircraft missile trials ship. Abaft the after funnel a new deckhouse was built, on top of which were deck projections reaching out to the ship's sides and supported by stanchions. It was on these projections that the Seacat launchers, holding four missiles each, were fitted. Although the Seacat guided missile system had been extensively proved on missile ranges ashore, these tests in early 1960 would be the first carried out at sea. The missile system had been designed as a replacement for the 40mm Bofors anti-aircraft gun, and originally it had been intended to fit the new Rothesay-class frigates with the missiles. In the event, however, this was not possible and the first ships to be equipped with them were the County-class destroyers, the first of which, HMS *Devonshire*, was launched in June 1960.

By the spring of 1960 work on *Decoy* was nearing completion and on 2 May her new commanding officer, Captain E. F. Hamilton-Meikle MBE RN, joined the ship. Three weeks later, manned by a much reduced ship's company, the destroyer put to sea for four days of post-refit trials, but on 27 May she returned to Devonport Dockyard and her steaming crew moved back to the accommodation at the Royal Naval Barracks. During the first week of July 1960 a full ship's company moved on board, and at 0945 on 8 July *Decoy* was commissioned for Home Sea service and for Seacat missile trials, the event being marked by a ceremony on the forecastle. Three days later she sailed for an extensive period of steaming and machinery trials, and on 20 July the C-in-C Plymouth, Admiral Sir Richard Onslow, spent the day on board carrying out his sea inspection. In early October 1960, with her sea trials completed, *Decoy* began her programme of Seacat firings at targets which were usually pilotless drones. With her missile trials under way *Decoy* quickly became a magnet for VIP visitors,

and it was said that during the course of each week the ship would play host to more VIPs than would normally be carried during a whole commission. During the course of the autumn and winter of 1960 and early 1961 the ship rarely ventured further than the Channel and the South-West Approaches of the Atlantic Ocean. There were a few port visits, such as Belfast in September and Nantes during the second week of November.

Christmas and New Year were spent alongside at Devonport, and on 12 January 1961 the missile trials began once again. For operational reasons this phase of the trials involved *Decoy* day running from Devonport, and early every forenoon she would embark a group of civilian scientists, who quickly became known to the ship's company as the 'Boffins', as well as a number of radio-controlled pilotless target aircraft. Later each day, when the programme of trials had been completed, she would return the 'Boffins' to Devonport Dockyard and replenish her stock of target drones and Seacat missiles. On 6 February there was a break from this daily routine when, after hoisting the flag of the C-in-C, Plymouth, Vice-Admiral Sir Charles Madden,

*Decoy* left Devonport for official visits to the French naval bases at Brest and Cherbourg. In March she made a weekend visit to Liverpool, but she spent the remainder of the month day running as the manufacturer's trials of the Seacat weapon system continued.

At the end of April *Decoy* took part in a Territorial Army Reservists exercise when she carried the advance party of 30 officers and men of the 4th Battalion, The Devonshire Regiment, from Devonport to their mobilisation base at Dover. During the 24-hour passage up Channel *Decoy* was subjected to mock submarine and air attacks and on 30 April, as she steamed through the early morning mist into Dover Harbour, her decks were manned by both Army and Navy personnel. Following this brief diversion, however, *Decoy* continued her guided missile trials, but in mid-May the routine was interrupted when, on 15 May, she again embarked Admiral Sir Charles Madden and sailed for Kiel. During the passage the C-in-C carried out his formal sea inspection, on completion of which he transferred by jackstay to *Paladin* and following his departure *Decoy* began her passage of the River

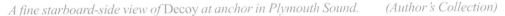

*A fine starboard-side view of* Decoy *at anchor in Plymouth Sound.*     *(Author's Collection)*

*Decoy leaving Portsmouth during the Seacat trials of 1962. The missile launchers and the specially built deck projections on which they were fitted can be seen aft of the second funnel.* (Portsmouth Royal Naval Museum)

Elbe and the Kiel Canal, arriving alongside the Tirpitz Mole of the German naval base during the evening of 17 May. Once alongside she hoisted the flag of Rear-Admiral M. S. Townsend, the NATO Commander of Allied Naval Forces Northern Area, Central Europe (COMNAVNORCENT). Admiral Townsend assumed control of a NATO operation which also involved West German, Danish and Norwegian naval and air force units. After leaving Kiel *Decoy* made an overnight passage to Aarhus where she joined 40 other NATO naval units for the exercises and for a farewell steam past to the outgoing C-in-C of NATO in Europe, and at one stage she had on board five Admirals and five Generals. The steam past in Aarhus Bay took place in perfect weather, and on completion *Decoy* set course for Stockholm where she arrived on 20 May. During the destroyer's six-day visit she was the main focus of attention for Sweden's senior naval officers and Defence Ministry officials, for the Seacat missile system was on the 'shopping list' for the Swedish Navy. *Decoy* left Stockholm on 26 May to return

via the Kiel Canal to Devonport where, once again, she began a monotonous day-running routine of Seacat trials. This time, however, she was engaged on the second phase of the trials which would see the missile system accepted for use in the fleet. During the latter half of 1961 there were few opportunities for foreign visits, with only a weekend alongside in Santander. In October the destroyer fired the 600th Seacat missile, and in mid-December the final firings took place prior to the ship's return to Devonport for leave and maintenance.

On 16 January 1962 *Decoy* left Devonport to restart the Seacat trials, and once again began the tedious routine of day running from Devonport. In March there was a visit to St Nazaire, and on 10 April she assisted in the search for two missing Gannet aircraft, which had disappeared from radar screens south of the Lizard during a joint RN-RAF exercise. At the end of May she called at Cherbourg, and from there she steamed north, via the Kiel Canal, to the southern Swedish port of

Karlskrona before retracing her route for a three-day call at Wilhelmshaven, after which she returned to Devonport.

*Decoy*'s final missile trials were carried out in July 1962 following short visits to Dover, Calais and Cherbourg. At the latter port she embarked 300 Royal Marines who had been on exercises in France which made for very cramped conditions on board for the seven and a half hour passage to Portsmouth. On 19 July Admiral Sir Charles Madden spent the day aboard watching the day's missile firings. Two days later, at 1450 on 21 July, *Decoy* secured alongside No.5 wharf at Devonport Dockyard. It was the end of her period as a trials ship, but not quite the end of the commission. During the first weekend of August *Decoy* was opened to the public for Navy Days, and at 0900 on 10 August Captain J. E. Pope RN assumed command of the destroyer.

In September she joined *Belfast* and the newly converted commando carrier *Albion* for the latter's work-up. For *Decoy* the commission ended on 20 September 1962, and ahead lay a six-month refit.

By the spring of 1963 *Decoy*'s refit had been completed and on 4 March she sailed to carry out a series of machinery trials, before returning to Devonport later in the month. At 1100 on 22 April, at a ceremony on the jetty alongside the ship, *Decoy* was recommissioned under Captain Pope, for a General Service Commission. Next day she left Devonport to begin her work-up at Portland, and in early May she carried out amphibious exercises with detachments of Royal Marines, first embarking and disembarking them at Slapton Sands, and then embarking them at Cherbourg and disembarking them in Plymouth Sound. During the remainder of May and for the first two weeks of June *Decoy* continued her work-up exercises at Portland, with only a short break when she took part in Navy Days at the Dorset base. In the third week of June, with her work-up successfully completed, she steamed north to the Clyde area to carry out anti-submarine exercises with *Bulwark* and *Grampus*. On 7 August, after carrying out maintenance at Devonport, giving leave and taking part in Plymouth Navy Days, *Decoy* hoisted the flag of the

C-in-C Plymouth and sailed for NATO exercises in the Atlantic Ocean. Also taking part were the cruisers *Belfast* and *Tiger*, and for the former it was to be the last operational exercise of her long naval career. During the course of the exercise *Decoy* acted as planeguard escort to the US Navy aircraft carrier *Independence*, and she also operated with the guided missile destroyer *Long Beach*. On 23 August, with both the C-in-C and the First Lord of the Admiralty aboard, *Decoy* led *Belfast* and *Tiger* up harbour into Devonport Dockyard.

During September and October *Decoy* exercised in home waters, operating with *Hermes* and *Tiger*, and as planeguard to the Dutch aircraft carrier *Karel Doorman* in the North Sea during the NATO exercise 'Flak Track'. In November, with *Tiger*, she paid a four-day visit to Lisbon, spent a long weekend in Gibraltar and in early December, with *Hermes*, *Hampshire*, *Berwick* and *Falmouth*, she took part in 'Exercise Limejug'. By mid-December *Decoy* had returned to Devonport for leave and maintenance prior to sailing for the overseas leg of the commission.

On 27 January 1964 *Decoy* left Devonport for two days of training at Portland and a short visit to Portsmouth, before steaming south to Funchal and Gibraltar whilst taking part in 'Exercise Magic Lantern', followed by anti-submarine exercises in the Clyde area. By 21 March she had returned to Devonport to undergo four weeks of maintenance, and during this period, on 2 April, there was a change of command when Commander J. K. Stevens took over from Captain Pope. Just over two weeks later, on 18 April, *Decoy* sailed for the naval base at Ireland Island, Bermuda, via Ponta Delgada arriving there some nine days after leaving Devonport. During her break at Bermuda *Decoy* hoisted the broad pendant of the Senior Naval Officer, West Indies Station, and four days later she steamed into the warm waters of the Caribbean.

By the mid-1960s many of HM ships had had air-conditioning installed in the accommodation for both officers and ratings, but the Daring-class destroyers relied on the old punkah louvre fresh air system of ventilation and, whenever possible, wind

scoops which provided welcome gusts of fresh sea air and, on occasions, more than just fresh air. As Commander Ian Inskip, who was a midshipman in *Decoy* during this period remembers:

'In terms of comfort *Decoy* was a definite step up from the Cadets' accommodation in *Wizard* and other ships of the Dartmouth Training Squadron. Even so I found myself, along with two other midshipmen, crammed into a very small two-berth cabin located directly above the ship's after fuel tanks, which the engineers seemed to regularly overfill with thick, black and pungent furnace fuel oil. In the days before air-conditioning was a common feature in HM ships, in hot climates we relied on wind scoops for fresh air ventilation and these were put out of the scuttles at every opportunity. On one occasion, when we were steaming downwind, one of my fellow midshipmen was ordered to give the ship a blow through. He duly piped the order, "Out wind scoops forward", and then turned the ship. He should, of course, have turned the ship first before opening the scuttles. As the ship's company were busy cleaning the messdecks for Captain's Rounds, they put out their wind scoops, and half a minute later they were drenched as the water rushed in. He was not popular. One afternoon in the Caribbean, like any good midshipman, I was lying stripped to the waist on my bunk when a lighted fag end, glowing red hot from the wind, blew into my cabin via the wind scoop and landed on my chest. I jumped out of my bunk pretty quickly, but had I not been there we would have had a serious fire in the cabin – atop the fuel tanks. On another occasion, as I was packing my kit for return to the UK, the ship was again turned hard without warning. Water flooded in through the wind scoop and all over my kit, which had to be packed damp. Imagine how my kit looked and smelt a month later when I was finally able to unpack my gear.'

During the first two weeks of May *Decoy* visited San Juan and Grenada, and on 12 May paid a five-

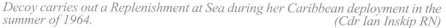

*Decoy carries out a Replenishment at Sea during her Caribbean deployment in the summer of 1964.* (Cdr Ian Inskip RN)

*It can be rough in the Caribbean. Decoy takes it green during her summer deployment.*
*(Cdr Ian Inskip RN)*

day visit to Georgetown, British Guiana (Guyana), the small British enclave on the continent of South America, where labour unrest on the large sugar plantations and racial tensions between people of African and Indian descent were causing problems at a time when the colony was moving towards independence. During *Decoy*'s first visit, however, there was no trouble and when she was opened to the public over 2,000 people took the opportunity to visit and take a tour round her. On 17 May *Decoy* left Georgetown to make a 24-hour passage to the Chaguaramas naval base on the island of Trinidad, some ten miles west of Port of Spain, to carry out maintenance. Four days later, however, the political situation in British Guiana deteriorated with further labour unrest and racial strife, resulting in murder, arson and rioting. Some 24 people were killed and 343 injured, and in order to reinforce the permanent garrison of 116 officers and men of the Devon and Dorset Regiment *Decoy* was ordered to Georgetown where a state of emergency had been declared. Leaving Chaguaramas at just before midnight on 22 May, the destroyer arrived at Georgetown some 15 hours later where her landing

platoons were deployed to assist the civil police patrol the capital. Three days later, with the situation having quietened, *Decoy* was ordered to the Bahamas area to patrol the southern banks between the islands and Cuba, where armed groups of political dissidents had been using the uninhabited islands as bases from which to enter Cuba.

*Decoy*'s first patrol began during the evening of 30 May and the following morning she anchored off Cay Sal, just 40 miles from the coast of Cuba. Once a landing party had searched the island and declared it to be free of inhabitants the rest of the day was devoted to banyan leave, with the long sandy beaches providing an ideal location for recreational pastimes. On 1 June *Decoy* was once again on patrol off the islands, and during the forenoon her landing parties searched Lobos Cay to find it all clear. At 1550 that afternoon the destroyer anchored off Anguilla Cay, 45 miles north of Cuba, and an armed landing party was put ashore to investigate what appeared to be wreckage on the beach, which turned out to be arms and ammunition. As they were searching the area a 25ft motor launch was spotted leaving the island at high speed and

*Decoy* hurriedly weighed anchor and set off in pursuit. After a chase of almost two hours covering some 12 miles, during which A turret and the Bofors guns were manned, *Decoy* overhauled and stopped the launch and its five occupants were arrested. After hoisting the launch inboard it was found to be carrying detonators and fuel. *Decoy* immediately returned to Anguilla Cay to put another landing party ashore who subsequently arrested three more people, and discovered an ammunition dump containing thousands of rounds. After all the arms and ammunition had been collected *Decoy* set course for Freeport, where the prisoners were landed the next day and the ship then continued her patrol. It later transpired that one of those arrested was the head of a Cuban revolutionary junta which had been conducting long-range guerrilla raids against the Castro regime in Cuba. Among the others arrested were two American freelance photogra-

phers. The destroyer had foiled a planned raid on Cuba and all those arrested appeared before magistrates in Nassau, before being handed over to immigration officials.

During the remainder of the month *Decoy* continued to patrol the islands off the Great Bahamas Bank, and on 7 June off Cay Sal she rescued three Cuban refugees from a waterlogged dinghy, subsequently handing them over to a US Coastguard vessel. During the patrol there were overnight fuelling stops at the US naval base of Key West and banyans on the sun-drenched, uninhabited islands, but on 21 June she returned to Chaguaramas to complete the interrupted maintenance period. During the second week of July *Decoy* exercised with *Whirlwind*, and began her second Bahamas patrol, during which she detained another group of Cuban refugees, this time landing them at Nassau. During the first week of August there was time for a short break at

*Decoy secured alongside at Newport Rhode Island, during her 'America's Cup' visit in September 1964.*

*(Ken Kelly)*

Chaguaramas before a third Bahamas patrol, on completion of which she steamed north to Bermuda and the naval base at Ireland Island where she underwent a three-week maintenance period.

When *Decoy* left Bermuda on 7 September she set course for the US mainland and the highlight of the commission, visits to the ports of Baltimore and Newport, Rhode Island. At 1600 on 9 September the destroyer arrived alongside Pier 4 at Baltimore, which coincided with celebrations to mark the 150th anniversary of the writing of the American National Anthem, '*The Star Spangled Banner*', composed by lawyer John Key who, in 1814, witnessed an assault by a British Fleet upon Fort McHenry. As dawn broke on the morning after the battle he observed that the US flag was still flying proudly, thus inspiring the composition. As *Decoy* steamed past Fort McHenry she fired a national salute of 21 guns, which was returned by a shore battery whose gunners were clad in the ceremonial garb of their predecessors from 150 years before. Unfortunately, a spell of unseasonable wet weather caused the cancellation of a parade in the city, but an unscheduled visit to the ship by comedian Bob Hope was appreciated by all on board. From Baltimore *Decoy* steamed by way of the Chesapeake-Delaware Canal to Newport, Rhode Island, where she acted as the British guardship during the America's Cup yacht races between the US defender *Constellation* and the British challenger *Sovereign*. During the six-day visit the destroyer was also the focal point for local society, with the British Ambassador to the United States holding a reception for 200 guests on board, and with over 500 people watching the yacht races from her decks. The memorable visit ended on 21 September when *Decoy* sailed for another series of Bahamas patrols, during which she detained a number of Cuban refugees on the island of Cay Sol.

In early November, flying the broad pendant of Commodore E. B. Ashmore, there was a break from patrolling when *Decoy* paid flag-showing visits to Bridgetown, Barbados; Rossau, Dominica; Castries, St Lucia; Gustavia, on the French island of Barthelemy, and San Juan, Puerto Rico, as well as

carrying out training exercises with the frigate *Rothesay*. By 18 November, however, she was back on the Bahamas patrol which, in company with *Rothesay*, is where she remained until early December. *Decoy*'s last day on that patrol was 8 December, and after refuelling at Key West she set course for Bermuda. Four days later, at Hamilton, 90 ratings who would form a skeleton crew during the ship's subsequent lay-up joined and on 11 January 1965, after spending Christmas and New Year at Bermuda, *Decoy* left Ireland Island to carry out her last Bahamas patrol. This ended in February with a visit to Port Everglades and a return to Bermuda.

At 0930 on 16 February *Decoy* left Bermuda bound for the Azores and Portsmouth, where she was to be paid off for a period in Reserve and a refit which would last for 20 months. The return passage was marred when, at 0810 on Sunday 21 February, the ship's NAAFI manager, Mr J. F. Mitchelmore, was found to be missing. He had last been seen at 2345 the previous evening, and it was clear that he had been lost overboard. The ship was some 200 miles south-south-west of the Azores and despite the impossible odds of his body ever being found, Commander Stevens retraced the ship's overnight track. Finally, however, at 1745 the search was abandoned and *Decoy* set course for Ponta Delgada where she refuelled. Finally, at 2130 on Thursday 25 February, *Decoy* anchored at Spithead and next forenoon, with her paying-off pennant flying and her decks manned, she steamed up harbour to secure alongside Fountain Lake Jetty. It would be more than 18 months before she put to sea again.

During the remainder of 1965 and for almost the whole of 1966 *Decoy* lay alongside No.3 basin, or in No.14 dry dock at Portsmouth Dockyard, as she underwent a modernisation refit. On 22 January 1966, as she was being moved to a new berth in the basin, she collided with the submarine *Tapir*, which was awaiting her final voyage to the shipbreaker's yard, and then struck the jetty, stern to, causing some damage to her hull. On 24 October, under the command of Commander G. I. Pritchard RN, a

reduced ship's company moved on board from the Royal Naval Barracks and four weeks later *Decoy* sailed to carry out machinery trials, which continued on into January 1967. In early February she paid a visit to Le Havre and this was followed by a two-month docking period at Portsmouth. On 2 May *Decoy* left Portsmouth to continue her machinery and ship handling trials, and in mid-June she exercised with the new guided missile destroyer *Glamorgan* off Scotland's east coast. This was followed by a five-day visit to Dundee where she secured alongside the city's Queen Elizabeth Wharf. On 3 July she left Dundee to make the return passage to Portsmouth, arriving alongside Fountain Lake Jetty the following day.

Originally it had been intended that, once her trials were completed, *Decoy* would be laid up in Reserve at Portsmouth, which in effect meant the end of her operational career in the Royal Navy, but a change of mind at the Admiralty gave her a new lease of life and one further commission. On 31 July Commander J. R. Symonds-Taylor RN took over command of the ship, and just over two weeks later, at 1100 on 16 August, *Decoy* was recommissioned for service with the Western and Far East Fleets. Later that month, at Navy Days, *Decoy* attracted over 9,000 visitors, after which she sailed for Portland to begin her work-up, a busy period which took from early September to mid-November, having been disrupted during October by a three-week maintenance period at Devonport. Although in naval terms *Decoy* was now one of the fleet's 'old ladies', one rating who joined the ship at this time was suitably impressed; ex-Junior Seaman Keith Sowerby remembers:

'I was thrilled when I saw *Decoy* for the first time. At 16 years of age and fresh from training at *Ganges* and *Vernon,* she still had the appearance of a sleek, triple-turreted destroyer and she looked a magnificent ship. I felt very proud. However, practical problems soon came to the fore and struggling up the gangway carrying both my holdall and kitbag, under the gaze of a number of spectators who were watching my progress, was a real effort. However, I managed to get over the brow and throw down my kitbag to salute the quarterdeck. It seemed that I had passed the first big test. I then turned to the quartermaster, a three-badged Chief Petty Officer who, to my young eye, looked very elderly. He held out his hand in my direction and I immediately grasped it and shook it heartily, immediately perking up at what appeared a kind gesture. I was soon put in my place when he said, "It's not your hand I want lad, it's your draft chit." It was my first mistake and I felt rather foolish. I later got to know the "Buffer", CPO Les (Scouse) Reynolds, who was an ex-Second World War sailor who had served in the cruiser *Dorsetshire* during the *Bismarck* action, and we often laughed at the "handshake" incident.'

*Decoy*'s final inspection began on 13 November and ended the next day at midnight when she anchored at Spithead, steaming up harbour later in the day to secure alongside the North Wall. It was duly noted that she had been away from her base port for 11½ weeks, but at no time had she got any further than 250 miles away from it. On 20 November *Decoy* left Portsmouth for the Clyde area where, with *Aurora*, *Falmouth* and *Hardy* and assisted by the submarine *Oracle*, she took part in anti-submarine training exercises. Keith Sowerby remembers this period well, for:

'Having completed my training as a Junior Seaman at *Ganges*, and having been drafted to *Vernon* for further training on the Mk 10 Mortar, we were solemnly assured that the Mortar's predecessor, the Squid, was obsolete and our chances of ever having to operate one were very remote. Imagine my surprise when, on receiving my draft chit for *Decoy* the instructor at *Vernon* glibly said, "I hope you know your Squid Drill, you'll need it in *Decoy*." Nevertheless, I soon learned all about the obsolete Squid, and spent two

Decoy *at sea in 1967. This aerial view shows to advantage the revised layout of the superstructure following the removal of the torpedo tubes.* (Syd Goodman Collection)

happy years in the old destroyer.'

By the first week in December *Decoy* had returned to Portsmouth for maintenance and leave and by the first week in January 1968 she was once again ready for sea. On 3 January she left Portsmouth as part of the First Western Fleet Division under the command of Admiral Sir John Bush, C-in-C, Western Fleet, led by the guided missile destroyer *London* which was returning to home waters from Simonstown, and in company with *Aisne*, *Falmouth* and *Juno*. After detaching from *London*, *Decoy*, *Aisne* and the two frigates set course for the Caribbean and, steaming via the Azores, *Decoy* arrived at St Kitts on 22 January. On 31 January, after visiting Nevis and San Juan, she embarked two Bahamas police officers and began a

ten-day patrol of the Grand Bahamas Bank which, unlike her previous patrol of the area, passed uneventfully. In mid-February she visited Jamaica, Curacao, the Colombian port of Barranquilla and Antigua, as well as taking part in a squadron exercise, code-named 'Caribex', which also involved the Dutch destroyer *Rotterdam* and ships of the Colombian Navy. On 1 March she arrived at the Chaguaramas Naval Base in Trinidad to undergo a 12-day maintenance period before rejoining *Aisne*, *Falmouth* and *Juno* for the passage back to the UK. On 28 March *Decoy* arrived in Portsmouth where, during three weeks alongside in the dockyard, she gave leave and underwent maintenance.

On 23 April she left Portsmouth for Gibraltar to join *Falmouth* and *Juno* in the NATO exercise 'Dawn Patrol', which involved units from six

nations in a major amphibious exercise, with landings at Messara Bay, Crete. During the course of the exercise there were no opportunities for shore leave and on 16 May, after collecting mail from Malta, *Decoy* sailed west for Gibraltar. During her six days alongside the colony's south mole she underwent her harbour inspection by Captain (D) and on 28 May, while en route for Rosyth, her sea inspection was carried out. After joining *Hampshire* and other units for Rosyth Navy Days *Decoy* steamed south again to spend the latter half of June day running from Portsmouth, during which she carried guests for Sea Days in company with *Hampshire*, *Danae*, and *Jaguar*. On 12 July she once again set course for Gibraltar to take on the role of guardship. During the forenoon of 1 August, while *Decoy* was alongside the south mole, an urgent request for assistance was received from the 5,388-ton British cargo vessel MV *Kinross*, which was in the Mediterranean and heading for Gibraltar. Her master had reported trouble among his Chinese crew members, who had been holding rowdy and threatening political meetings and he felt that the safety of his British officers and the ship was threatened. The crew's behaviour mirrored the political turmoil in China at that time, when Mao Tse-tung's controversial 'great proletarian cultural revolution' was causing massive upheavals in the country and, occasionally, amongst expatriate Chinese nationals. As soon as the signal was received, *Decoy* came to immediate notice for steam and sailed at 1145. At 2150 *Decoy* sighted the merchant vessel in a position Lat 36°32'N/Lat 00°56'W, and an hour later she took up station one cable off *Kinross*'s port side, with a fully armed boarding party ready to transfer to the ship if required. By this time, however, the situation on board the merchantman had stabilised and *Decoy* escorted the vessel to Gibraltar, illuminating her upper deck with a searchlight every 15 minutes. Fortunately there were no further problems and at just before midnight on 2 August *Kinross* and *Decoy* anchored off Gibraltar's harbour mouth where the civil police were waiting to board the merchant ship.

*Decoy* remained in the area off Gibraltar until the

last week of August when she returned to Portsmouth, via Lisbon, to carry out a nine-week maintenance period. At 1600 on 31 October 1968, after a 24-hour delay due to a faulty turbo alternator, *Decoy* left Portsmouth bound for the Far East. After a 48-hour pause at Gibraltar she sailed south for Simonstown and seven days later a full Crossing the Line ceremony was held on the iron deck. At 1312 on 19 November, when the destroyer was still some 300 miles north-west of Cape Town, and steaming through heavy seas, a red flare was sighted just a few miles ahead. Seven minutes later *Decoy* located a small, 158-ton Dutch merchant ship, the MV *Wuta*, which was listing dangerously to starboard. The vessel, which was carrying a cargo of sand, had been rolling heavily and this had caused her cargo to shift, resulting in the severe list. To add to her troubles her engines had failed and she was taking in water. On board *Decoy* a boarding party of engineers and seamen armed with shovels was assembled, all under the command of the gunnery officer. Once aboard the *Wuta* the seamen set to work to level out and readjust the cargo while the engineers tackled the engines. Meanwhile *Decoy* took the merchantman in tow and slowly continued her course to Simonstown. However, with the *Wuta* continuing to take in water, the list kept worsening and at 0100 on 20 November, some eight and a half hours after beginning the tow and despite the fact that weather conditions had improved, it suddenly increased dramatically. A Gemini dinghy was quickly dispatched from the destroyer to take off *Wuta*'s crew and most of the boarding party, leaving just enough personnel to manage the tow. It soon became apparent that the *Wuta* was unlikely to stay afloat long enough to reach Cape Town, and course was altered towards nearby Saldanha Bay where it was hoped that the small vessel could be beached in shallow water. However, as the list continued to increase rapidly, at 1605 the towing party was brought back to *Decoy* and less than half an hour later, as *Decoy* towed her charge into the bay, *Wuta* began to roll over. As the merchantman slipped beneath the waves the tow line was slipped. *Decoy*'s diving team spent more

than two hours searching the sunken wreck and they finally managed to recover the destroyer's 40-ton portable pump. At 2000 the destroyer was able to resume her passage and she secured alongside Simonstown Dockyard next forenoon, where *Wuta*'s crew were landed.

Having been delayed by the attempts to salvage the *Wuta*, *Decoy*'s visit to Simonstown was limited to just 24 hours and during the forenoon of 22 November she left harbour and set course into the Indian Ocean for her stint on the Beira Patrol. Two days after leaving Simonstown *Decoy* rendezvoused with her sister *Defender* to carry out a mail transfer before commencing her first patrol off the Mozambican port of Beira, aimed at enforcing the oil blockade of Rhodesia. During *Decoy*'s two-week patrol inter-ship sports and uckers competitions were arranged with *Manxman* and *Naiad* for the much-prized and highly painted and polished 'Beira Bucket'. During the second week of December, sailing by way of Farquhar Island and Gan, *Decoy* made her passage to Singapore, arriving alongside the naval base during the forenoon of 24 December, just in time for Christmas and New Year celebrations.

At 1715 on 4 January 1969 there was a final change of command for *Decoy* when Commander J. J. Black MBE RN, who had flown out from the UK, took over from Commander Symonds-Taylor. For the destroyer there were still two weeks of essential maintenance to complete, and on 27 January she sailed to take part in the annual 'FOTEX' exercise. Also present were *Hermes*, *Diamond*, *Aurora*, *Grenville*, HMAS *Duchess* and *Derwent* and HMNZS *Blackpool*. After the first phase of night encounter and air defence exercises the fleet anchored off the idyllic island of Pulau Langkawi to exercise the ships' divers and, of course, to make the most of banyans on the beautiful unspoilt beaches, which in the late 1960s were still largely beyond the reach of mass tourism from Europe and Australia. During the forenoon of 2 February the exercises got under way once again but just 20 minutes later *Decoy* suffered a major lubricating oil failure to her starboard main gearbox. It marked the

end of her participation and later that day she was detached from the exercise to return to Singapore.

The passage through the Strait of Malacca on the port engine, with 17 degrees of helm, was slow and it was the forenoon of 4 February before she arrived alongside Singapore Naval Base. Work began immediately to ascertain both the cause and extent of the damage, which turned out to be serious. Fortunately, spares could be flown out from the UK and the engine room department and the dockyard toiled to get the ship ready for sea by the end of February. Having missed the FOTEX exercises *Decoy* was ready just in time to participate in the fleet's programme of visits to Australia, and she left Singapore at 1100 on 20 February, first to run brief trials on the repaired gearbox and then to set course for Auckland. *Decoy* made the passage by way of Townsville in Australia which she reached on the last day of February. Four days later she arrived at Auckland's Devonport Navy Yard, on the north side of the harbour, for what was to be a very successful six-day visit. After leaving Auckland *Decoy* steamed north into the Pacific Ocean to pay short visits to a number of islands, including Vanuatu, the Solomon Islands where she anchored off Kirakira, and Auki. The very nature of the islands and the anchorages meant that shore leave was restricted to organised banyans and local hospitality invitations. One of the latter took the form of an invitation to 50 members of the ship's company to attend a traditional Solomon Islands feast. Having left the Pacific islands *Decoy*, *Danae* and *Tidespring* carried out training exercises while en route to Hong Kong, and during the afternoon of 27 March they arrived in Victoria Harbour, where *Decoy* secured alongside the North Wall of Hong Kong Dockyard. *Decoy*'s arrival in Hong Kong marked the beginning of a very busy ten days for the destroyer's ship's company as preparations were made for their harbour and sea inspections, the latter taking place on 5 April as *Decoy*, *Albion*, *Danae* and *Lincoln* were en route to South Korean ports. *Decoy* made a two-day visit to the South Korean port of Chinhae, just west of Pusan, followed by further exercises with *Albion*, *Danae* and *Lincoln* as they

made their way from South Korea to the Japanese port of Kobe for a much-publicised goodwill visit led by *Albion*, which was wearing the flag of Vice-Admiral A. T. F. G. Griffin, FO2 Far East Station. From Kobe coach parties were organised to the former ancient capitals of Japan, Kyoto and Nara, and on 19 April, after five days in Kobe, *Decoy* steamed across Japan's busy Inland Sea to the smaller port of Takamatsu where, in a less formal situation, officers and men were warmly welcomed. In his autobiography Admiral Black nostalgically recalls a civic reception for the officers at which he led a 'Conga' style dance at the City Hall. When the ship opened to the public over 4,000 people visited her during just one afternoon, which was a measure of the success of the five days at the small Japanese port.

After leaving Takamatsu during the forenoon of 24 April *Decoy* rendezvoused with *Danae* and *Lincoln* to set course for Okinawa and exercises with the US Navy, and by the end of April the destroyer was back alongside in Hong Kong. By now *Decoy*'s deployment in the Far East was drawing to a close as she left Hong Kong on 6 May to return to Singapore. In mid-May she carried out a series of gunnery training exercises, interspersed with the ever-popular recreational leave on the island of Pulau Tioman. Finally, after a four-week maintenance period at Singapore, at just after midday on Monday 23 June, *Decoy* left Singapore Naval Base to steam via Gan and Farquhar Island for the Beira Patrol. During the evening of 3 July she relieved *Dainty* off Beira, and the latter set course for home and decommissioning. *Decoy*'s second Beira Patrol lasted for four weeks before, on 2 August, she was relieved by *Rothesay* and she too set course for the passage home, via Simonstown.

After an enjoyable six days alongside the South African naval base, on 11 August *Decoy* left harbour to rendezvous with *Naiad* for the long passage north. The voyage was broken by a refuelling stop at Freetown and a weekend visit to Funchal on the island of Madeira. Finally, at 0730 on 28 August, *Decoy* anchored at Spithead and four and a half hours later she was secured alongside Portsmouth

Dockyard's Fountain Lake Jetty, where she was welcomed by families and friends. Although she was home it was by no means the end of *Decoy*'s commission, and on 6 October she left Portsmouth for Gibraltar where, for nearly three months, she would perform the duties of the colony's guardship. During the final phase of *Decoy*'s career with the Royal Navy there was a visit to Tangiers, a major exercise, 'Emery Cloth', with *Blake* and *Hampshire*, a ten-day maintenance period in Malta and finally, on 11 December, a four-day visit to Livorno. At just after midnight on 19 December *Decoy* left Gibraltar to return to Portsmouth, and at 1130 on Tuesday 23 December she arrived alongside North Corner Jetty to give leave and to undergo maintenance. On 28 January 1970 she left Portsmouth to return to Gibraltar for further duties as the colony's guardship. This time, from her arrival until the first week of February, she was kept busy shadowing the Soviet helicopter carrier *Moskva* and her accompanying group, which included a Sverdlov cruiser, two Kotlin destroyers, three submarines and two support ships. *Decoy*'s role was to gather intelligence on *Moskva* for which cameras had been specially set up in order to get good photographs of her while operating aircraft. During the evening of 3 February, as *Decoy* was shadowing *Moskva*, one of the Soviet submarines surfaced very close to the destroyer, but fortunately no harm was done. Three days later *Decoy* secured alongside in Gibraltar, but within days she was back at sea exercising with *Hermes*, *Ajax*, *Charybdis* and *Lincoln*. At one stage the C-in-C, Western Fleet, transferred by jackstay from *Lincoln*, leaving four hours later by helicopter which hovered over the destroyer's quarterdeck. During the third week of February *Decoy* operated with *Ajax* and *Lincoln* while day running from Gibraltar, but on 21 February she left Gibraltar to return home to Portsmouth. After anchoring at Spithead during the morning of 25 February she steamed up harbour during the forenoon to secure alongside the South Wall at 1100. This time it was the end of her operational career with the Royal Navy.

For 14 days *Decoy* lay alongside at Portsmouth as

*Still recognisable as a former Daring-class ship, the Peruvian Navy's destroyer* Ferré.

*(Lt Cdr J. R. Asti, Peruvian Navy)*

she was de-ammunitioned and de-stored, and on 6 March Commander Black left the ship as the First Lieutenant took command. Five days later, at 1000 on 11 March, manned only by a steaming crew, *Decoy* left Portsmouth to make a 27-hour passage through strong winds and blizzards to Birkenhead. She arrived alongside the outer basin of Cammell Laird's shipyard during the afternoon of 12 March, and at noon the next day she was paid off for disposal.

Both *Decoy* and her sister *Diana* had been sold to the Peruvian Navy, and the refitting of the two ships, at a cost of £4.5million, would last for three years. Work carried out during this refit included the rebuilding of the mast for the installation of new Plessey AWS-1 air-search radar and the fitting of eight Exocet MM-38 missile launchers, which took the place of the blind fire director forward of X turret. Finally, on 28 April 1973, having been renamed

*Ferré*, after Diego Ferré, a war hero who died at the Battle of Angamos during the 'War of the Pacific' between Peru and Chile in 1879, she began her service under the Peruvian flag. While serving with the Marina de Guerra del Peru further modernisation work was carried out and in the mid-1970s the Squid ASW Mortar was removed and a helicopter landing deck fitted. Later in the 1970s her gunnery systems were modernised, but she was still recognisable as a 'Daring-Class' destroyer. In the later 1990s, during the course of a visit to Peru, the Type-42 destroyer HMS *Edinburgh* met up with *Ferré*, but whether any 'old stagers' among her senior rates ever served in her at the start of their naval careers is not recorded.

*Ferré* was decommissioned in 2005, more than 50 years after she had first entered service. She was the last of the eight 'Darings' in operational service.

**HMS *Decoy*
Commanding Officers**

| Name: | Date Appointed: |
| --- | --- |
| Captain R. H. Maurice DSO DSC RN | 7 April 1953 |
| Captain M. N. Tufnell DSC RN | 16 August 1954 |
| Captain P. J. Hill-Norton RN | 10 February 1956 |
| Captain F. P. Baker DSC RN | 27 August 1957 |
| Captain E. F. Hamilton-Meikle MBE RN | 2 May 1960 |
| Captain J. E. Pope RN | 10 August 1962 |
| Commander J. K. Stevens RN | 2 April 1964 |
| Commander G. I. Pritchard RN | 24 October 1966 |
| Commander J. R. Symonds-Taylor RN | 31 July 1967 |
| Commander J. J. Black MBE RN | 4 January 1969 |

**Battle Honours**

| Ashantee 1873-74 | Greece 1941 |
| --- | --- |
| Alexandria 1882 | Crete 1941 |
| Mediterranean 1940 | Libya 1941-42 |
| Calabria 1940 | Malta Convoys 1941-42 |

Atlantic 1942

# Part Seven

# HMS DELIGHT

## October 1953 - August 1967

*HMS* Delight *manoeuvring at sea.*                                                                    *(MoD/Crown Copyright)*

**D**isdain was to have been the name of the destroyer whose keel was laid on 5 September 1946 at the Govan shipyard of the Fairfield Shipbuilding Company on the River Clyde, however, three months before this event it was changed to *Delight*, which revived memories of the destroyer of that name which, on 29 July 1940, had been bombed and sunk off Portland. In the austere post-war years of the 1940s, with shortages of steel and skilled labour, it would be four years before the vessel was ready for launching. The ceremony took place on Thursday 21 December 1950, when Lady Lesley Jowitt, the wife of the Lord Chancellor in Attlee's Government, sent her down the slipway into the River Clyde. Although the launch freed the slipway for merchant ship tonnage,

it was to be almost another three years before *Delight* was commissioned. In the summer of 1951 the first key naval personnel were appointed to travel north to Glasgow to stand by the ship as she was fitting out, and two years later, on 30 June 1953, *Delight*'s first commanding officer, Captain H. J. F. Lane OBE RN, was appointed. By this time building work on the destroyer was nearing completion, and she was lying in Fairfield's basin just off the Govan Road. During the early hours of Saturday 14 September 1953, a patrolling watchman discovered a fire in *Delight*'s direction-finding room and raised the alarm. Four units of Glasgow's fire brigade were quickly on the scene, and after an hour the blaze was extinguished. Fortunately, damage was confined to electrical equipment, timber panelling

and to radio valves. As *Delight* was fitted with the latest anti-aircraft and anti-submarine weapons, prompt security measures were taken, with all entrances to the shipyard being sealed and special guards mounted. In addition the Glasgow City Police launched a full investigation, but it was soon ascertained that the fire had been caused by an electrical fault and that there was no question of sabotage.

In the first week of October, with fitting-out work almost completed, the main body of the ship's company joined the ship and during the forenoon of Friday 9 October *Delight* slipped her moorings to steam downriver to carry out a day of machinery trials in the Firth of Clyde. Later in the day, at 1640, just off Greenock, the ship was stopped and at a small ceremony she was accepted from the builders, commissioned for the first time, and the White Ensign was hoisted. Twenty minutes later she anchored off the Tail of the Bank.

During the week following her acceptance *Delight* carried out further machinery trials, but on 18 October she slipped her mooring buoy at Greenock and set course, via the Irish Sea and Channel, for Chatham, arriving alongside No 3 basin two days later. For three weeks after her arrival at her new base port the destroyer loaded stores and ammunition, and her ship's company was brought up to full strength. Finally, on 14 November she left Sheerness for Spithead and Portland where she spent two weeks on further trials and a mini work-up. On completion of these, on the last day of November *Delight* left Portland to sail via Gibraltar for Malta where, on 10 November, she joined the Mediterranean Fleet. The destroyer's first weeks operating from Malta were spent mainly day running as she worked up to full operational efficiency with other units, including her sister *Daring* and the aircraft carrier *Glory*, for whom she acted as planeguard. On 18 December she returned to Grand Harbour for the Christmas and New Year break.

During the first three weeks of 1954 *Delight* continued day-running exercises from Grand Harbour taking part, along with *Glasgow*, *Cheviot*, *Daring*,

*Wakeful*, *Magpie* and *Mermaid*, in 'Exercise Janex 4', which was designed to test the fleet's air defences, but also included a rehearsal for a ceremonial meeting with the royal yacht *Britannia* in early May. Meanwhile the gunnery department staged a full-calibre bombardment of the range on Filfa Island just south of Malta. On 21 January, with the exercise over, *Delight* set course for Port Said where, during the afternoon of 24 January, she secured stern to on Navy Wharf, to carry out three and a half weeks of guardship duties. During her stay leave was granted to the ship's company, but the security situation meant that it expired at 2200 each day. There were sighs of relief when, on 17 February, *Delight* steamed out of harbour to rendezvous briefly with her sister *Daring* in order to carry out a jackstay transfer before returning with her and *Glasgow* to Grand Harbour, where she secured alongside *Gambia* at Parlatorio Wharf. After undergoing a two-week maintenance period in Malta *Delight* returned to Port Said where, as guardship, she spent the rest of March and the first week of April. The period was broken by three days at sea during which she gave a number of Army personnel from the Suez Canal Zone a taste of life at sea with the Royal Navy. The thankless task of guardship at Port Said ended on 6 April when, after embarking 162 Royal Marines and their equipment which made the ship's main passageway almost impassable, she sailed for a choppy and uncomfortable 56-hour passage to Malta where she disembarked her passengers.

On 1 May *Delight* left Malta to join with other ships of the Mediterranean Fleet, including *Eagle*, *Bermuda*, *Gambia* and *Glasgow*, to make a rendezvous with the new royal yacht *Britannia* which had steamed out from the UK with Prince Charles and Princess Anne, who were meeting their parents on return to Malta from their Commonwealth tour. Most of the world voyage had been made in the passenger liner *Gothic*, but on 30 April, after flying from Entebbe to Tobruk, the Queen and Prince Philip joined *Britannia*. At 1045 on 2 May the units of the Mediterranean Fleet sighted the royal yacht, and led by *Glasgow*, flying the flag of the C-in-C

Mediterranean Fleet, Admiral Lord Mountbatten, they fired a coordinated 21-gun salute before steaming past *Britannia* in line ahead formation and manning and cheering ship. After the steam past the fleet took up stations around *Britannia* and escorted her to Malta, arriving off Grand Harbour the next forenoon and making a ceremonial entry. For *Delight* there then followed another maintenance period after which, on 5 June, she sailed with *Bermuda* and *Daring* for exercises off Cyprus. The two Darings followed these up with a three-day visit to Famagusta where they both manoeuvred into the small harbour to secure alongside. On 12 June, together with *Bermuda*, *Daring* and *Whirlwind*, *Delight* secured alongside Beirut's Eastern Mole at the start of a five-day official visit. It was only the second official visit to the Lebanese port by the Royal Navy since the end of the Second World War, and had been arranged in an attempt to improve relations following, what was to the Arab peoples of the Middle East, the very unpopular British policy of allowing mass Eastern European Jewish immigration into the adjoining land of Palestine. These same immigrants had waged a particularly vicious terrorist campaign against the British Mandate authority before seizing political power and forcibly expelling a million Palestinians so that they could set up the State of Israel - a political problem which is still with us today. There is no doubt that, in the short term, the visit succeeded in improving relations with the regime that was in power at the time. When the squadron sailed *Bermuda* had on board President Shamoun of Lebanon who, as guest of Vice-Admiral J. P. L. Reid (FO2 Mediterranean), was treated to three and a half hours of high-speed manoeuvres and an impressive gunnery display by *Daring*. On completion of the display and after disembarking the President, the squadron left for Turkish waters which, for *Delight*, included visits to Iskarderam and Izmir. The Eastern Mediterranean cruise ended with a five-day visit to Athens before the whole squadron returned to Grand Harbour on 5 July.

In mid-July *Delight* exercised with *Cumberland* off Malta, before moving to Italian waters to visit Taranto and Augusta and to take part, with Italian and Greek units, in joint exercises. On 23 July, however, after returning to Grand Harbour, *Delight* de-ammunitioned and prepared for dry-docking and a six-week, dockyard-assisted maintenance period, which came to an end in early September with FO2's inspection of the ship. Four days later, on 6 September, *Delight* left Grand Harbour and set course for home, making a two-day stop at Gibraltar en route and arriving at Devonport on 14 September. Less than 24 hours later, however, she was back at sea and with her sister *Daring* was heading north for Invergordon and a series of exercises, which took place in the North Sea and off the Norwegian coast. On 5 October she returned to Chatham to undergo a further docking and maintenance period. During this period long leave was limited for on 3 November the ship was due to sail for a major NATO anti-submarine exercise off the coast of Scotland, which would involve British, French, Dutch, Norwegian and US ships. Following the exercise *Delight* was scheduled to visit Londonderry before returning to Chatham in early December to give seasonal leave. However, on 3 November, just hours before she was due to sail, sand was discovered in an oil feed system of her steering machinery. It was apparent that this was a deliberate act of sabotage, and although it was discovered before any real damage was done to the steering gear, cleaning out the system was a long process which meant that the ship's sailing and involvement in the NATO exercise had to be cancelled. During the subsequent police investigation 200 members of the ship's company were interviewed and although the identity of the offender was not definitely established, eight men, including the prime suspect, an Electrical Mechanic, were removed from the ship and drafted. On Saturday 20 November, again shortly before the ship was due to sail, there was another suspicious incident when auxiliary machinery valves which should have been open were found to be closed, but this was not a serious problem and next day *Delight* sailed for Londonderry, from where she operated for the rest of the month. Having spent the first week of

December at Portland *Delight* then returned to Chatham to give leave. During the period she was alongside the destroyer received visits from her sponsor, Lady Jowitt, and from a delegation of British and German Members of Parliament.

On 7 January 1955 there was a change of command when Captain F. M. A. Torrens-Spence DSO DSC AFC RN, a distinguished naval aviator, took over from Captain Lane, and by the third week of the month the ship was ready for sea once again.

*Delight* left Chatham on 20 January to carry out a mini work-up at Portland, before joining *Bermuda*, *Apollo* and *Virago* on the passage to Gibraltar and on into the Mediterranean for joint Home and Mediterranean Fleet exercises, during which she acted as planeguard escort to *Albion* and *Centaur*. There were visits to La Spezia and Malta, and the ship herself was visited by the radio and television broadcaster Wynfred Vaughan Thomas who, with the First Sea Lord, transferred by jackstay from *Centaur*. On 22 March, after an eight-day maintenance period at Malta, *Delight* joined *Centaur*,

*Saintes*, *Defender* and HMNlS *Karel Doorman* for the passage home which took the form of a series of exercises. On the last day of March she arrived at Chatham to give leave. The final leg of the commission began on 15 May when the destroyer put to sea again to steam to Portland and then north to Invergordon. After leaving Portland during the morning of 20 May, during her passage up Channel she rescued the navigator of an RAF Meteor jet aircraft from RAF Tangmere, which had crashed in the sea off Selsey Bill. Sadly, although the man was quickly transferred to Haslar Hospital at Gosport he later died. *Delight* continued her passage north into Scottish waters where, with *Apollo*, *Sparrow* and *Tyne*, she took part in a 12-day air-defence exercise which ended at Rotterdam. It was the ship's last foreign visit of the commission, and on 2 June she returned to Chatham where, 11 days later, she paid off and the main body of her ship's company moved into shore accommodation at the Royal Naval Barracks.

*Delight*'s second commission began 12 days after

HMS Delight *at anchor in Venice Lagoon during her visit of September 1955, which coincided with the Venice Film Festival.*
*(Harry Whiteside)*

*A touch of glamour on board. Two notable visitors to* Delight *were the actress Mary Ure and the actor James Robertson Justice. The two were in Venice for the release of their film 'Storm Over the Nile', which also starred Laurence Harvey and was an adaptation of A. E. W. Mason's novel 'The Four Feathers'.* (Harry Whiteside)

the end of the first when, at 1020 on Tuesday 14 June 1955, her commissioning party arrived on board and, ten minutes later, the Commissioning Service was held on the forecastle. Two weeks later the destroyer left Chatham to steam south for Gibraltar and the Mediterranean Fleet at Malta. She arrived on 11 July and secured to buoys in Grand Harbour's French Creek. The ship's first weeks on station were spent working up on day-running exercises, which included acting as planeguard to *Eagle*, and bombarding the gunnery range at Filfa. In mid-September, with her work-up completed, *Delight* underwent a 17-day maintenance period

before participating in an official fleet visit to Italian ports as part of a force which included *Sheffield*, *Defender*, *Delight* and *Surprise*. *Delight*'s itinerary took her to Venice with the other ships, to Ancona and, after a short break at Malta, to Cagliari for bombardment training exercises. The end of September saw *Delight* secured alongside at Naples, and during October she took part in fleet exercises and paid a four-day visit to Algiers. On 28 October, however, she left Malta to steam east to Gibraltar where she underwent a three-month refit. *Delight* had been experiencing overheating problems to her plummer block bearings, and the refit at

Gibraltar included a long spell high and dry in No.2 dry dock. By the second week of November living conditions on board had deteriorated to the extent that the ship's company was moved ashore into dockyard accommodation, much of which was only a slight improvement on that on board ship. With Christmas and New Year having been spent at Gibraltar, on 3 February 1956, the ship's company moved back on board, and four days later she put to sea for post-refit trials. Within three days, however, she was back in dry dock, a process which was repeated twice during February. It was, in fact, the last day of February before *Delight* was fully operational once again, just in time to join the joint Home and Mediterranean Fleet exercises.

On 5 March the C-in-C, Home Fleet, Admiral Sir James Eccles, who had arrived in Gibraltar by air from Valencia, hoisted his flag in *Delight* and next day the destroyer sailed for the first of the joint exercises, code-named 'Cascade'. Among the other units taking part were *Birmingham*, *Ark Royal*, *Defender*, *Reward* and the submarines *Sanguine* and *Taciturn*, as well as the Home Fleet flagship *Tyne*, to which the C-in-C and his staff transferred

during the first afternoon at sea. Also taking part was the royal yacht *Britannia* with the Duke of Edinburgh and the Second Sea Lord, Admiral Sir Charles Lambe embarked. Soon after leaving Gibraltar the ships of the combined fleets steamed westward to welcome *Britannia* into the exercise. As the royal yacht appeared over the horizon they broke into two files of four in line ahead, and dressed with masthead flags and with their ships' companies manning the upper decks the two files turned outwards, one towards Spain and the other towards North Africa. Once they had completed the manoeuvre and were steaming eastward with *Britannia* at their centre they fired a simultaneous 21-gun salute. The exercise proper began at midnight and took place over five days between Gibraltar and Sardinia. Although it eventually included 31 ships, owing to the Mediterranean Fleet's commitments off Cyprus, the scale of the exercise was reduced. For *Delight* it ended at Gibraltar on 12 March and six days later FO2, Mediterranean, Vice-Admiral Richmond, bade farewell to the destroyer which, two days later, sailed for the final exercise of the commission.

*The Royal Yacht* Britannia *in Stockholm Harbour, June 1956. In the background is* Defender. *(Harry Whiteside)*

*During the forenoon of 11 June 1956, the Queen and Duke of Edinburgh posed on* Delight's *forecastle with Captain Torrens-Spence, his officers and ship's company for the ship's official photograph.* (Harry Whiteside)

This time *Delight* was to be part of the major NATO exercise 'Dawn Breeze', which also included Dutch and Portuguese vessels, as well as French and American aircraft. The principal object of the exercise was to train NATO navies and air forces in coordinated attacks on submarines and in the escorting of convoys, with the royal yacht *Britannia* acting as a merchant ship. Aircraft from *Ark Royal*, to which *Delight* acted as planeguard, were to have 'attacked' targets between Start Point and Portsmouth, but severe Atlantic weather hampered flying from the carrier which at one point went to the aid of a German merchant ship in distress. For *Delight* the exercise ended during the evening of 25 March, and next day she returned to Chatham.

On the last day of April 1956, having undergone a short refit and having recommissioned, *Delight* moved out to a buoy off Sheerness in preparation for sailing the next day to start a short work-up at Portland. This was finally completed in mid-May, having included a weekend break at the French port of Brest after which she steamed north to Invergordon where she joined *Defender* and *Tyne* for anti-aircraft training with Seahawks from RNAS Lossiemouth. On 1 June, in company with *Defender*, she steamed south to Hartlepool from where, three days later, the two destroyers and HMCS *St Laurent* escorted the royal yacht *Britannia* on a State visit by the Queen to Stockholm. The Trinity House vessel *Patricia* led

*Britannia* to the mouth of the River Tees, where she was met by the three warships for the four-day passage into the Baltic Sea. After steaming through gale force winds and heavy seas the four vessels arrived in Stockholm during the late forenoon of 8 June, to be welcomed by large crowds and a flypast by 32 formations of SAAB 275 jet fighters of the Swedish Air Force. On the third day of the visit the Queen and Duke of Edinburgh visited the three escort ships, and on board *Delight* they sat with the officers and men for the ship's official photograph. The Scandinavian sojourn ended at 0900 on 18 June, when *Delight* left Stockholm to set course for Kiel where she spent five days, before transiting the Kiel Canal and arriving at Devonport on 28 June.

*Delight* was making a rare visit to the West Country naval base in order to embark a large detachment of Royal Marines and their equipment from Stonehouse Barracks, together with Land-Rovers, trailers and stores, for assault landing exer-

cises in Scottish and Norwegian waters. The main body of Royal Marines joined the ship during the early morning of 5 July and soon afterwards, with living space on board at a premium, the destroyer set sail. The first amphibious landing took place at Lamlash, with the Marines completing their disembarkation and assault of a deserted beach during the late evening of the next day. On 7 July they were re-embarked and that evening, in company with *Comet* and *St Kitts*, *Delight* made a crowded and uncomfortable passage round Scotland's north coast to the Norwegian port of Harstad where, once again, the Marines were disembarked for nine days of training exercises in Norway's rugged terrain. While the men were ashore the three destroyers visited various Norwegian ports, including Andalsnes and Narvik, before *Delight* returned to Harstad on 20 July to re-embark her Marines and their equipment. Five days later, having returned them to Devonport, the destroyer sailed for Chatham to give

*Delight dips her nose into a heavy sea as she exercises off Filfa Island, Malta, in April 1957.*     (A.F. Sell)

leave and undergo maintenance. In early August she took part in the port's Navy Days and over the three days attracted 7,770 visitors.

For much of the fleet the Suez crisis dominated the autumn months of 1956, but *Delight* was not involved in the campaign. However, when she left Chatham in early September she took part in training exercises with other units which were deployed on the operation, including her sister *Daring* and the cruiser *Glasgow*, which was in her final few weeks of operational service. On 1 October *Delight* secured alongside Portsmouth's Middle Slip Jetty, where she would undergo six weeks of maintenance. It was during this period that there was another change of command when Captain L. E. D. Walthall DSC RN took over from Captain Torrens-Spence.

On 13 November, following the end of her refit, *Delight* steamed round to Chatham where she was recommissioned for service on the Mediterranean Station, and on 10 December she arrived in what was, following the ill-fated Suez invasion, a very busy Sliema Creek. Within days of her arrival she was quickly involved in two weeks of intensive work-up exercises in local waters, often in company with her sister *Defender*, and with only a short break for the Christmas holiday period. Sailing again on 27 December the exercise period continued into the new year of 1957. During the second week of January *Delight* joined *Albion, Jamaica, Daring, Defender, Manxman, Wizard, Whirlwind* and *Woodbridge Haven* for fleet manoeuvres which ended on 24 January with visits to Naples and Taranto. On 6 February, when *Delight* left Taranto, she joined *Defender* and set course for Cyprus to begin her first patrol of the island's coastline which was aimed at enforcing the arms blockade. For six weeks *Delight* steamed slowly round the coast of Cyprus, stopping and boarding vessels on a regular basis. There were short breaks at anchor off Dhekalia, or secured alongside RFA *Wave Knight* for refuelling and storing, but any shore leave was confined to organised sports parties and the canteens in the Army base areas. This routine continued into March, but finally on 26 March *Delight* left

Dhekalia Bay arriving back in Malta two days later to undergo a 14-day maintenance period. In the last week of April, in company with *Albion* and *Birmingham, Delight* steamed into the Western Mediterranean to carry out joint exercises with the French Navy, which culminated in visits to Marseilles and Toulon. In early May she took part in 'Exercise Medflex', during which she acted as planeguard to *Albion*. The exercise ended at Gibraltar in mid-May when *Delight* began a 15-week refit, including six weeks in dry dock when the ship's company was accommodated ashore. It was Tuesday 20 August when she was ready for sea again. During the course of her post-refit trials that day she was one of a number of ships which went to the aid of the 25,000-ton Liberian-registered tanker *World Splendour*, which had suffered an engine room explosion and fire some 30 miles east of Gibraltar. The tanker had been in ballast and on passage between Fawley and the Persian Gulf when the accident occurred and *Delight* was able to rescue some 40 members of her crew and land them at Gibraltar. Nine days later, with her refit completed *Delight* sailed for home, calling briefly at Cadiz to disembark Flag Officer, Gibraltar. She arrived alongside at Chatham on 2 September, but for the ship's company there was only a brief respite, for within a week she was due to begin the Home Sea Service leg of the commission.

On Saturday 7 September *Delight* slipped her buoy at Folly Point to head north for Rosyth to join *Sheffield, Bulwark, Alamein, Undaunted* and other units to rehearse for a forthcoming NATO exercise code-named 'Strikeback'. The exercise was to involve some 100 ships, including the 60,000-ton USS *Forrestal* and a particularly strong British carrier force which included *Ark Royal, Eagle, Albion* and *Bulwark*. The primary objective of the exercise was to test and improve the combat readiness of the NATO forces, as well as their anti-submarine defence procedures, from points as far north as the Arctic Circle and south almost to the equator. For three days *Delight* exercised off Scotland's east coast before making her passage of the Pentland Firth in order to join the main exercise which was

due to begin on 19 September. On 13 September, after refuelling from RFA *Olna*, the destroyer secured alongside Greenock's Princes Pier for what was to be a short break before joining the exercise. However, in September 1957 an extremely virulent form of influenza was sweeping the country and all four aircraft carriers were badly hit, with hundreds of men confined to sickbays and messdecks. By 19 September, when the exercise began, over 40 members of *Delight*'s ship's company had succumbed to the virus and had been admitted to hospital in Greenock, while many others were suffering from various degrees of the illness. As a result *Delight* was withdrawn from the exercise and placed under quarantine restrictions at Greenock. That afternoon she was shifted to Customs House Pier. Any hopes that the destroyer might belatedly take her part in 'Exercise Strikeback' were dashed completely

when, at 1935 on 20 September, the tug *Forager* collided with *Delight*'s stern, tearing a large hole extending from some 14 feet from deck level to six inches below the waterline. Water poured into *Delight*'s steering gear compartment and only prompt action by the engine room department, who checked the inrush with canvas awnings until shipwrights could plug the hole with a temporary cofferdam prevented the whole compartment from being flooded. Unable to sail until more permanent repairs had been made *Delight* was de-ammunitioned and moved into dry dock at the nearby Barclay Curle shipyard. It was 9 October before *Delight* put to sea again, and then she steamed directly to her home base at Chatham to give leave to the ship's company. On the last day of October she steamed north once again to take part in Home Fleet manoeuvres with *Sheffield*, *Bermuda*, *Daring*

*Delight (nearest), in company with sister ships* Dainty, Daring *and* Defender *in January 1958.*

*(MoD/Crown Copyright)*

and *Defender*. These took her to Rosyth and off Scotland's east coast, then round to Londonderry where she spent the last week of November and the first few days of December. By 9 December, however, she had returned to Chatham where leave was given and the ship underwent maintenance.

When *Delight* left Chatham in the new year of 1958 she steamed round to Portland where she joined other units of the Home Fleet, including *Maidstone* (flag Admiral Sir John Eccles, C-in-C, Home Fleet), *Bulwark*, *Bermuda*, *Ceylon*, *Daring*, *Dainty*, *Defender*, *Barfleur*, *Camperdown*, *Ulster*, *Troubridge* and the submarines *Tiptoe* and *Turpin*, to rehearse exercises in the Channel before the Home Fleet began a programme of joint exercises in the Western Atlantic combined with a spring cruise to the Caribbean. During this period *Delight* acted as planeguard escort and anti-submarine screen to *Bulwark*. Following visits to Belize, Kingston, Grenada and the island of Bequia, the ships of the Home Fleet steamed north to Bermuda before beginning 'Exercise Maple Royal' with Canadian units, including HMCS *Bonaventure*. At the end of the exercise the final port of call was Halifax, Nova Scotia, and on 18 March, in company with *Maidstone*, *Daring*, *Ceylon*, *Camperdown* and *Barfleur*, *Delight* set course for home. She arrived at Devonport in early April and paid off before undergoing an eight-month modernisation refit.

In October, during the course of the refit, *Delight*'s new commanding officer, Captain P. C. G. Dickens DSO DSC MBE, was appointed to the ship and in late January 1959 the destroyer was recommissioned. During the spring of 1959 *Delight* carried out training exercises from Portland as the ship was worked up to full operational efficiency and in May, in company with *Dainty*, she steamed out to Malta where she joined the Mediterranean Fleet. The first weeks on the station were occupied by day-running exercises in local waters and in June, together with *Birmingham* and *Diamond*, she took part in exercises in the Western Mediterranean with visits to Barcelona and Palmas Bay. The return passage to Malta took the form of

a simulated nuclear explosion, with *Delight* steaming through fallout in order to test the prewetting system. At 0913 on 6 July *Birmingham* led *Delight*, *Defender*, *Battleaxe*, *Blackpool*, *Ulysses*, *Armada* and *Camperdown* to sea for exercises and the passage to Istanbul. At 1750 the same day *Delight* manoeuvred alongside *Birmingham*'s starboard side to carry out a heaving line transfer. However, before the evolution could begin the two ships drifted towards each other and collided, causing minor injuries to one rating and slight damage to both ships. As a precaution, however, both vessels stopped in order to check and take soundings of double bottom compartments. It was at this point that tragedy struck on board *Birmingham* when an engineer officer and three ratings were overcome by toxic fumes in one of the compartments. Sadly, two of the ratings died from suffocation. It was 2150 that evening before the ships were able to get under way once again, and next forenoon as the force approached the Turkish coast, all ships stopped as a mark of respect while *Birmingham* conducted a funeral service and the bodies of the ratings were committed to the deep. During the afternoon of 8 July, with the force having reached the mouth of the Dardanelles, it stopped so that *Delight* and *Birmingham* could make repairs to and paint the damaged ships' sides. Next forenoon they anchored off Istanbul to begin their five-day official visit to the Turkish city, followed by exercises in Greek waters.

In August, again in company with other units of the fleet, *Delight* anchored in Augusta Bay, Sicily, for the annual three-day fleet regatta. This routine was much as it had been in pre-war days and reflected the end of a more relaxed age which was disappearing quickly, as many Crown Colonies gained independence and the overseas bases were no longer required. The regatta, as was customary, ended with the cups and prizes being awarded to the winning teams by the C-in-C.

In September, with *Gambia*, *Daring* and *Dainty*, *Delight* took part in joint exercises with Italian units from Taranto, which included visits to Taranto itself, Venice and Trieste. In the closing weeks of

*Delight leaving Devonport in March 1959.* (Author's Collection)

1959 *Delight* and other units of the Mediterranean Fleet joined the newly arrived cruiser *Tiger* which, wearing the flag of the C-in-C, Admiral Sir Alexander Bingley, led the fleet in a ceremonial meeting just north of Malta with USS *Des Moines* which, in company with USS *Essex,* was carrying President Eisenhower from Athens to Toulon as part of the President's 20-day tour of Europe, Asia and North Africa. The upper decks of all units were manned and a coordinated 21-gun salute was fired in honour of the American President.

In mid-January 1960 *Delight* underwent a maintenance period and dry docking at Malta, and in mid-March, after running several days of post-refit machinery trials, she left Maltese waters to steam west for Gibraltar. It was the start of her passage home, but before she left for the UK she took part in the NATO exercise code-named 'Dawn Breeze V'. After calling at Algiers for a five-day visit, *Delight* arrived in Gibraltar on 22 March to join *Tiger, Dainty, Tyne, Daring, Solebay, Bermuda, Battleaxe* and *Apollo,* which were also gathered for the exercise scheduled to begin the next day in the Western Mediterranean. As was usual in those days, once at sea Soviet warships and trawlers bristling with radio aerials took a close interest in proceedings which, as well as 18 Royal Navy units,

involved ships from the French, West German, Dutch and Portuguese navies. By the end of March the exercise had moved into the Eastern Atlantic where severe weather conditions, with gales and heavy seas, slowed down most of the ships involved. One interesting aspect of the exercise was the involvement of the West German frigates *Graf Spee* and *Hipper* (ex-HMS *Flamingo* and *Actaeon*) which took on the role of 'Red Force' surface raiders attacking a 'Blue Force' convoy, of which *Delight* formed part of the escort. At one point, in the heavy seas, a Petty Officer was washed overboard from HMS *Teazer,* but, fortunately, he was quickly rescued. The exercises closed with a simulated nuclear explosion, testing all the pre-wetting systems, after which *Delight* arrived at Devonport on 1 April. This was to be her new base port for the rest of the commission, but first she had to be dry docked for repairs to her Asdic equipment which had been damaged in the severe Atlantic weather.

When *Delight* left Devonport on 25 April she headed north through the Irish Sea to Icelandic waters to carry out a fishery protection patrol. For 19 months, ever since Iceland had declared a 12-mile limit to its territorial waters, Britain had been in dispute with the Icelandic Government over fish-

ing rights and the Royal Navy had the difficult task of protecting the trawler fleet from harassment by Icelandic gunboats. During her patrol *Delight* virtually acted as 'nursemaid' to the trawler fleet, collecting and delivering mail, treating sick and injured fisherman and in return being presented with freshly caught cod, which were quickly prepared and served by the galley staff. The destroyer's patrol ended in late May when she steamed south to Londonderry for an eight-day break before beginning Home Fleet anti-submarine exercises in the Clyde and Eastern Atlantic areas during which she, *Blackwood* and *Daring* stalked *Thermopylae*, *Truncheon* and *Sentinel*. This series of exercises continued into June, with a weekend break at Wallasey and a two-day bombardment of the gunnery ranges at Cape Wrath. In July *Delight* moved south into the Channel to act as planeguard escort to *Centaur* during 'Shop Window' demonstrations which saw the destroyer day running from Portsmouth.

At the end of August, after giving leave and taking part in Devonport's Navy Days, *Delight* sailed back to Icelandic waters for her second fishery protection patrol, which ended in mid-September when there were also hopeful signs of a political settlement to the dispute. Leaving Iceland *Delight* steamed south to Rosyth from where, with *Ark Royal*, *Gambia*, *Defender*, *Camperdown*, *Eastbourne* and *Whitby*, she took part in a NATO exercise involving units from the USA, France and Portugal, which ranged from the Norwegian Sea to the Bay of Biscay. *Delight*'s role in the exercise ended at Portsmouth on 2 October, but there was only a short break before the destroyer was operating from the Clyde and stalking the submarine *Amphion*. Later in the month she took part in a convoy escort exercise in the Atlantic, before returning to Devonport for a short break. The last four weeks of *Delight*'s commission were spent in the North Sea, with visits to Wilhelmshaven, Hamburg and Rotterdam. On 26 November she left the Dutch port to return to Devonport, where she arrived the following day. Three days later, on the last day of November 1960, *Delight* paid off into Reserve, and

it would be almost four years before she put to sea again.

By the summer of 1964 *Delight* had been towed to Rosyth, and in mid-July she was briefly reactivated for ten days of machinery trials which were dogged by boiler feed water contamination; after a full-power trial in the North Sea she returned to Rosyth. Four months later, on 20 November 1964, under the command of Commander P. Maslen MVO RN, *Delight* was recommissioned at Rosyth. Three days later a fire broke out in A boiler room which took two hours to extinguish and delayed her sailing for almost a week so that it was nearly the end of November before she began her sea trials from Rosyth. At just after midday on 8 December she left her anchorage in the Firth of Forth to go to the assistance of the Hull trawler *Arctic Adventurer* which had suffered a serious explosion in her engine room, killing three members of her crew and leaving her adrift, without steering, lighting or power, in heavy seas some 130 miles east-north-east of Flamborough Head. In the event the stricken vessel was taken in tow by another trawler which was close by, but that evening *Delight* sighted the two ships and stood by until the forenoon of the next day when the two trawlers reached the safety of the River Tyne. With her rescue mission complete *Delight* returned to Rosyth to continue her machinery and weapons trials, which ended in mid-January 1965. Fourteen days later the destroyer was again paid off and her commanding officer transferred to *Dainty*, which was at Portsmouth preparing to recommission.

*Delight* remained laid up at Rosyth for six months until mid-July 1965 when, under the command of Commander G. A. F. Bower RN, she steamed south to Portsmouth to begin a three-month refit on 19 July which would render her operational again. During the period in Portsmouth Dockyard *Delight*'s after bank of torpedo tubes was removed and replaced with a deckhouse to provide additional accommodation, and all her main propulsion machinery received a thorough overhaul. The refit ended on 11 October and whilst day running from Portsmouth, *Delight* began a series of trials which

continued until mid-December. In the new year of 1966 she steamed west to Portland to begin a gruelling six-week work-up period, which ended with the ship's final inspection off The Lizard on 23 February. Next day *Delight* secured alongside No 1 wharf of Devonport Dockyard to give foreign service leave and to prepare for service on the Far East Station.

In the spring of 1966 the Confrontation with Indonesia, which reflected that country's opposition to the British-sponsored Federation of Malaysia, had been under way for more than three years, spiralling from a local revolt in Brunei in December 1962. The lengthy conflict, at a time when Britain had been reducing its military commitment in South-East Asia, had resulted in a huge build-up of forces at all the military bases in Singapore, including the naval base on the north shore of the island where *Delight* would be based. Leaving Devonport on 2 April to steam via Gibraltar, Suez, Jeddah and Aden, where she arrived on 17 April, *Delight* paused for only 24 hours before proceeding to the more hospitable port of Mombasa. During the passage south there was time to celebrate 'Crossing the Line' in the traditional manner and Mombasa provided four days of relaxation. On 26 April, however, the destroyer left Kilindini Harbour to head south for the coast of Portuguese Mozambique to take her turn on the Royal Navy's other major commitment east of Suez, the Beira Patrol. Three days after leaving Mombasa *Delight* relieved *Puma* off Beira to begin her first ten-day patrol in company with *Ark Royal*. In mid-May there was a welcome eight-day break at Mombasa and on the last day of the month she left Beira to set course for Gan where, in the lagoon, she refuelled from the hulk *Wave Victor* before continuing her passage east to Singapore. Finally, on 10 June she arrived alongside the heavy repair ship *Triumph* to undergo a three-week maintenance period.

*Delight*'s arrival in Singapore coincided with diplomatic meetings between British and Indonesian government ministers in Bangkok, which would, within a few weeks, formally end the Confrontation with Indonesia, but with continuing

Indonesian incursions into what was Malaysian North Borneo, the military operations continued. On 9 July she left the naval base for exercises in the South China Sea, and on 25 July, after a week in the Admiralty Floating Dry Dock at the naval base, she sailed for a patrol of the waters off North Borneo, between Labuan in the north-west and Tawau on the east coast. *Delight*'s patrol lasted for three weeks, during which she refuelled at both Labuan and Tawau where there were very limited facilities for liberty men. On 11 August an agreement ending the Confrontation was signed by British and Indonesian Foreign Ministers at Jakarta, and, in return for the cessation of the Indonesian incursions into Malaysia, it provided for the withdrawal of British troops from Malaysian Borneo by the end of September. *Delight*'s patrol duties ended on 14 August, when she left her anchorage at Tawau and returned to the naval base at Singapore, to secure alongside the maintenance ship *Mull of Kintyre* for work to be carried out on an overheating steering motor. On 26 August *Delight* arrived in Hong Kong and next day there was a change of command when Commander J. M. Child MVO RN, took over from Commander Bower.

After leaving Hong Kong on 10 September *Delight* steamed to the US Navy's exercise areas at Subic Bay where she acted as planeguard to *Victorious* during joint manoeuvres. On 21 September she was detached from the exercises to return to Singapore, and on the last day of the month left the Strait of Johore to begin her passage home. This was marked in the Indian Ocean by a major steam leak in A boiler room which necessitated her lying hove to for three hours as repairs were carried out. On 15 October, after very brief refuelling stops at Gan and Aden, *Delight* made her northbound transit of the Suez Canal, and three days later called at Malta. During the passage there was a 42-hour stop at Gibraltar, and during the late forenoon of 28 October she arrived alongside at Devonport where she would undergo a five-week maintenance period and give leave to the ship's company.

The last eight months of *Delight*'s commission

*An excellent bow view of Delight taken in 1966.* (Syd Goodman Collection)

were to be spent in home and European waters, and during early December she was based at Londonderry from where she carried out anti-aircraft exercises in the Irish Sea and Atlantic. Like the other Daring-class destroyers, however, her machinery was becoming ever more unreliable and for three weeks in December and early January 1967 Devonport Dockyard was called upon to carry out major maintenance work on the ship. During the first week of January *Delight* sailed for exercises in the Channel and North Sea, and during the course of the month there were visits to Newquay, a weekend in Portsmouth and five days at Rotterdam. During the latter visit, when the destroyer was opened to the public, over 5,000 Dutch people turned out to visit her. In late February, after a period alongside at Devonport, *Delight* rendezvoused with the newer destroyer *London*, which had just returned from the Caribbean, *Aurora*, *Pellow*,

*Phoebe* and the Dutch ships *Pizeven*, *De Zeven Provincien*, *Zeeland* and *Noord Brabant*, for a series of Anglo-Dutch exercises in the Western Approaches. *Delight*'s part in the manoeuvres ended during the early hours of 3 March when she detached from *London* for a weekend break at Devonport. Four days later, in company with *Mohawk*, RAN *Oxley* and *Odin* she carried out anti-submarine exercises off Scotland's west coast and on 21 March her seaboat rescued a crew member of a crashed naval Wessex helicopter. Next forenoon, however, she was ordered south to Falmouth to prepare for a very different salvage operation. Two days earlier, on 19 March, the 61,263-ton oil tanker *Torrey Canyon* had run aground on the Seven Stones Reef, between Land's End and the Scilly Isles. Initially it was thought that the stranded tanker would be towed safely off the reef and there was little concern shown about the first light films

*A starboard-side view of* Delight *taken in 1967.*                *(Portsmouth Royal Naval Museum)*

of oil which started to seep from the stricken vessel. However, it was not long before heavy seas began battering the *Torrey Canyon* and the rocks of the reef soon penetrated some 17 feet into the bottom of the ship, allowing hundreds of tons of heavy crude oil to gush from the ship's cargo tanks. In turn the wind and tides began pushing the thick black toxic slicks towards the beaches of the Scilly Isles and mainland Cornwall. It was clear that unless some drastic measures were taken the oil would create both a major natural and economic disaster. The first Royal Navy warship to arrive on the scene was HMS *Barrosa*, quickly followed by *Delight*, bringing spraying equipment and detergent which she had embarked in Falmouth. At 0700 on 24 March, just two hours after leaving Falmouth, *Delight* sighted *Torrey Canyon* and began spraying detergent on the oil slicks. Next day *Delight* steamed in close to the wreck in an attempt to transfer a salvage team to the tanker, but in the heavy seas which were running this was not possible and spraying operations continued. As well as attempting to disperse the oil slicks both *Delight* and *Barrosa* had to enforce a seven-mile exclusion zone around the wreck which, by 26 March, had broken its back on the rocks. With the problem of toxic oil pollution reaching proportions never seen before on the British coastline it was decided to bomb the tanker hopefully to release the remaining oil and to set fire to the main oil slicks, an operation undertaken by Royal Navy Buccaneers which dropped high explosive bombs; they were followed by RAF Hunter fighters which dropped petrol bombs in order to spread the fierce fires which were burning. Three times during the operation *Delight* returned to Falmouth in order to refuel and to replenish her detergent stocks, the last occasion being the evening of 29 March when, with her part in the clean-up operation over, she landed her spraying equipment before returning to Devonport to give leave and undergo maintenance.

On 30 April *Delight* left Devonport to make the overnight passage to Spithead where, next day, she escorted the royal yacht *Britannia* through the Solent and Needles Channel as the Queen Mother began a tour of Devon and Cornwall. The first stop was Penzance, followed by Falmouth, Plymouth and Brixham. Finally, on 6 May, she escorted *Britannia* to Cherbourg, from where the Queen Mother made a private visit to Normandy. Next day, with the royal visitor having re-embarked at St Malo, *Delight* escorted *Britannia* back to Portsmouth Harbour where on 8 May she secured alongside Fountain Lake Jetty. Eight days later she joined *Glamorgan*, *Zulu* and the submarine *Token* for a five-day official visit to Amsterdam. *Glamorgan* was flying the flag of the C-in-C Home Fleet and inevitably the visit was dominated by formal functions, but after leaving the Dutch port *Delight* steamed north to make a much more informal 'Meet the Navy' visit to Middlesbrough, where she attracted some 8,000 visitors, and to Lerwick where, despite being anchored offshore, some 500 visitors arrived in the space of one afternoon. After leaving the Shetland Islands *Delight* made what were to be her final foreign visits, the first to the Danish port of Esbjerg, and the second to the picturesque Norwegian Sandelfjord Inlet.

On 14 June, after leaving Norwegian waters, *Delight* steamed through the Pentland Firth to spend a weekend off Rothesay, before joining *Malcolm* for exercises in the Irish Sea and a return to Devonport for a two-week maintenance period. When she left Devonport on 10 July she rendezvoused with *Eagle* in the Irish Sea and for four days she acted as planeguard to the carrier, before putting into Belfast for a weekend break. On 17 July, after leaving Bangor Bay, *Delight* steamed the short distance to the Firth of Clyde where, for the rest of the month, she took part in a major anti-submarine exercise in the Atlantic Ocean which, as well as the conventional submarines *Alcide*, *Cachalot*, *Olympus*, *Otter* and *Thermopylae*, also involved the newly built Polaris submarine *Resolution*, which was undergoing her builder's trials at the time. During this exercise period there were short breaks at Rothesay and Faslane, but for most of the time the exercises were intensive and at one stage were observed by a Government Minister. They finally ended on 2 August when *Delight*

*A series of images of* Delight *at the shipbreaker's yard, Inverkeithing, in October 1970. She is alongside the hulk of what used to be HMS* Adamant. (T. Ferrers-Walker)

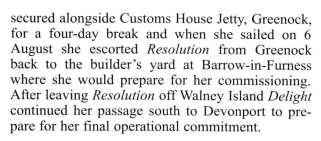

secured alongside Customs House Jetty, Greenock, for a four-day break and when she sailed on 6 August she escorted *Resolution* from Greenock back to the builder's yard at Barrow-in-Furness where she would prepare for her commissioning. After leaving *Resolution* off Walney Island *Delight* continued her passage south to Devonport to prepare for her final operational commitment.

On 11 August, after leaving Plymouth Sound in the early hours of the morning, *Delight* steamed east to Portsmouth where her ship's company was able to enjoy a change of scenery before embarking a Royal Marines Detachment and Band and sailing for the French port of Dieppe. She was to be the Royal Navy's representative at the 25th anniversary commemoration of the disastrous 'Dieppe Raid' in

August 1942. During the two days of ceremonies the Royal Marines and an Honour Guard from the ship played a prominent part in the parades, but on 21 August she left Dieppe to return to Portsmouth where her Royal Marines contingent was disembarked. That same evening she sailed for Devonport, arriving alongside No.1 wharf of the dockyard at 0800 on 22 August, and de-ammunitioning began at once. Four days later she took part in Navy Days where, despite her age, she attracted some 8,000 visitors. On Tuesday 29 August, with Navy Days over, *Delight*'s ship's company moved into shore accommodation at the Royal Naval barracks, and two days later the destroyer was paid off into Reserve.

Originally it had been planned that *Delight* would recommission in September 1967, for an 18-month General Service Commission which was to have been phased as Home, West Indies and finally Home Service. In fact, by the spring of 1967 many Royal Naval and Royal Marines personnel had received their draft chits to join HMS *Drake* for service in *Delight*. However, in the words of one such member, '...there was something in the air and eventually I went instead to HMS *Rhyl*'. It had, in fact, been decided that some of the older destroyers of the Cambrian and Daring classes were to be phased out of service earlier than had been originally expected, with *Delight* and *Daring* being among the first casualties. In the event *Delight* was laid up at Devonport until September 1970, when she was sold to Thomas Ward & Sons and broken up at Inverkeithing.

*A sorry sight.* Delight *at the shipbreaker's in May 1971, some eight months after her arrival. All her upperworks have been stripped away and work is beginning on the hull.*
*(Maritime Photo Library)*

**HMS *Delight***
**Commanding Officers**

| Name: | Date Appointed: |
|---|---|
| Captain H. J. F. Lane OBE RN | 30 June 1953 |
| Captain F. M. A. Torrens-Spence DSO DSC AFC RN | 7 January 1955 |
| Captain L. E. D. Walthall DSC RN | 20 November 1956 |
| Captain P. C. G. Dickens DSO MBE RN | 3 February 1959 |
| Commander P. Maslen MVO RN | 26 October 1964 |
| Commander G. A. F. Bower RN | 30 June 1965 |
| Commander J. M. Child MVO RN | 22 August 1966 |

**Battle Honours**

Armada 1588      Cadiz 1596
Norway 1940

# Part Eight

# HMS DIANA

## March 1954 - October 1969

Originally to have been named *Druid* the contract for the construction of the last Daring-class destroyer went to the Clyde shipbuilding company of A. Yarrow and Co. who, in 1908, had moved from the narrow confines of the Thames where it had flourished. On 3 April 1947, when her first keel plates were laid at the company's Scotstoun shipyard, hers was the sixth of the eight hulls to be laid down. However, building work was slow and it was 8 May 1952 before she was launched, with the ceremony being carried out by Lady Gwendoline McGrigor, the wife of the First Sea Lord. Unfortunately, the day was marred by a tragic accident when one of the shipyard workers was killed by a loose wire hawser as the newly named *Diana* was sliding down the slipway into the River Clyde.

Following her launch *Diana* was towed to Dalmuir Basin on the Clyde for fitting out, and in April 1953 the first naval personnel joined the ship. In early 1954 work on the new destroyer was nearing completion and on 23 February her first commanding officer, Captain C. R. L. Argles RN, arrived on board. Two weeks later the main body of the ship's company joined. The journey north to Glasgow is remembered by ex-AB John Millward thus:

'We all mustered in the drill shed at HMS *Drake*, Devonport, and there was much activity as we loaded our kit bags, hammocks and pussers' suit-cases onto handcarts, before pushing them to nearby Keyham railway station where a special train was waiting. There must have been 200 of us travelling to join the ship and after loading our kit we piled onto the train. On reaching Crewe we all piled off again and into the station buffet where we were served with a hot meal,

*HMS* Diana *in late 1953 undergoing trials on the Clyde.*                    *(Maritime Photo Library)*

*A port-bow view of Diana at anchor off Portland during 1954.* (Maritime Photo Library)

before we reboarded for the second leg of the journey. However, instead of setting off for the north our train was shunted into a siding for a few hours, and needless to say under such uncomfortable conditions it was difficult to get any sleep. Eventually we got going again to make an overnight journey from Crewe to Glasgow where, in the early hours of 9 March, we left the train and climbed into a fleet of five-ton trucks which drove us to Yarrow's shipyard, and to the company's canteen where we got a very nice breakfast, together with a boarding card which showed our Mess Number, Watch, Part of Ship and Locker Number, together with other essential information. Finally, after break-fast we marched to the ship where we embarked our kit and then ourselves.'

At 0900 on Wednesday 10 March 1954, *Diana*, which was still flying the Red Ensign, slipped her moorings and steamed down the River Clyde to carry out her builder's full-power trials. Despite initial faults with turbo generators, by the afternoon the trials had been completed successfully and at 1600 the ship stopped off Greenock for a formal

handing over and Commissioning Ceremony. All ship's company members not on watch mustered on the quarterdeck where, in the pouring rain, Captain Argles accepted the ship from Sir Harold E. Yarrow, the chairman and managing director of the shipbuilding company, who had accompanied the ship on her trials. With the ceremony over the new HMS *Diana* steamed back upriver to secure once again alongside Dalmuir Basin.

For 19 days *Diana* lay alongside the Clyde berth while the builders completed repairs to the faulty generator, and on 29 March she embarked on a series of trials over a six-day period, anchoring each evening off Greenock. During the afternoon of 4 April, with the trials completed, the ship set course for Devonport, arriving alongside in the dockyard two days later. For the rest of April *Diana* remained firmly alongside at Devonport, during which time she was visited by a steady stream of VIP visitors, including her sponsor Lady McGrigor, who was accompanied by her husband and sons. In early May *Diana* steamed east to Portland to begin her trials and work-up, but these were interrupted on 11 May when she joined *Vanguard* and other units of the Home Fleet in Tor Bay in order to rehearse

manoeuvres for 'Operation Loyalty', a ceremonial meeting with the newly commissioned royal yacht *Britannia*, which was bringing the Queen back to the UK after her Commonwealth Tour that had started in November 1953. For three days the ships of the Home Fleet rehearsed the meeting and steam past ready for *Britannia*'s return to home waters.

*Britannia* had left Malta on 7 May with a close ocean escort which had changed at Gibraltar and a week later, during the morning of 14 May, she entered the Channel. At just before 0900 *Diana* joined *Duchess* and *Vanguard* as part of the escort and two hours later off Start Point, the training carrier *Triumph* and other units of the Home Fleet Training Squadron, with their upper decks manned, ceremonially steamed past the royal yacht. At 1730 the Home Fleet escort, including *Diana* and *Vanguard*, detached to Portland where, two hours later *Diana* secured alongside. For the rest of that month and during the first two weeks of June *Diana* operated from Portland, carrying out her work-up, but in the latter half of June there was a break from this arduous routine when the destroyer sailed for the Baltic. Together with *Aisne* she had been chosen to take part in a well-publicised visit to Finland, Denmark and Iceland. Leaving Portland on 17 June *Diana* steamed north and two days later made a five-day visit to the Scottish port of Stonehaven. On 23 June she left for a three-day passage into the Baltic Sea to Helsinki. In the mid-1950s the visit of a Royal Navy warship to Finland was still quite a novelty, and the local newspapers gave the event a great deal of coverage, taking a particular interest in what they considered to be an 'eccentric' British tradition - the daily rum ration. Before leaving Finland *Diana* put on a magnificent firework display and the traditional children's party was held on board.

From Helsinki she steamed west to visit the port of Helsingar on the Danish coast of Zealand, from where she returned to Portland. During the last weekend of July she sailed north to act as the emergency ship in case an accident should befall the airliner which had taken off from Tangmere in Sussex carrying the Duke of Edinburgh to Ottawa for a three-week visit to Canada, during which he would attend the Empire Games at Vancouver. After refuelling at Reykjavik, and seeing the aircraft safely overhead, *Diana* returned to Devonport at the end of her trials and work-up period. This concluded the first half of the commission.

During the ship's six-week maintenance period alongside at Devonport she took part in the port's Navy Days, attracting thousands of visitors, and the second half of the commission began in earnest on 10 September when, at 0934, in company with *Diamond* and *Duchess* she left for the Mediterranean. The three destroyers paid a brief visit to Gibraltar, arriving in Grand Harbour on 18 September. For what remained of the month they carried out joint training exercises with other units of the Mediterranean Fleet, including *Glasgow*, *Barfleur*, *Chaplet*, *Childers* and *St Kitts*. In early October, the fact that both *Diana* and *Chaplet* had to return to harbour with machinery problems led to press speculation that the two destroyers might have been sabotaged, and the Admiralty had to issue a statement to the effect that there was 'nothing sinister' involved. In fact, *Diana* had lubrication problems with the main engines and, as a result of a leaky condenser, *Chaplet* had suffered feed water contamination. In *Diana*'s case it would be the end of October before she was ready for sea again. On 9 October the C-in-C Mediterranean Fleet, Admiral Lord Louis Mountbatten, visited the ship and spoke to the ship's company, and next day FO2, Mediterranean, Vice-Admiral J. P. L. Reid, took the salute at Ceremonial Divisions. When *Diana* returned to sea on 1 November she continued with training exercises in local waters. On 2 November a Dragonfly helicopter, hovering over the destroyer's quarterdeck, lifted an officer from the ship and transferred him to shore. In the mid-1950s this was still a revolutionary evolution, but it was a clear indication of the potential for the future of helicopters in the fleet, and particularly operating from smaller ships. On 6 November *Diana* hoisted the flag of FO2, Mediterranean for two weeks of anti-submarine training with *Teredo* and *Trenchant*. During the last week of the month *Diana* acted as

*A midships detail view of* Diana *showing the enlarged funnel casing she sported during her early career.* (T. Ferrers-Walker)

planeguard to *Albion*, the first day of which was marred by a fatal flying accident from the carrier. On 24 November, with *Albion*, she secured alongside Molo Angioino at Naples for a six-day visit, which was followed by joint exercises with the Italian Navy before returning to Malta for local day running and Christmas and New Year breaks.

For *Diana* the new year of 1955 got under way on 4 January when, with *Jamaica* and *Diamond*, she left Malta for night encounter exercises and a seven-day visit to Algiers. During the third week of January *Diana* began a five-week docking and maintenance period at Malta's Dockyard Creek, returning to sea on 1 March for two days of post-refit trials. On Wednesday 9 March *Diana* received a visit from her sponsor, Lady McGrigor, who was visiting Malta, and next day the destroyer left to carry out five days of anti-aircraft and convoy escort training off the North African coast. During the morning of 15 March the final evolution of the exercise programme involved a ceremonial steam past of the royal yacht *Britannia*, which was bringing the Duke of Edinburgh to Malta for an official

visit. Eight days later, with other units of the fleet, *Diana* left harbour to make another ceremonial steam past as the fleet bade farewell to *Britannia*. Visits to Naples and Toulon followed and on the return passage to Malta exercises were held with *Centaur*, *Agincourt* and *Diamond*. Later in the month *Diana* was involved in amphibious landing exercises which took her to Tripoli, and at the end of April, to the Algerian port of Arzew, east of Oran. During the five-day visit a detachment of the ship's company marched in the French parade to commemorate the 12th anniversary of the Allied liberation of North Africa. On conclusion of the visit *Diana* carried out training exercises with the French cruisers *Jeanne d'Arc* and *Georges Leygues*, which included bombarding the French Navy's gunnery range at Oran with her main armament. On conclusion of the gunnery exercises *Diana* returned briefly to Arzew for another three days and, as the ship's company enjoyed the run ashore, her senior officers attended wash-up conferences with their French counterparts. After leaving Arzew in the early hours of 9 May *Diana* made a fast passage to

Tripoli to embark a detachment of Royal Marines and return them to Malta, arriving back in Grand Harbour during the afternoon of 11 May.

On Sunday 22 May, led by the cruisers *Sheffield* (flying the flag of Admiral Sir Guy Grantham, C-in-C Mediterranean) and *Jamaica* (flag FO2, Mediterranean), *Diana*, *Decoy*, *Diamond* and *Duchess* left Malta for training exercises and visits to Eastern Mediterranean ports. The first visit, to Istanbul, lasted for four days, after which the force was joined by *Battleaxe* and *Scorpion* for further exercises. On 1 June the fleet dispersed to various ports, including Larnaca, Limassol, Kerikes and Alaya, with *Diana* steaming south to Alexandria. During her four days in the Egyptian port a coach trip was arranged to the British war cemetery at El Alamein, where one member of the ship's company was able to visit his brother's grave. After leaving Alexandria *Diana* steamed north to Limassol and on to the Turkish port of Marmaris where, on 15 June, the fleet reassembled in the sheltered bay for the Mediterranean Fleet regattas. On 19 June, with the prize-giving over, the fleet left harbour for the final phase of exercises, in which they were joined by Indian naval units. Three days later *Diana* returned to Grand Harbour to prepare for her passage home and subsequently during the forenoon of 24 June sailed for Gibraltar. The final evening in Malta had not been without incident when a fire in the forward switchboard almost postponed sailing, but hard work by the electrical department ensured that she sailed on time and joined *Decoy*, *Diamond* and *Duchess* for the passage. With only a short break at Gibraltar *Diana* arrived in Plymouth Sound late in the evening of 30 June, and next forenoon she steamed up harbour to secure alongside No.6 wharf at Devonport Dockyard. Less than an hour later the first long leave party were on their way to their homes.

The final phase of the commission began on Wednesday 31 August when, in company with *Glasgow*, *Decoy*, *Urania* and *Loch Fada*, *Diana* sailed north for Home Fleet exercises off Scotland's east coast. For two weeks she and the other units rehearsed for the major NATO exercise code-named 'Sea Enterprise', which would also involve the four aircraft carriers *Eagle*, *Albion*, *Bulwark* and *Centaur*, as well as the Canadian carrier *Magnificent*. On 13 September, during the rehearsals whilst an engine room rating was being transferred from *Diana* to *Chaplet*, the latter collided with *Diana*'s starboard bow. Fortunately, the damage was confined to some dents to *Diana*'s bow plating, and at 0755 on 20 September 'Exercise Sea Enterprise' began.

*Diana* was one of ten destroyers in the exercise, most of which took place off the Norwegian coast, with the most important aspect being the use of carrier-borne aircraft in mock attacks on targets in Norway. Another aspect was an anti-submarine operation during which *Diana* and HMAS *Queenborough* were commended for the skilful way they hunted down and 'sank' a submarine which had earlier 'sunk' *Glasgow*. During the course of the exercise there were breaks and opportunities for runs ashore at Trondheim and Rosyth. On 6 October *Diana* and *Decoy* secured alongside at Copenhagen to await their rendezvous with *Triumph*, *Apollo*, *Chieftain* and *Chevron*, for the C-in-C, Home Fleet's high-profile visit to Leningrad (St Petersburg).

The visit to the Soviet Union had been arranged at the highest political level during the 'Four-Power Conference' in Geneva, and it was agreed that a simultaneous exchange of visiting naval squadrons would take place. At the same time that the Royal Navy's squadron visited Leningrad, a Soviet squadron, led by the cruisers *Sverdlov* and *Alexandr Suvorov*, would visit Portsmouth. During the forenoon of 10 October *Diana* and *Decoy* rendezvoused with *Triumph* and the other units outside Copenhagen Harbour to set course across the Baltic, arriving off the Leningrad Light Vessel at 1400 on 12 October, where they were met by the Soviet destroyer *Odaryonny*, which escorted *Triumph* up the swept channel and into the Neva River. The remainder of the squadron anchored until the late afternoon, and at 1726 with the remaining hour of daylight fast receding, *Diana* weighed anchor and began her long passage upriv-

*An aerial view of* Diana *in a choppy sea.*

er. One member of the ship's company remembers the occasion thus:

'The river was well illuminated from the tall street lights ashore, and we saw massive buildings interspersed with wide streets reaching nearly the length of the port bank, with the Russian Admiralty building, a huge domed structure, and more buildings on the starboard bank. On the jetty there was what appeared at first sight to be a wide "black wall" stretching as far as the eye could see. Suddenly, we realised that the "wall" was actually people, crowded ten to 15 deep on the river bank. They had waited patiently and silently for our arrival and it was their first glimpse of a British warship for 13 years.'

It was midnight before *Diana* secured to her buoys in the Neva River, close to the Schmidt Bridge, but even at that late hour people were still lining the river banks to greet her. Throughout the visit the city authorities made arrangements for large numbers of the ship's company to be entertained daily, and as one of them remembers:

'When the time came to go ashore, some of us went on organised outings, and others went ashore independently, but we all had to run the gauntlet of the effusive and friendly crowds who were always there. Many wanted to exchange souvenirs and they swapped badges, matchbox-

es, emblems, postcards and Russian roubles, for cigarettes, British currency, 'nutty' (sweets and chocolate bars) and even copies of the latest pop chart hits. Most of the people could speak some English and when we were in conversation with them our remarks were often loudly translated for the benefit of the large crowds who were gathered.'

During the last two days of the visit strong winds hampered the movements between ship and shore and prevented some people from being able to visit *Diana* when she opened to the public, but when she sailed at 1255 on Monday 17 October everyone on board remembered the warmth of the greeting from the local citizens.

After leaving Leningrad *Diana* steamed to Rosyth, from where she carried out exercises with *Bulwark* and *Diamond*. In early November she made a six-day visit to Middlesbrough before steaming round to the Clyde for seven days of anti-submarine exercises, followed by a four-day visit to Belfast. Finally, on Thursday 24 November, she returned to Devonport to begin a 13-week refit to prepare her for a very different kind of commission.

In late November, shortly after *Diana*'s return to Devonport, it was announced that for her next commission Captain O. N. Bailey RN would be the destroyer's new commanding officer, and at the end of December the ship herself was high and dry in No.3 dry dock.

During her 13 weeks in the hands of Devonport Dockyard *Diana* was made ready for her next commission, which was to be a special and top secret assignment to Australian waters where she would join a task force off the Monte Bello islands, situated some 60 miles off the coast of Western Australia, for the testing of Britain's hydrogen bombs. To fit her out for this sinister and potentially deadly mission a comprehensive pre-wetting system was installed, the seals to her airtight citadels were renewed and she was also equipped with a large metal fin which would be fitted with scientific instruments and towed in a vertical position from the forecastle. At the end of January 1956 *Diana*

was shifted from dry dock to No.4 non-tidal basin where she was inspected by the Third Sea Lord. During the third week of February, however, shortly before she was due to recommission, Captain Bailey was injured and at very short notice Captain J. R. Gower DSC RN, who was the Royal Navy's Director of Physical Training and Sports, received a 'pierhead jump' to join *Diana* at Devonport 'forthwith' and take command.

At 0815 on Tuesday 28 February 1956 the ratings remaining on board from the previous commission left, and were replaced by an advance party from the Royal Naval Barracks. At 0915 Captain John Gower joined the ship and at 1130 the main body of the ship's company arrived on board from the barracks. No sooner were they aboard than *Diana* was recommissioned and her Ensign hoisted. Captain John Gower remembers this important, but unrecorded occasion thus:

'The ship's company were the last West Country crew to commission a Devonport ship before central drafting was introduced. What a fine lot they turned out to be; additionally I was blessed with good officers.'

In mid-March *Diana* was shifted to the sea wall at No.1 wharf, and soon afterwards the ship's company moved temporarily back to barracks in order that the dockyard could carry out important closing down trials to test the effectiveness of the citadel. Two days later, with everyone back on board, a Senior Government Scientific Officer and a team of physicists joined the ship and on 22 March *Diana* sailed for the first machinery, pre-wetting and closing trials. Captain John Gower remembers the problems encountered with the specially designed 'fin':

'Those of us familiar with streaming paravanes considered the design to be unworkable, and so it proved. It invariably under-ran the ship and was recovered only with difficulty. We replaced it with polythene sheeting and weights designed jointly by the Gunnery Officer and the

Scientific Officer.'

Finally, on 29 March the destroyer sailed for Gibraltar on the first leg of her passage to Australia. *Diana*'s passage south and on into the Mediterranean was made independently, which set the pattern for most of the commission, although on her arrival in Malta on 9 April she briefly joined two other members of her squadron, *Decoy* and *Duchess*. Two days later *Diana* left Malta and made her southbound passage of the Suez Canal on 13/14 April, and called briefly at Aden to refuel. After leaving Suez Captain Gower informed the ship's company that *Diana* had been ordered to be off Monte Bello by 3 May, and that they were to play a very active part in the forthcoming nuclear tests on the islands. As Captain Gower remembers:

'It was only years later that I read the illuminating power politics which formed the backdrop to our adventures. Since the end of the Second World War America had kept the results of her nuclear tests to herself, leaving Britain out in the cold. The purpose of all our nuclear tests at that time was to show Washington and Moscow that we were a full member of the "nuclear club". Time was running out before a worldwide ban was imposed and Britain wanted the Hydrogen Bomb. Perfection of an operational trigger device[1] was a matter of great urgency and this task had to be completed at Monte Bello in 1956 to ensure a satisfactory detonation of the H-bomb at Christmas Island in 1957. "Mosaic I" and "Mosaic II" (as the Monte Bello tests were code-named) were organised with great urgency. More immediately, but unknown to me at the time, since 1953 the Chiefs of Staff had wanted to know what effect an atomic explosion would have on ships, their contents, equipment and men. How much radioactivity could a ship withstand and remain operational? HMS *Diana*, her officers and men, were made

*Diana alongside Devonport Dockyard's No4 Basin in June 1957. Three weeks earlier she had undergone Admiral's inspection and her paintwork is looking immaculate.*
*(Maritime Photo Library)*

---

[1] An H-bomb can only be detonated by the explosion of a special kind of atomic bomb.

available to provide the answers.'

Not including fuelling stops the destroyer had just 11 working days to prepare for the ordeal and intensive training began immediately. During the training the engineers in both boiler and engine rooms had the most difficult time in the stifling heat of the Red Sea and Indian Ocean. Their sealed plastic suits were connected to a filtered air supply which, when inflated, gave the wearers the appearance of 'Michelin Men', and in the tropical conditions caused them to sweat profusely. The remainder of the ship's company wore working rig with seaboots, and carried gas masks. Captain Gower remembers:

'We had a young medical officer on board, his first seagoing ship who, rather than telling us what might happen, gave us reassuring lectures. We were also shown unreleased films of Hiroshima and Nagasaki.'

During the training exercises everyone except the boiler and engine room watchkeepers were shut down in inside two citadels, the forward one accommodating 207 and the after one 95. Initially some suffered fatigue, faintness, headaches, respiratory distress, abdominal discomfort and claustrophobia, but these problems were alleviated with practice. In order to create a reasonable scenario the ship simulated being faced with a nuclear attack and so the ship's company were at Action Stations, from where they went to Shelter Stations. The pre-wetting was switched on and checked by the close-range gun crews, and as this proved only 80% efficient, arrangements were made to cover the anti-aircraft guns and the bridge with canvas screens during the time spent in the fallout area after the real explosion.

After leaving Aden *Diana* set course for Colombo where she remained just long enough to refuel, before continuing her passage to Singapore, arriving alongside the naval base on 26 April. Just 48 hours later *Diana* was at sea again and heading directly for Monte Bello. Twenty-four hours after leaving Singapore, and almost within sight of Krakatoa Island, the Crossing the Line ceremony was held, and on 1 May the last full-scale 'Mosaic' rehearsal was held. At 0940 on 2 May *Diana* anchored off Flag Island, one of the small islets of the Monte Bello group, where she joined the special squadron which included *Alert*, *Narvik*, HMAS *Fremantle* and HMAS *Junee*. Captain John Gower's memories of the occasion make interesting, but unsettling reading:

'We had steamed 11,000 miles in five weeks to arrive at our destination on time. We anchored three miles outside the parting pool because our draught would not allow entry. I called on the Commodore of the task force, CTF 308, Commodore H. C. Hortell, flying his pendant in *Narvik*. He sent some of his scientific staff over to report progress. Their report, which I did not see at the time, read "General impression was everybody understood the basic problems and how to tackle them but they have fallen short in the apparatus and tools to do the job." This was followed by the disclaimer: "We cannot, however, assume any direct responsibility for the radiological safety of *Diana* since this is outside our terms of reference." So doubt did exist.'

It is apparent from the scientists' disclaimer that *Diana* and her company were being used as expendable guinea pigs. However, as Captain Gower recalls, 'We were eventually supplied with 600 overshoes and gauze masks.'

In the event, with delays to the atomic weapons-tests, *Diana* was allowed to take a short break at Fremantle, and the ship's company spent an enjoyable four days at the West Australian port, which itself was only two days steaming from the test site. By the afternoon of Monday 14 May she was back at her anchorage off Flag Island. The first of the nuclear tests, code-named 'Mosaic I', was scheduled for 16 May, and after weighing anchor at 0415 that morning an eventful day lay ahead for *Diana*. The first bomb was a 15-kiloton device mounted on a tower and before it was detonated *Diana*'s seamen

had to lower and anchor a whaler full of scientific instruments, a task which was completed by 0630, stream the fin with its scientific instruments, and prepare the ship for the inevitable radioactive cloud it would have to steam through. The bomb itself was detonated at 1151 local time, when the ship was some 51 nautical miles away, and within minutes A engine room and B boiler room were evacuated so that the ship was steaming on the starboard propeller shaft only. The two remaining machinery spaces were manned by just four watchkeepers wearing protective suits and taking alternate 35-minute watches which, under the appalling conditions down below, was the longest period which could be endured. At 1220 the ship's company went to Action Stations and at 1305, as the ship approached the main radioactive cloud, to Shelter Stations. Once again Captain John Gower remembers events:

'The expected arrival of 95% fallout was 1325. First readings, however, showed us as being only on the fringe of the fallout. No real effect was experienced until 1915 and fallout readings ceased at 2100. The monitoring staff, fully protected, left the citadel at 2135, switched off the pre-wetting and took readings at selected positions on the upper deck which had been marked by white paint. Most readings indicated 5 milliroentgens, and at 2230 the decontamination parties were dispatched to hose and scrub the upper decks. All canvas coverings were ditched overboard and by 0100 the upper deck was considered safe.'

By this time personnel in the two citadels had been closed down for over 12 hours and were suffering the effects of cramped conditions, heat and humidity. Many of the smokers were feeling the strain of the smoking ban in force and the limitations on food and drink affected everyone. Despite the threat of the deadly but invisible radiation, and the trying conditions, as Captain Gower recalls, *'Morale was high and we were still alive!'*

It was 0610 on 17 May before work began to recover the scientific instruments from the anchored whaler but it was so 'hot' that the small craft was rammed and sunk. When the main engine condenser cooling water filters were examined it was found that the debris and seaweed which had accumulated was also 'hot' with radiation contamination. Finally, however, after a very tense 24 hours, at 0831 *Diana* anchored off Flag Island. That forenoon Captain Gower spoke to his assembled ship's company on the forecastle to explain that with 'Mosaic I' completed it had been hoped that the ship could return to Fremantle, but the Australian Government had 'blacked' *Diana*, and as a result she would have to steam back to Singapore.

At 1600 on 18 May *Diana* weighed anchor and, steaming by way of Christmas Island where she paused just long enough to embark mail, she made the four-day passage to Singapore. Although there was work to be carried out in order to prepare the ship for the second 'Mosaic' nuclear test, scheduled for June, the destroyer's 12 days at the naval base on the north shore of Singapore Island provided the ship's company with a welcome break. However, at 0900 on Sunday 3 June, she sailed from Singapore and set course for Monte Bello again. Once again she steamed by way of Christmas Island where, at 0830 on 5 June, she paused to unload stores for the Naval Weather Station; she anchored off Monte Bello at 1630 on 7 June.

The second nuclear test off Australia's coast involved a much larger device than the first, but following *Diana*'s return to the area there was a 12-day delay before it went ahead. It appeared that weather conditions were not exactly right, but political pressure on the scientists to construct a trigger which was urgently needed for the H-bomb was such that to cancel or postpone would involve a waste of a lot of time and money. During this period of waiting *Diana* remained at anchor off Flag Island and as Captain Gower recalls,

'We now waited patiently for the next test to commence since, after several false starts, the ship's company were beginning to get bored in this Scapa of the southern hemisphere. To coun-

teract this we staged every conceivable dog watch pastime to while away the time.'

Finally, however, despite the risk of adverse weather conditions, it was decided to go ahead with the test, and at 0415 on Tuesday 19 June, *Diana* weighed anchor at the start of what was to be a hectic, tense and uncomfortable 36 hours.

At 1014 that forenoon the second atomic bomb was detonated and, despite the fact that *Diana* was some 97 miles away, the spectacular explosion was clearly visible with the huge mushroom cloud being seen as far away as Port Hedland, some 265 miles to the east. At Roebourne, 150 miles away from Monte Bello, a dull rumbling sound heralded two loud, vicious cracks, heard about a minute apart. Once again Captain John Gower takes up the story:

'The fireball was twice the size of "Mosaic I" and climbed a lot faster. The explosion when it came was a colossal double crack heard 200 miles away in Australia.'

Unknown to the officers and men aboard *Diana* this second bomb was, in fact, the most powerful device detonated in any of the 1950s' atomic weapons tests, and it was only in 1985 that the British Government finally admitted that it had yielded 98 kilotons - seven times more powerful than the bomb dropped on Hiroshima. However, events did not go entirely to plan and the radioactive cloud moved over the Australian mainland. This is hardly surprising given the fact that the people of Onslow, a coastal town some 80 miles south of the test site, said that the explosion, 'jolted the town and the fireball was the biggest and deepest orange'.

Back on board *Diana* the Commodore signalled the ship to expect fallout at 1330. Action Stations were sounded at 1225 and followed almost immediately by Shelter Stations. The first traces of fallout were detected at 1325 and just over an hour later radiation in excess of ten milli-roentgens was recorded. By 1845 the level had dropped to 0.4, and four hours later decontamination parties were

dispatched from both citadels. This time, with the benefit of the previous experience, they had completed their task in one and a half hours, but in one area where a pre-wetting pipe had severed, high radiation readings were still showing, which required a great deal of washing and scrubbing by the decontamination parties. Some areas, where high readings could not easily be reduced, were roped off and equipment was ditched overboard. At 1100 the anchored whaler was sunk by rifle fire and at 1210 on 20 June *Diana* anchored off Exmouth Gulf. Three days later, with her role in 'Operation Mosaic' over, the destroyer sailed for Singapore, arriving alongside the naval base during the morning of 30 June.

After her arrival in Singapore the dockyard carried out work to remove radiation-contaminated paintwork, and repair the damage caused by the constant use of the pre-wetting system. One of the ship's boilers, which was still contaminated by radioactivity, was re-bricked by the dockyard and the whole ship was painted overall, one side by the ship's company, the other by the dockyard. Having taken a leading role in an event of national importance, one would have thought that the officers and men who, without being give any choice in the matter, were deliberately exposed to radioactive fallout from two nuclear explosions and then required to serve in the ship, parts of which were still unacceptably radioactive, would have been given some official recognition. In the event, however, they did not even receive a congratulatory signal.

On 10 July 1956, having been ordered to rejoin her squadron at Malta, *Diana* left Singapore bound for the Mediterranean. With no urgent deadlines to meet, Captain Gower was able to choose the destroyer's itinerary, and she made a leisurely passage west by way of Penang, Madras and the picturesque naval base at Trincomalee. On 24 July *Diana* continued her passage from the island of Ceylon (Sri Lanka), and two days later as she steamed through the Arabian Sea, President Nasser of Egypt announced to an ecstatic crowd at Alexandria that he was nationalising the Suez Canal Company, a joint British and French Corporation,

and that his Government was taking over forthwith the operational day-to-day running of the waterway. For the British Government, coming hard on the heels of Iran's nationalisation of the Anglo-Iranian Oil Company, it was seen as a deliberate attempt to humiliate Britain, and the Prime Minister Anthony Eden, despite a warning from the Lord Chancellor that it would be illegal, made the decision to invade Egypt to regain control of the canal and to topple Nasser. Given the serious internal security problems which had dogged the British bases on the Suez Canal right up to the withdrawal of British forces just a few weeks earlier, it is difficult to see what Eden's long-term plans for relations with Egypt were. His decision to use military force would, however, prove to be an unmitigated disaster.

During the afternoon of 30 July, the day after Nasser's dramatic announcement, *Diana* arrived in Aden Harbour where, after refuelling, she secured alongside the homeward-bound cruiser *Kenya*. Both ships soon received the order to remain at Aden until further notice, and as anyone who has visited Aden will testify, this rocky, barren port with its sweltering heat and inhospitable terrain is not a pleasant part of the world to be indefinitely detained in without air-conditioning. For *Diana*'s officers and men there was little in the way of recreation beyond the Combined Service Clubs, with their hot, sandy beaches, the anti-shark netting and tepid beer, but she remained at the port for over two months, during most weeks putting to sea with *Kenya* on day-running exercises. In early September she carried a detachment of the Aden Police to the island of Perim and in mid-September she spent 48 hours at the French colonial port of Djibouti which, as far as an inhospitable climate goes, is Aden's equal. Following this visit *Diana* and *Kenya* exercised at the southern end of the Red Sea, and on 28 September *Newfoundland* relieved *Kenya* at Aden, the latter returning home. On 10 October there came some temporary relief from the stifling heat when *Diana* left Aden to steam south, and five days later she secured to a buoy in Kilindini Harbour for a welcome week-long visit to

Mombasa. On 22 October, with the joint British, French and Israeli invasions of Egypt drawing closer, *Diana* returned to Aden where she spent just three days before, on Sunday 28 October, in company with *Newfoundland* and *Modeste*, she left harbour to steam north into the Red Sea. Captain Hamilton of *Newfoundland* became Commander of the Red Sea Task Force, which comprised *Newfoundland*, *Diana*, *Crane*, *Modeste*, the French frigates *La Perouse* and *Gazelle*, together with the minesweeper FS *Jasmin* and RFA *Wave Sovereign*. During the afternoon of Monday 29 October, when the Task Force was some 100 miles north-east of Massawa, news came of the Israeli attack on Egyptian forces in the Sinai and, as the British-French-Israeli collusion was known to only a few Government Ministers in each of the three countries, it came as a complete surprise to the Task Force. It was followed almost immediately by a joint British-French ultimatum to both Israel and Egypt to cease hostilities and withdraw from an area ten miles on either side of the Suez Canal. It went on to state that in the event of either country rejecting the ultimatum, British and French forces would intervene in order to safeguard the canal itself and it was presented in such a way as to guarantee rejection by Egypt. As expected, this is exactly what happened and on 31 October the first British and French air attacks on Egyptian targets began (some French aircraft were actually operating from Israeli airfields). The British air attacks were conducted from the aircraft carriers *Eagle*, *Albion* and *Bulwark*, and in addition the RAF carried out a few high-level raids by Canberra bombers.

Meanwhile, in the Red Sea, the Task Force commanded by *Newfoundland* was, by midday on 31 October, off the coast of Egypt, some 150 miles north of the border with Sudan and steaming north towards the area where the Gulfs of Suez and Aqaba meet. Their main duty was to protect British and French merchant shipping in the area from retaliatory action, and at 2030 that evening they passed through the Strait of Gubal into the Gulf of Suez to search for Egyptian warships. Between

Diana *off Portsmouth in 1957. By now she had reverted to a standard funnel.* *(Portsmouth Royal Naval Museum)*

0100 and 0115 *Diana*'s radar detected an aircraft in the vicinity, and at 0120 as the two ships were checking a group of merchant ships which were on an opposite course, they noticed another vessel close behind them. Although she was showing her navigation lights she was otherwise darkened. As she came abeam of *Newfoundland* Captain Hamilton decided to investigate her identity and the cruiser altered course, swung under her stern and steamed close to her, only seven cables from her starboard beam. He illuminated the ship by searchlight and immediately revealed the Egyptian Navy's frigate *Domiat*.[2]

Captain Hamilton's primary aim was to capture rather than sink the *Domiat*, and he at once signalled, 'Stop or I Fire'. This was acknowledged by *Domiat*. However, when further ordered to 'Report when Stopped', the frigate switched off her navigation lights, increased her speed and trained her guns

on *Newfoundland* with the obvious intention of engaging. Before she could do so both *Newfoundland* and *Diana* opened fire at a range of 1,500 yards, with the latter firing 17 rounds from A and B turrets. The fire from the two ships was so accurate and devastating that *Domiat*'s brave attempt to turn and ram *Newfoundland* was stopped dead in its tracks as at 0133, badly damaged and ablaze, she sank in a position Lat 28°28.7'N/Long 33°04.5'E. Captain Gower remembers:

'Any feelings of anger during the action were replaced by sympathy for the Egyptian sailors, many of whom had been trained in England. It seemed tragic that men like these - the *Domiat*'s Captain was clearly a brave man - should suffer and die in such circumstances.'

In fact, during the brief, one-sided action, *Domiat*

---

[2] *Domiat* was the ex-River class frigate HMS *Nith*, built in 1942 and sold to Egypt in 1948.

had opened fire and two of her shells had hit *Newfoundland*. Although damage was not serious one member of her ship's company was killed and five were injured. Both the cruiser and *Diana* lowered boats to search for survivors, and in spite of the choppy sea the destroyer rescued over 70 Egyptian sailors, including some who were seriously hurt. It was gone 0300 before the rescue mission was concluded, and with only a few hours before daylight it was important that *Newfoundland* and *Diana* steamed south so that they would be clear of the Gulf of Suez by daylight when air attacks might be expected. By 0800 they were back in the more open waters of the Red Sea. During the remainder of the day *Newfoundland* and *Diana* continued to search for Egyptian naval units which might endanger shipping, and with interrogation of *Domiat*'s survivors indicating that she had been carrying mines, there was a new urgency to the search. At 1030 that forenoon one of the wounded *Domiat* seamen (Able Seaman Altu el Said Hussan) died of his wounds, and later that day his body was committed to the deep. This indicated clearly the need to land the survivors as soon as possible, and during the afternoon watch all but the most seriously injured were transferred to *Newfoundland*. That night *Newfoundland* and *Diana* returned to the Gulf of Suez where they extricated the British tanker MV *Borus*, owned by the Shell oil company, from Egyptian waters. As the tanker had an Egyptian crew her master was ordered to make for Aden, and to remain in radio contact.

*Diana* and *Newfoundland* continued their patrols, and at noon on 2 November the cruiser sent an armed boarding party to *Borus*, whose crew were threatening to run the ship aground. During the day *Diana* refuelled from the cruiser, whose surgeon was transferred to the destroyer to assist in an operation on one of the injured Egyptian naval ratings. That evening radar contacts suggested that an MTB attack against *Diana* and *Newfoundland* was developing, but after making smoke and training their guns on the radar contacts, which had closed to a range of two miles, the situation became confused and by 2230 the threat was over. During the early hours of 3 November another Egyptian prisoner on board *Diana* (Able Seaman Ali Oman) died of his wounds, and during the forenoon his body was committed to the deep. Later that day, at 1745, the frigate *Crane*, which was patrolling close to *Diana* and *Newfoundland*, was attacked by Egyptian jet aircraft and was hit on her starboard side aft by seven rockets. Fortunately, she suffered no serious damage or casualties and she recorded one of the aircraft as 'possibly shot down'. During the forenoon of 4 November *Diana* rendezvoused with the frigate, and later in the day came a much-needed replenishment from *Wave Sovereign*. Also that day the *Domiat* prisoners were transferred back to *Diana* from *Newfoundland* and during the late afternoon of 6 November, when the destroyer put into the port for four hours, they were landed into French custody at Djibouti. In the early hours of 7 November the destroyer put into Aden's outer harbour to refuel, but it was not long before she was steaming north again to her patrol area in the Red Sea.

At midnight on 6/7 November a United Nations' ceasefire came into effect, and within seven weeks this was to be followed by a complete withdrawal of British and French forces from Egypt, leaving Nasser in complete control of the Suez Canal. After the last withdrawal of British forces in mid-December both *Diana* and *Newfoundland* continued their patrols at the northern end of the Red Sea. For *Diana* the Suez operations finally ended on 13 December when she returned to Aden. Six days later she sailed for home which, with the Suez Canal well and truly blocked, meant steaming via Mombasa, Dar es Salaam[3], Durban and Simonstown. On 11 January 1957 *Diana* left South Africa for the long Atlantic passage north, fuelling en route at the Angolan port of Luanda and at Freetown. On 29 January she arrived in Gibraltar, but her three days alongside were clouded by the death of a ship's company member (M(E)1 Mason

---

[3] At Dar es Salaam Captain Gower was able, for the first time, to meet his nephew David, the son of the District Commissioner. David Gower would, of course, eventually captain the England cricket team.

who was found dead at 0130 in Gibraltar Dockyard). Finally, after leaving Gibraltar on 1 February, *Diana* anchored in Plymouth Sound during the late evening of 3 February and next forenoon she steamed up harbour to secure alongside *Decoy* at No 1 wharf.

For eleven months *Diana* had carried out duties of great national importance, and as far as the Suez operations were concerned she received an acknowledgement from the C-in-C Middle East congratulating her officers and men for their service during the short campaign. In respect of 'Operation Mosaic' there was no recognition whatsoever. As Captain Gower recalls:

'This was not an easy peacetime task, nor was the very lucid report prepared by my Gunnery Officer, a most able and capable officer, ever acknowledged - despite the fact that it later became the "bible" for the atomic defence of ships.'

For three months after her return from the Middle East *Diana* underwent a refit in Devonport Dockyard, and in mid-June she put to sea again for a week of trials which ended with a visit to Southend-on-Sea. During the first week of July, together with *Maidstone* (flag C-in-C, Home Fleet), *Albion*, *Gambia*, *Jamaica*, *Scarborough* and the Norwegian destroyer *Trondheim* (ex-HMS *Crozier*), she took part in 'Exercise Fairwind II' in northern waters. Afterwards, following a weekend break at Rosyth, *Diana* sailed for anti-submarine exercises which saw her acting as a 'clockwork mouse' for the submarines *Anchorite*, *Subtle*, *Termagent* and *Totem* to stalk. These manoeuvres took her round Scotland's north coast to Cambeltown and the Clyde, before returning to Devonport on 24 July.

In early August *Diana* took part in Plymouth Navy Days, and on Thursday 22 August she paid off. Captain Gower left for his new appointment which would take him, via Greenwich, to South America where, as Naval Attaché at the British Embassies in Lima, Bogota, Quito and Panama, he

helped to negotiate the sale of HMS *Newfoundland* to the Peruvian Navy. It was the end of *Diana*'s most momentous commission.

At 1700 on Monday 26 August, *Diana*'s new commanding officer, Captain J. T. Kimpton DSC RN, joined the ship and at 1145 next day, during a short ceremony on the forecastle, the destroyer was recommissioned. Eight days later, on 4 September, *Diana* left Devonport to join her sister *Decoy* for the short passage to Portland where the two ships were scheduled to carry out a mini work-up before sailing for the Mediterranean. Later that day, however, as they arrived in Portland Harbour, *Decoy* grounded herself on the outer breakwater close to the harbour entrance. Despite the best efforts of a number of tugs it was late evening before she was refloated and safely alongside Portland's Coaling Pier and so the programme of exercises was cancelled. On 6 September *Diana* escorted her damaged sister ship back to Devonport, a passage which took just over 24 hours, and on 8 September she left Devonport alone, bound for Gibraltar. Once again the passage took longer than usual, this time because she was escorting the paddle tug *Director*. After a short break at Gibraltar *Diana* steamed east for Malta and during the afternoon of 21 September she anchored in Marsaxlokk Bay and joined the Mediterranean Fleet's Fifth Destroyer Squadron, which also included *Diamond*, *Duchess* and *Decoy*. Following her arrival *Diana* carried out two days of exercises in local waters before, on 25 September, she entered Grand Harbour for the first time since April 1956. On the next day the squadron was joined by the delayed *Decoy*.

Throughout the first two weeks of October, together with her sister ships and *Birmingham*, *Cavalier*, *Undine* and the submarine *Sanguine*, *Diana* was employed on day-running work-up exercises. On 18 October, however, she returned to Grand Harbour to undergo a five-week maintenance period, which included ten days in No.3 dry dock. By 25 November she was once more operational and her programme of day running from Malta continued. *Diana*'s first 'foreign' visit of the commission came in early December when, with

*Birmingham*, she paid a five-day visit to Naples. On leaving the Italian port she set course for Cyprus to begin an 18-day patrol searching for weapons smugglers. During her period on patrol she intercepted and searched countless small merchantmen and fishing vessels, but although the Royal Navy was keeping a tight blockade round the island, weapons, ammunition and explosives continued to be supplied to the EOKA guerrillas, which ceased only when the British Government finally conceded independence to Cyprus in 1959. On 17 December, when *Diana* was anchored off Limassol, there was a change of command when Captain P. W. W. Graham DSC RN took over from Captain Kimpton. Christmas Day was spent slowly patrolling the coast. The patrol ended during the forenoon watch of New Year's Eve when *Diana* secured to a buoy in Grand Harbour's Dockyard Creek, and the ship's company was able to get ashore to Strait Street to celebrate in style.

During the first three weeks of January 1958 *Diana* underwent maintenance in Malta, but at the end of the month she steamed west to Gibraltar to join *Ark Royal*, which was beginning a six-month deployment to the Mediterranean. For the remainder of the month and until early June *Diana* regularly acted as planeguard escort for the carrier, but there were breaks in the intensive training exercises when the destroyer called at Savona and, with *Sheffield*, at Split and Trieste. On 30 April, in company with other units of the Mediterranean Fleet at anchor in Aranci Bay, she underwent FO2's harbour inspection and, next day, his sea inspection. In mid-May *Diana* took part in 'Exercise Medflex Fort', which took place between Malta and Cyprus. During the exercise, at 2130 on 19 May, while night flying from *Ark Royal* a Sea Venom ditched on launching. Within three minutes of the accident *Diana* had rescued the pilot, and begun a search for the observer, Sub-Lt Michael Goodwin, but sadly, despite continuing the search into the early hours of the next morning, no trace could be found of him. That night, with serious political unrest in Lebanon, the units of the Mediterranean Fleet were put on alert to evacuate British subjects should it prove

necessary. During this period *Diana* stayed close to the island of Cyprus, anchoring off Limassol where some very limited shore leave was granted. During the forenoon of 17 June, while the ship was anchored off Dhekalia, *Diana*'s divers assisted in the search for one of their colleagues from *Diamond* who had gone missing in a heavy swell. On 28 June *Diana* left Cyprus to return to Malta, and two days later she arrived in Grand Harbour. On 4 July, with her deployment to the Mediterranean over, she left Malta to return home by way of Gibraltar and, during the morning of 11 July, anchored in Plymouth Sound. Five hours later she steamed up harbour to secure on *Decoy* at Devonport Dockyard's No.1 wharf.

It was on Tuesday 16 September that *Diana* and *Decoy* put to sea again, this time to head north for Icelandic waters to carry out a fishery protection patrol. Iceland, in an effort to preserve fish stocks, had unilaterally declared all waters within a 12-mile radius of the island to be territorial waters, but the British Government did not accept this declaration and the two destroyers had been dispatched north to protect British trawlers which were continuing to fish outside the former four-mile limit. During *Diana*'s 17-day patrol she was continually required to prevent the Icelandic Coastguard 'gunboats' *Odinn* and *Thor* from harassing British trawlers, but there were no incidents as serious as those encountered during the later 'Cod War' of the 1970s. Ironically, on 20 September *Diana* had to steam close inshore to the small town of Vatneyri on the north-west coast of Iceland in order to land a member of her ship's company who had been taken ill with acute appendicitis. Five days later a crew member from the Grimsby trawler *Paynter* was also taken ill with appendicitis and was transferred to *Diana*. Once again the destroyer was granted permission to land the man, but whilst this was in progress *Odinn* and *Thor* stopped the *Paynter* and sent boarding parties across to the fishing vessel. As soon as the sick man had been landed at Patreksfjoerdur, close to Vatneyri, *Diana* raced back to patrol area to find that although *Odinn* and *Thor* had left the scene, their boarding party had

disabled the trawler's engine. Fortunately, the destroyer's engineers were able to get the fishing vessel under way once again. Finally, on 4 October, to everyone's relief, *Diana* set course south, arriving at Londonderry forty-eight hours later. Two days later, after an overnight passage down the Irish Sea, the destroyer arrived alongside Swansea's Prince of Wales Dock, to make a four-day goodwill visit to the Welsh port. From Swansea she retraced her route down the Bristol Channel before rounding Land's End and steaming up Channel to Rotterdam, where she spent six days alongside the city's Parkade Jetty. The visit ended on 20 October when, at 0815, the destroyer left harbour to rendezvous with *Birmingham* and *Decoy*, before setting course for Gibraltar, where she arrived on 24 October.

The final weeks of *Diana*'s commission were to be spent on major Home Fleet and NATO exercises, starting off Gibraltar and ending in the Channel off Plymouth. First, however, there was a short break in the form of a four-day visit to Casablanca before the exercises began on 10 November. *Diana* formed part of a group consisting of *Birmingham*, *Apollo*, *Duchess*, *Diamond* and *Decoy*, and they all encountered some severe Atlantic storms during the manoeuvres. On 25 November, with the end of the exercises in sight, *Diana* steamed into the mouth of the River Tagus to land a rating for compassionate leave, and four days later put into the small Spanish port of Avilés for a short break. The exercises ended during the afternoon of 8 December, and that same evening the destroyer anchored in Plymouth Sound. Next forenoon she steamed up harbour to a buoy in the Hamoaze, and by the end of the afternoon she had been secured alongside Devonport Dockyard's No.4 basin. Nine days later, at 0800 on 18 December 1958, *Diana* was paid off into dockyard control and it would be almost two years before she put to sea again.

For 18 months *Diana* was laid up in Reserve at Devonport, but in the summer of 1960 work began to refit the ship for sea once again. On 28 September that year the new commanding officer, Captain G. J. Kirby DSC RN, arrived on board, and on 28 November *Diana* put to sea for preliminary

sea trials which lasted for three days before she returned to Devonport Dockyard for further work on her machinery. Finally, however, on Saturday 21 January 1961, *Diana* was recommissioned and three days later started another series of sea trials which lasted until the end of February.

During these trials, at 0120 on Wednesday 8 February, having left Devonport the previous forenoon, *Diana* was off Start Point when she received an urgent signal for assistance from the small, 386-ton German coaster *Robert Meyhoefer* which was in difficulty off Land's End. Caught in gale force winds and heavy seas the coaster, which was carrying a cargo of aluminium sulphate from Antwerp to Westport on Ireland's west coast, had suffered engine failure and was drifting helplessly at the mercy of the elements. *Diana* immediately increased speed and set course for the merchantman, which was in a position Lat 50° 26'N/Lat 07°06'W. By 0246 the destroyer was off the Eddystone Light and soon afterwards the engineers were able to connect the second boiler. At 0613 *Diana* rounded the Scilly Isles, and at 0745 she sighted *Robert Meyhoefer* wallowing beam on in the heavy seas. Preparations began at once to take the coaster in tow, but it took an hour and a half before the first lines were passed to her. With both ships rolling and pitching heavily it was a difficult operation, but by 1000 *Diana* had begun the tow. With the weather showing no signs of abating progress was slow, and it was 2000 before the two ships had rounded Wolf Rock. Fortunately, as the evening wore on the high winds and heavy seas moderated, and by 0752 on 9 February *Diana* had brought her charge safely into Falmouth Bay, where a local tug took over the tow and guided *Robert Meyhoefer* into the safety of Falmouth Harbour. *Diana* herself anchored in the bay while Captain Kirby visited the merchantman to complete the salvage formalities. The destroyer eventually weighed anchor at 1110 and set course back up Channel, and by early afternoon was secured alongside at Devonport Dockyard.

On 13 February, four days after towing the stricken German coaster to safety, *Diana* left Devonport

for training exercises in the Portland area, and to carry out radar calibrations. At 1340 that afternoon she entered Portland Harbour to disembark the calibration team before returning to sea. Just over three hours later, at 1658, *Diana* received another distress signal, this time from the 262-ton Dutch coaster *Anja*, which was on fire some ten miles east-north-east of Start Point. The vessel had been carrying a cargo of coal from Blyth to Plymouth when fire broke out in the engine room at the after end of the ship, and had quickly spread out of control. A number of ships in the area, including the Torbay lifeboat, attended the scene and the Dutch oil tanker *Frans van Seumeren* prepared to take *Anja* in tow. *Diana* arrived on the scene at 1830 to find the coaster well alight. Her fire parties quickly rigged up firemain hoses and water was sprayed onto the vessel's stern. At 1915, with the first tow having parted, *Frans van Seumeren* managed to get another tow in place, but it was clear that the coaster's crew were unable to control the blaze and that they needed the expert help of *Diana*'s well-trained firefighters. The destroyer's seaboat was lowered and, while water continued to be sprayed onto the coaster's stern, Petty Officer Wise and his fire party clambered aboard and, suitably clad in asbestos suits and wearing breathing apparatus, made their way to the seat of the fire with a high-pressure hose. Working in complete darkness and intense heat, the situation being aggravated by thick smoke, they toiled to bring the fire under control and, by 2234, *Diana*'s fire party had succeeded in extinguishing it completely. Ten minutes later the destroyer anchored off Dartmouth to retrieve her fire party and equipment from *Anja*, which had been towed into Kingswear. There is no doubt that the destroyer's fire party had been in a very dangerous situation, but with hard work and determination they had saved the vessel and her crew.

During the second half of February and throughout March and April *Diana* continued her trials and work-up, finally completing the latter on 11 May. Next day, in company with *Duchess*, she steamed north to Rosyth for Navy Days before returning south again, and on 26 May she anchored off Felixstowe for a two-day visit. Shortly before leaving the East Anglian port one of her former commanding officers, Captain John Gower, who was the Commanding Officer at HMS *Ganges*, the boys' training establishment at Shotley, was able to visit his old ship and join her for the overnight passage to Spithead. On 3 June, having spent four days in Portsmouth Dockyard, *Diana* left harbour to rendezvous with *Duchess* and set course for Invergordon and training exercises off Scotland's east coast. Also taking part were *Bermuda*, *Puma*, *Diamond*, the Dutch aircraft carrier *Karel Doorman* and the Norwegian destroyer *Oslo*. For *Diana* the exercises ended with a weekend at Aarhus, followed by a passage into the Baltic for a four-day visit to the port of Turku in Finland. On leaving Finland during the evening of 2 July *Diana* made the return passage to the North Sea by way of the Kiel Canal, and on the morning of 6 July she anchored in Jennycliffe Bay where tenders brought out families and friends for the short sea trip round the Eddystone Light and the return passage up harbour to secure alongside in Devonport Dockyard.

Following her return to Devonport *Diana* underwent a short maintenance period before sailing, on 25 July, to join *Diamond* and *Duchess* for the passage south to Gibraltar where she underwent a 16-day docking period before continuing into the Mediterranean to call at the Spanish island of Ibiza. *Diana* spent five days alongside during which time over 2,000 local people visited the ship, but the football team went down 8 - 1 to a very good local side. After leaving Ibiza *Diana* carried out training exercises with the submarine *Sea Devil* and, upon arrival in the Malta exercises areas, with *Tiger*, *Battleaxe* and *Totem*. Finally, during the afternoon of 1 September *Diana* secured to a buoy in Malta's Sliema Creek.

During the days which followed her arrival on the Mediterranean Station *Diana* underwent her work-up, often in company with *Lion* and *Talent*, but on Friday 15 September, having embarked large quantities of stores, she left harbour to make a west-

---

[4] The squadron also included *Plymouth (*Leader*), Diana, Dido, Cambrian* and *Salisbury.*

bound passage to Gibraltar from where, after a short refuelling stop, she steamed south to Freetown, arriving alongside the Kissy refuelling jetty on 23 September. *Diana* had been temporarily detached from the Mediterranean Fleet on an unusual 55-day cruise to mid-Atlantic ports of West Africa in order to be present at the Independence Ceremonies of the British Trust Territory of the Southern Cameroon, which was part of the former German colony of Kamerun, which Britain and France had split between them in 1919 as part of the Versailles Armistice Treaties. On gaining independence the territory was actually reunited with its former neighbour to create the Federal Republic of Cameroon.

After leaving Freetown on 25 September *Diana* made a four-day passage into the Gulf of Guinea to the port of Bota (formerly Victoria, and now

Limbe), where she arrived early on Friday 29 September to join the troopship *Devonshire* which was waiting to embark the outgoing garrison of Grenadier Guards. One member of the ship's company remembers the West African port thus:

'We soon made our first acquaintance with the bumboatmen, who were offering strange carvings, bananas and even monkeys, in exchange for money, old clothes and cigarettes.'

Meanwhile, at the stroke of midnight on 29 September, following the Independence and Reunification Ceremony, the outgoing British Colonial Commissioner and his wife were given a ceremonial send-off by Honour Guards from the Cameroon Army and the Grenadier Guards on the jetty when, at 1530 on 30 September, they

Diana *and* Crossbow *exercising off Portland in November 1962.*          *(Imperial War Museum Neg. No. MH27490)*

*An undated photograph of* Diana *during a 4.5-inch gunnery shoot.* (T. Ferrers-Walker)

embarked in *Diana*. At 2300 that evening the destroyer left harbour and set course for the Nigerian port of Lagos where, on 3 October, the VIP passengers were disembarked. That afternoon *Diana* sailed for Santa Isabel (now Rey Malabo) on the mountainous Spanish island of Fernando Po (now Bioko) which, although only 240 miles north of the equator, was at that time a province of Spain.

The ship's company were offered traditional Spanish hospitality and at 1400 on each of the five days the destroyer was alongside, buses arrived alongside to take the sailors on tours of the banana and cocoa plantations, returning them to the ship at 1930. During these coach trips it was said that the islanders were most intrigued by the bus passengers' renditions of the West Country 'Oggie Song' - a song well known to all Plymouth 'Janners'. From Santa Isabel *Diana* made an overnight passage to Douala, the capital of the Cameroon Republic, where the destroyer's 21-gun salute was returned by an ancient nineteenth-century gun which emitted fearsome noises, showers of sparks and clouds of smoke. With some civil unrest in the former French colony all shore leave ended at 2130, but this did

not prevent groups of ship's company members visiting the local brewery, and the civic authorities hosted a lavish reception for 150 officers and ratings from the ship.

*Diana*'s final visit on the West African coast was to Libreville, the capital of the Gabon Republic, where Captain Kirby and a group of 22 officers and ratings visited Dr Schweitzer's renowned mission hospital at Lambaréré. In order to get to the hospital the Gabon Government laid on a DC-3 aircraft, and on their arrival at the hospital the party was met and shown round by Dr Schweitzer himself. Before leaving Captain Kirby presented the hospital with a donation from the ship's welfare fund. *Diana* left Libreville on 20 October and steamed south to cross the equator early next day - Trafalgar Day. The event was to have been marked by the traditional ceremony, but strong, gale-force winds and heavy seas ruled this out. However, a belated ceremony was held with the captain, who, in his 25 years seagoing career, had only ever crossed the line by air, being the first victim to be dunked. During the passage north the ship put into Freetown for fuel and four days later, on 28 October, she secured

alongside Franco Jetty, Las Palmas, Grand Canaria, for what was an excellent 'duty free' run ashore.

*Diana* left Las Palmas on 1 November to make a refuelling stop at Gibraltar two days later, before continuing her return passage to Malta. At 0930 on Monday 6 November, however, when she was steaming through gale-force winds and heavy seas off the Tunisian coast, she received an SOS signal from the owners of the British cargo steamer SS *Clan Keith* which had suffered a massive explosion on board. The vessel had left Middlesbrough on 14 October with a cargo of chemicals, steel pilings and cast iron pipes, bound for Aden, but off Tunisia she encountered the storm and it is thought that in the early hours of 6 November her deadly cargo of chemicals shifted, causing the huge explosion. Meanwhile, in the same storm *Diana* was being buffeted by what were now storm-force winds and raging seas which, at one stage, smashed and washed away her whaler, but as soon as the emergency signal was received she set course for the last known position of the merchantman. At 1305 she sighted the frigates *Plymouth* and *Rhyl* which, with the cruiser *Blake*, were also involved in the search for survivors, but *Diana* recovered only the body of one unidentified seaman from the area where *Clan Keith* had disappeared. At 1655 it was brought on board and at 2005 was committed to the deep. In all 61 crew members from *Clan Keith* were lost, with only seven survivors being rescued by nearby merchantmen. At 2318 the search was called off and *Diana* arrived in the Marsaxlokk anchorage during the evening of 7 November.

During the last three weeks of November *Diana* underwent a maintenance period alongside the heavy repair ship *Ausonia* in Lazaretto Creek, and in early December she was involved in Mediterranean Fleet exercises with *Victorious*, *Blake*, *Duchess* and *Crossbow*, before spending the Christmas and New Year holidays in Malta. The first weeks of 1962 were spent exercising in local waters off Malta where *Diana* acted as planeguard to *Ark Royal* and took part in anti-submarine training with *Talent* and the Italian submarine *Evangelista Toricelli* (ex-USS *Lizardfish*). In early

March, with *Blake*, *Battleaxe*, *Crossbow*, *Diamond* and *Berwick*, *Diana* took part in NATO exercises in Greek waters, which included a six-day visit to Athens and was followed by the destroyer's sea inspection. By the end of March *Diana*'s deployment to the Mediterranean was drawing to a close, and on Monday 26 March, steaming in line ahead with *Battleaxe*, *Crossbow* and *Duchess*, she left Sliema Creek and set course for Gibraltar and Plymouth, arriving at anchor in Jennycliffe Bay during the late evening of 5 April. Next forenoon she steamed up harbour to secure alongside in Devonport Dockyard.

After returning to Devonport *Diana* underwent a four-week maintenance period, and it was 3 May before she sailed to complete the final months of the commission. She paid a nine-day visit to Milford Haven and later in the month, in company with *Diamond* and *Duchess*, she visited Stockholm and Helsinki. In June she took part in training exercises off Scotland's east and north coasts, with the gunners bombarding the Cape Wrath ranges with the main armament. The month ended with the NATO exercise 'Fairwind VII', during which she took on the role of convoy escort between Invergordon and Bergen. Finally, after a weekend in Bergen, *Diana* returned to Devonport, arriving alongside on 4 July to begin a 15-week refit.

In late October *Diana* underwent her post-refit trials and carried out anti-submarine training in the Portland area. On 12 November she steamed north to the Clyde where, after a five-day visit to Glasgow, she, *Agincourt* and *Crossbow*, provided targets for the submarine *Orpheus* to stalk. On 1 December she returned to Devonport and just over two weeks later she made her final seagoing foray of the commission when she steamed west to The Lizard and returned at speed with the passage being made under full power, arriving back in Devonport during the forenoon of 18 December 1962. Two days later over half the ship's company left for seasonal leave and *Diana* was paid off.

At 0845 on 2 January 1963 *Diana*'s new commanding officer, Captain D. J. Kent RN, joined the ship and that same afternoon the recommissioning

party moved on board from the Royal Naval Barracks. At 1530 the next day the ship was recommissioned, and on 14 January the destroyer put to sea to undergo machinery trials. During February, and into March, *Diana* carried out her work-up training at Portland, culminating in her Sea Inspection on 7 March. Subsequently she was based at Londonderry, from where, with the brand new *Leander*, she was deployed on anti-submarine training with *Hardy*, *Salisbury*, *Yarmouth* and the submarines *Talent* and *Truncheon*. During April she continued to operate from Northern Ireland, and from Portland, with weekend visits to Liverpool and Portsmouth, but on 26 April she returned to Devonport to undergo maintenance and to give leave. On 30 May Captain Kent left *Diana* to take command of Plymouth as Captain (D) 22nd Escort Squadron[4] which was being formed in the Far East; in his place Commander H. J. Startin RN took command of *Diana*.

In the Far East the formation of the Federation of Malaysia from the former British Commonwealth Crown Colonies and Protectorates had led to political unrest in Brunei and an outright military 'Confrontation' with Indonesia, whose leader President Sukarno was vehemently opposed to the new union and it became apparent in London that urgent military reinforcements were required in the area. On 4 June 1963, in company with *Plymouth*, *Diana* left Devonport bound for the Far East Station at Singapore. Steaming by way of Gibraltar and Malta, they transited the Suez Canal on 14/15 June and arrived in Aden five days later. On 21 June they left Aden to join *Salisbury* and to set course for Gan where they refuelled from *Wave Victor* before continuing eastwards. During the passage they rendezvoused with *Ark Royal* for training exercises, and at 1515 on 4 July, as they approached the Nicobar Islands, *Diana* was diverted to the aid of the Norwegian oil tanker SS *Credo* which had a badly injured crewman on board. That same evening the man was transferred by whaler to *Diana* and an hour later by helicopter from the destroyer's quarterdeck to *Ark Royal*. Next day *Diana* anchored briefly off Penang before beginning anti-submarine exercises with other units of the Far East Fleet, including *Hermes*, *Ark Royal*, *Caesar* and the two Australian Darings HMAS *Vampire* and the ill-fated *Voyager*. The major naval exercises at the northern end of the Strait of Malacca and in the southern Andaman Sea were designed to send an unequivocal political message to President Sukarno that Britain was determined to uphold its treaty obligations to the newly created Federation of Malaysia, which was composed of the former British-administered territories of Malaya, Singapore, North Borneo and Sarawak. The exercises ended at just before midnight on 9 July and 32 hours later *Diana* arrived alongside the Singapore Naval Base to begin a seven-week dockyard-assisted maintenance period.

On 27 July, with the ship having been dry-docked, the ship's company moved ashore to the spacious and comfortable accommodation at HMS *Terror*, with its swimming pools, sports facilities and canteen, and they did not return to the ship until the end of August. As for *Diana*, she did not return to sea until 2 September when she carried out post-refit trials in the South China Sea. However, after four days it became clear that there were problems with the plummer blocks and a further docking period was necessary. On 11 September the ship's company moved back into HMS *Terror*, which brought no complaints from the men, and the ship herself was moved back into AFD No 10. In the event it was 23 September before *Diana* was ready for sea and early next morning, having embarked a number of Malaysian police officers, she sailed for the Tawau area on the east coast of North Borneo, close to the Indonesian border, where she carried out a patrol intercepting and searching small craft in an area where Indonesian guerrillas had made deep incursions into Sarawak. During this period the destroyer operated with the Malaysian Navy's patrol boat *Sri Kedah*, and there was even time for a run ashore when *Diana* secured alongside the small port's main jetty. On 5 October there came a welcome break in the form of a five-day visit to Hong Kong, after which *Diana* returned to Singapore, carrying out anti-submarine exercises

with *Andrew* en route.

On the last day of October *Diana* left Singapore bound for Karachi and a goodwill visit to what was, in those days, still the capital city of West Pakistan. Three days into the passage, however, the starboard plummer blocks were found to be seriously overheating and for several hours the ship was stopped in order that temporary repairs could be carried out. It was late evening before she was under way again, but the mechanical problems persisted and on 6 November she put into Colombo to refuel before retracing her course back to Singapore, where she arrived five days later. With the Indonesian Confrontation having intensified, the strength of the Far East Fleet had grown enormously to levels which had not been seen since the days of the Korean War. This meant that dockyard facilities were at full stretch and *Diana* was sent on to Hong Kong for repairs to the plummer block bearings on her starboard propeller shaft. She arrived in the colony on 18 November and was sent to the commercial Taikoo Dockyard and Engineering Company, where the repairs took three weeks to complete. During the morning of 12 December, after trials on her newly repaired plummer blocks had passed without a hitch, *Diana* returned to the exercise areas in the South China Sea off Singapore, where she joined manoeuvres with *Barrosa* and *Duchess*, before returning to the naval base for the Christmas and New Year festivities.

With the Confrontation having escalated and regular soldiers of the Indonesian Army having been involved in the border fighting, during the first weeks of 1964 *Diana* operated in the Strait of Malacca with *Victorious*, *Caesar* and the New Zealand frigate *Taranaki*. It was imperative that the Royal Navy provided a real deterrent to any possibility of an Indonesian crossing of the Strait onto the mainland of the Malayan Peninsula's west coast. However, other post-colonial problems for Britain were arising in Africa, and on 18 January 1964, in company with *Victorious*, *Diana* was ordered to steam west 'with all dispatch' to Mombasa.

In East Africa the newly independent Protectorate of Zanzibar was experiencing its first civil unrest, with a popular uprising against the Sultan. The Royal Navy and a company of the Staffordshire Regiment were placed on standby in case Britain decided to intervene, or to evacuate British nationals from the island. In the event the British Government did neither, but on 20 January as *Diana* and *Victorious* were approaching Gan, units of the Tanzanian Army mutinied against their British officers, so when the two ships arrived in Mombasa's Kilindini Harbour the political situation in East Africa was tense and uncertain. *Diana* spent the last day of January anchored off Dar es Salaam as the Royal Marines of 45 Commando disarmed the mutinous Tanzanian troops in the city. Then, at the end of February, with the situation calmer, she and *Victorious* returned to the Andaman Sea to take part in 'Exercise Jet 64' with the Indian units *Vikrant* (ex-HMS *Hercules*) and *Rana* (ex-HMS *Raider*), and units of the Far East Fleet, including *Plymouth*, *Cambrian* and HMAS *Yarra*. Towards the end of the exercise, however, *Diana* began to experience plummer block overheating once again and on 15 March she put into Singapore Naval Base for more work to her troublesome propeller shaft bearings.

On 6 April, in company with *Plymouth*, *Diana* left Singapore to head north for a weekend visit to Bangkok, after which she returned to the Singapore exercise areas for exercises with *Centaur*. On 20 April, in company with *Cambrian*, she left Singapore to make her way home. On 24 April, in mid-Indian Ocean, she was forced to stop for several hours in order that the engineers could work on a badly leaking stern gland, and it was 2 May before she reached Aden. Six days later she began her northbound transit of the Suez Canal, and during the final leg of her homeward passage she made brief calls at Malta and Gibraltar. Finally, at 2200 on 21 May she secured to a buoy in Plymouth Sound. Next forenoon, having embarked a large group of relatives, *Diana* steamed up harbour to secure alongside Devonport Dockyard's No.8 wharf. It was the end of what had been a busy commission, dogged by mechanical problems, particu-

larly with the propeller shaft bearings and stern glands.

On Friday 5 June, as *Diana* lay high and dry in No.9 dry dock, her new commanding officer, Captain R. C. C. Greenlees RN, joined the ship and 12 days later the destroyer was recommissioned for a General Service Commission in the Home Fleet and east of Suez as part of the 29th Escort Squadron. In the event, however, she was destined to spend all but two of the next 18 months alongside in Devonport.

During the last six months of 1964, with her much reduced ship's company living in barracks accommodation, *Diana* spent the year firmly secured alongside Devonport's No.4 basin undergoing a long refit and it was 2 December when the ship's company moved back on board. In early January 1965 the ship was shifted to the sea wall, but it was to be 19 May before she put to sea for four days of machinery trials in the Channel. After a short break at Devonport the trials of her machinery and weapons were resumed, and they continued throughout June. On 29 June, however, after a week at Portsmouth she returned to Devonport, where she remained for the rest of the year.

On 1 November 1965 *Diana*'s next commanding officer, Commander P. I. F. Beeson RN, was appointed, and on 22 January 1966, for the first time in seven months, she came to eight hours' notice for steam. Two days later she left Devonport to begin four days of intensive machinery trials, often in severe weather conditions, after which she returned to Devonport Dockyard to secure alongside *Belfast* at No 6 wharf[5]. During February and in early March the dockyard worked on *Diana*'s main propulsion machinery, and it was 14 March before she returned to sea to begin her work-up at Portland. Unfortunately, this was dogged by mechanical problems in her main propulsion machinery, and on 25 March she returned to Devonport for further repairs and maintenance and three days later, while entering No.4 basin, she collided with the wharf, damaging both her hull and port propeller. Once again she was taken in hand by

the dockyard, which included three weeks' dry docking, and the work was not completed until mid-May. Finally, however, on 18 May *Diana* sailed to carry out further engine trials, and to resume her interrupted work-up.

For over two months the destroyer was put through Portland's gruelling work-up routine as the ship's company was brought up to a state of full operational and material efficiency which would enable her to face with confidence the duties and obligations that every ship may encounter during a commission. The exercises and evolutions included dealing with civil disturbances, assisting civil authorities after natural disasters such as earthquakes, and going to the aid of merchant ships in distress. With long hours having been spent at Action and Defence Stations it was with some relief all round that, on Wednesday 3 August, *Diana* underwent her final sea inspection by Flag Officer Sea Training and his staff. Next forenoon she anchored in Plymouth Sound to embark families and friends of the ship's company and treat them to a day at sea and lunch on board. Later that afternoon she secured alongside Devonport's South Yard to prepare for her first foreign service for two years.

At 1300 on Tuesday 30 August 1966 *Diana* left Devonport bound for the Far East Station and service with the 1st Destroyer Squadron. Sailing via Gibraltar and Malta she passed through the Suez Canal on 12 September and arrived in Aden four days later, pausing just long enough to refuel before continuing her passage via Gan. *Diana* arrived in Singapore on 26 September, when the Indonesian Confrontation was virtually at an end, although the fleet at Singapore was still on a high level of alert. Immediately following her arrival on station *Diana* underwent a ten-day maintenance period, following which she visited Hong Kong before returning to Singapore. In early November she patrolled the Strait of Malacca and visited Penang and later in the month, together with *Leopard*, *Londonderry*, HMS/m *Auriga* and HMNZS *Blackpool*, she took part in fleet manoeuvres in the exercise areas of the

---

[5] *Belfast* was in Reserve, and in May 1966 she was moved to Portsmouth as an accommodation ship.

South China Sea just north of Singapore, which included a weekend break at Pulau Tioman. On 24 November the destroyer returned to Singapore for two weeks of maintenance before steaming west to take her turn on the Beira Patrol.

On 31 December, having spent Christmas Day at sea in the Indian Ocean, *Diana* relieved *Falmouth*[6] on the Beira Patrol, which she carried out with *Sirius* and *Zulu* for almost three weeks before putting in to Kilindini Harbour, Mombasa, for a maintenance and rest period. On 1 February 1967 she sailed south for her second Beira Patrol, this time with *Nubian*. The patrol lasted for just two weeks. On completion she again returned to Mombasa, but this time just to refuel and set course for Aden on the first leg of her passage home. *Diana* passed through the Suez Canal on 26 and 27 February and

arrived in Malta on 1 March. Initially she was to have sailed within 48 hours of her arrival, but her departure was delayed for four days in order to carry out condenser repairs. She finally left Grand Harbour with *Dainty* on 7 March. The two ships remained in company for the passage home, and *Diana* arrived in Devonport during the afternoon of 15 March, when she was paid off.

Although *Diana* remained in dockyard hands for some six months, she was recommissioned for the last time on Thursday 13 April, but with the ship high and dry in No.8 dry dock at Devonport there was no ceremony to mark the occasion. On 4 July her new ship's company moved on board from barracks accommodation, and finally on 18 September the ship was shifted back alongside the sea wall, before starting her sea trials the next day. In early

*An excellent starboard side view of* Diana *at speed.*                    *(MoD/Crown Copyright)*

---

[6] The author was serving in *Falmouth* at the time.

November, for a period which lasted for seven weeks, *Diana* underwent her work-up at Portland, with a weekend break at Southampton in early December. By 20 December she had completed her final inspections and had returned to Devonport to give leave.

On 17 January 1968 she sailed for Gibraltar, for service in the Mediterranean. On 24 January, after a four-day break at Gibraltar, she sailed for Malta, but next day whilst on passage she was ordered to increase speed and make the journey with 'all dispatch' to assist in the search for the Israeli submarine *Dakar* which had been reported missing some 100 miles west of Cyprus and 150 miles north of Alexandria. *Dakar* was, in fact, the ex-Royal Navy submarine *Totem* which had been sold to Israel and commissioned in late 1967, and she was still undergoing sea trials for her new owners. *Diana* arrived in Grand Harbour at 2200 on 26 January, and after embarking a recompression chamber and refuelling she sailed after only six hours alongside to begin her search. In the event *Dakar* had been lost with all hands and the loss remained a mystery until the wreck was eventually located in May 1999. That evening at 2000 *Diana* received a distress signal from the Spanish oil tanker MV *Bahia Gaditana*, whose engine room was on fire. The tanker was in a position Lat 36°34'N/Long 19°02'E, some 70 miles north of *Diana*'s position. Despite heavy seas the destroyer arrived in the vicinity of the stricken tanker at just after 2130, but the severe weather precluded all chance of boarding the tanker that night and during the hours of darkness *Diana* circled the ship, keeping watch. At 0730 on 28 January conditions had eased somewhat and a firefighting team led by the first lieutenant, Lt Cdr Teague, and engine room personnel were put aboard by life-raft. By that time the fire had been burning for 18 hours, and it was clear that the tanker's own firefighting equipment was hopelessly inadequate. At 1040, despite the heavy swell, *Diana*'s seaboat was launched to carry a pump and other equipment to the tanker. Loading the heavy gear aboard the *Bahia Gaditana* was no mean feat as the boat was rising and falling by as much as 12 feet alongside

the tanker, but it was accomplished safely and by 1600 the team had made it possible to enter the engine room once again. *Diana*'s firefighting team remained on board to cool down the tanker's overheated bulkheads and prevent another outbreak of fire, and at just after midnight on 29 January a Dutch tug arrived to take over the oil tanker. Six hours later, with the firefighting teams and equipment back on board, the destroyer left to head for the area off Crete and continue the search for the *Dakar*, stopping briefly at Souda Bay to refuel.

During the evening of 31 January the search for the missing submarine was called off, and two days later *Diana* returned to Grand Harbour from where, over the next two weeks, she operated on a day-running basis. On Tuesday 13 February she put to sea to search for a Greek cargo ship which was on fire, but in the event her assistance was not required and she returned to Grand Harbour the next day. Three days later she left Malta to make the passage home via Gibraltar, and on 23 February she arrived alongside at Devonport.

On Tuesday 2 April *Diana* sailed for Gibraltar again to carry out four weeks' duty as the colony's guardship. On 6 May when this period ended she left in company with *Cavalier*, *Grenville* and *Troubridge* for the Far East Station. With the Suez Canal closed to shipping following the Arab-Israeli Six Day War her passage was made via the Cape of Good Hope, with a fuelling stop at Dakar. On 21 May she arrived at the South African naval base at Simonstown for a seven-day visit. On leaving South Africa *Diana* steamed north into the Indian Ocean and on the last day of May relieved *Aurora* on the Beira Patrol. *Diana*'s first patrol of the commission lasted for 16 days, before she had a break at Mombasa where, during her nine days in Kilindini Harbour, many members of the ship's company were able to get away for a break at Silversands leave centre, while others opted for safari trips to the nearby Tsavo National Park. Meanwhile, the messdecks filled up with wooden animal carvings, and it was said that many messdeck bulkheads were adorned with Masai shields and spears.

On 25 June she left Mombasa to return to the Beira Patrol, which was carried out in company with *Aurora* and *Grenville*. In order to beat the long days of boredom under the hot sun, dogwatch games were held on the upper deck, with the wardroom mess winning the shooting competition. Finally, on 20 July *Diana* left the patrol area to steam via Gan to the naval base at Singapore. Before entering harbour, however, she steamed round to the exercise areas off the east coast of the Malaya Peninsula to carry out a bombardment exercise with *Glamorgan*, with the added bonus of banyans on the island of Pulau Tinggi. During the evening of 29 July the exercise was concluded, and next forenoon *Diana* secured alongside the naval base to de-ammunition before a seven-week dockyard-assisted refit.

During this period high and dry in the dockyard's AFD No 10, the ship's company was accommodated in the comfortable and airy buildings of HMS *Terror*, but by mid-September the men were back on board and next day the ship was moved to the nearby armament depot for ammunitioning. On Sunday 15 September *Diana*'s last Royal Navy commanding officer, Commander E. D. L. Llewellyn RN, took over from Commander Tomlinson, and next day put to sea for eight hours of post-refit trials. On 18 September *Diana* put to sea for eight hours of trials and three days later, with *Hermes*, *Albion*, *Triumph*, *Glamorgan*, *Defender* and *Intrepid*, took part in what was, at that time, the biggest maritime and amphibious exercise ever held in eastern waters. The exercise was codenamed 'Coral Sands' and involved more than 50 ships[7] and 18,000 men, including 2,000 Royal Marines of No 3 Commando Brigade. Starting off Malaya's east coast the force moved south into an area ranging from the Solomon Islands to Sydney, with the main objective being to destroy an 'enemy force' consisting of 900 Gurkhas under a mythical leader 'Sultan Orangi', which had invaded Queensland in northern Australia.

For most of the exercise *Diana* was in company with *Hermes*, to whom she acted as planeguard, and *Glamorgan* and during the course of the manoeuvres they rendezvoused with the replenishment ships which, acting as the convoy, were escorted to the operating area at Shoalwater Bay where the amphibious landings took place. The exercise ended on 13 October, and next forenoon *Diana*, *Hermes* and *Glamorgan* secured alongside the Australian Navy's base at Garden Island, Sydney. After four weeks at sea the 17-day stopover at Sydney was a welcome break for the ship's company, but on 1 November *Diana* was back at sea carrying out gunnery exercises in the Jervis Bay area. Two days later she joined *Hermes* as planeguard escort and underwent FO2's sea inspection before setting course for Subic Bay and joint exercises with the US Navy, including the aircraft carrier USS *America*. From the Subic Bay area *Diana* and *Hermes* steamed to the US Navy's exercise areas off Okinawa, and during the forenoon of 23 November *Diana* anchored in Buckner Bay off Okinawa. Two days later she was ordered to weigh anchor and proceed 'with all dispatch' to join *Hermes* which had lost a Gannet aircraft. The Gannet, of the ship's 849A Flight, had been launched at 0800, but had ditched into the sea. Despite an intensive search by *Hermes* and *Diana* no trace could be found of the three crew members, but during the afternoon watch *Diana* recovered pieces of wreckage from the stricken aircraft. On 27 November, with *Hermes* having left for Hong Kong, *Diana* returned to Buckner Bay where the ship's company spent three days repainting the ship in preparation for a much-anticipated cruise of Japanese ports. Leaving Buckner Bay on the last day of November the destroyer rendezvoused with *Grenville* and at 1240 on 2 December they secured alongside Hiroshima's main harbour pier for a five-day stopover. From Hiroshima the two ships made a short, half-hour passage to the island of Etyjima, where they anchored off the Japanese naval acade-

---

[7] Other RN units taking part were *Hermes*, *Albion*, *Intrepid*, *Triumph*, *Forth*, *Glamorgan*, *Fife*, *Defender*, *Caprice*, *Euryalus*, *Puma*, *Onslaught*, *Cachalot*, *Andrew*, *Bossington*, *Kirkliston*, and *Maxton*, as well as RFAs *Fort Rosalie*, *Reliant*, *Tarbatness*, *Tidespring*, *Gold Ranger* and *Pearleaf*.

*On 1 April 1969* Diana *returned to Devonport from the Far East Station. Here, on a warm and sunny forenoon, she steams up harbour.* (Maritime Photo Library)

my for a 30-hour visit. During this period there was a constant stream of visitors to the warships which were of great interest to the establishment's cadets. After weighing anchor on 8 December both ships made a 12-hour crossing of Japan's Inland Sea to anchor off the picturesque hot springs resort of Beppu for an enjoyable visit to the town. Their departure during the forenoon of 11 December marked the end of the Japanese cruise, and after transiting the Taiwan Strait on 13 December, the two ships arrived in Hong Kong where *Diana* secured alongside the dockyard's North Arm.

*Diana*'s five-week maintenance period in Hong Kong Dockyard came at a time when, in mainland China, Mao Tse-tung's Cultural Revolution was at its height, and the ship's company became willing volunteers in efforts to prevent the worst of the civil strife which was gripping China from spreading to the small colony. On 18 December, carrying 236 local children, the ship put to sea for a 40-mile cruise round Hong Kong Island, followed by a tea party on board. Ashore a party of 50 ship's company volunteers were employed on Lantau Island for what was known as the 'Hearts and Minds' organisation, and spent eight hours a day building a concrete footpath for the coastal hamlet of Man Kok,

who had only a muddy path to take them five miles round a steep hillside to the nearest school and market. Each day the working party ferried themselves and numerous hundredweight bags of concrete and sand to the island for what was very arduous manual work, but on 16 January 1969, to the delight of the villagers, the new footpath was officially opened by the captain's wife, Mrs E. D. L. Llewellyn. Four days later *Diana* left Hong Kong to return to Singapore on what was to be the start of her passage home.

*Diana* left Singapore for the last time at 0945 on Saturday 1 February, and following the Great Circle Track she made a 27-knot passage to Gan where, in Gan Lagoon, she refuelled from *Wave Victor*. During the second part of her passage there was a brief pause off Agalega Island, and at 0900 on 11 February she relieved *Glamorgan* off Beira, where she operated with *Lincoln*. Two days into the patrol *Diana* embarked an urgent compassionate case from *Lincoln*'s ship's company and took him to Majunga (now Mahajamba) on the north-west coast of Madagascar, the location of the nearest airport from which he could be flown home. The destroyer then returned to the patrol area where she remained for another three weeks. Finally, on 7 March she

was relieved by *Jaguar* and set course for Simonstown and home.

After seven days at the South African naval base *Diana* left port to join *Hermes* and *Aurora* for the non-stop passage home to Devonport. In the early hours of 28 March they passed Gran Canaria. Three days later they rounded Ushant, where *Diana* was detached and 14 hours later, at 2200 on the last day of March, the destroyer anchored in Plymouth Sound. Next forenoon she steamed up harbour to secure alongside Devonport Dockyard, where she began a seven-week maintenance period.

The final phase of *Diana*'s service with the Royal Navy began on 19 May when she left Devonport to begin weapon training at Portland, and seven days later she joined *Eagle* in the Irish Sea to act as planeguard during trials of the F-4K Phantom aircraft. She remained with *Eagle* until the end of May, and after a weekend break at Devonport paid a three-day visit to Dartmouth for the town's commemoration of the 25th anniversary of the D-Day landings. After leaving Dartmouth *Diana* steamed

south to Gibraltar for a further three-week stint as the colony's guardship. On 7 July she returned to home waters and further weapon training at Portland before joining *Eagle* and other Home Fleet units in Tor Bay for the Queen's Review of the Western Fleet. Leaving Tor Bay on 29 July the destroyer paid a goodwill visit to Bognor Regis, before returning to Devonport to give seasonal leave.

On 2 September *Diana* put to sea to begin the final weeks of her operational career with the Royal Navy and on 7 September, after more weapon training at Portland, she rejoined *Eagle* in the Irish Sea. For three days, during intensive anti-submarine exercises, she acted as planeguard again, relieved by a short visit to Barry in South Wales. She then returned to *Eagle* to take part in the NATO exercise 'Peacekeeper' in the Western Approaches of the Atlantic. *Diana*'s part in the exercise ended on 25 September when she made a five-day visit to Lisbon. During late September that year the Spanish Government stepped up its campaign of

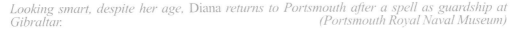

*Looking smart, despite her age,* Diana *returns to Portsmouth after a spell as guardship at Gibraltar.* (Portsmouth Royal Naval Museum)

*Armed with Exocet missiles, and with a small flight deck and hangar in place of the after turret, the Peruvian Navy's Palacios is still recognisable as a Daring-class destroyer.* (Lt Cdr J. R. Asti, Peruvian Navy)

harassment against Gibraltar, and an armada of Spanish warships, including the light aircraft carrier *Dedalo* (ex-USS *Cabot*), the cruiser *Canarias* and smaller units took up a provocative position in the vicinity of the stretch of water in Gibraltar Bay known as 'The Loop', which both Britain and Spain claimed as territorial waters. In addition to the naval presence there was a continuous flow of propaganda in the Spanish media insisting that Spain, if it wished, could completely isolate The Rock by interfering with shipping and aircraft movements. As a result, when *Diana* left Lisbon on 30 September she steamed south and next day joined *Llandaff* as guardship at Gibraltar. This time, however, the duty lasted only ten days and on 5 October, her last Sunday in harbour, she hoisted her paying-off pennant. Five days later, with *Llandaff*, she left

Gibraltar for the last time and at 2215 on 12 October anchored in Cawsand Bay. Next forenoon, at 0815, she weighed anchor and steamed up harbour to secure to No.1 buoy in the Hamoaze, where ammunition lighters came alongside to begin the process of de-ammunitioning. Later that afternoon the destroyer was moved alongside a berth in the dockyard and four days later she was shifted into the non-tidal basin. Those members of the ship's company remaining aboard faced the move into barracks accommodation, and on 21 October a sales meeting was held between officials from MoD and the Peruvian Navy in the wardroom.

Like her sister *Decoy*, *Diana* had been sold to the Peruvian Navy and as part of the contract a £4.5 million, three-year refit was awarded to Cammell Laird & Co at Birkenhead. During this long period

on the River Mersey the destroyer was equipped with eight Exocet MM-38 surface-to-surface missiles, which were fitted where the Close Range Blind Fire Director, forward of X turret, had once been. The foremast was also rebuilt and plated in for the installation of new Plessey AWS-1 air-search radar. The refit was completed in February 1973 and the destroyer was commissioned into the Marina de Guerra del Peru as the *Palacios*. During her service with the Peruvian Navy *Palacios* operated mainly from the naval base at Callao, and in 1977 the after 4.5-inch turret was removed and a helicopter-landing platform fitted. However, soon afterwards the hangar was removed and the 4.5-inch gun mounting was restored. *Palacios'* career with the Peruvian Navy ended in 1993, some 40 years after she had first commissioned.

## HMS *Diana*
## Commanding Officers

| Name: | Date Appointed: |
|---|---|
| Captain C. R. L. Argles RN | 23 February 1954 |
| Captain J. R. Gower DSC RN | 28 February 1956 |
| Captain J. T. Kimpton DSC RN | 26 August 1957 |
| Captain P. W. W. Graham DSC RN | 15 December 1957 |
| Captain G. J. Kirby DSC RN | 29 September 1960 |
| Captain D. J. Kent RN | 2 January 1963 |
| Commander H. J. Startin RN | 30 May 1963 |
| Captain R. C. C. Greenlees RN | 3 June 1964 |
| Commander P. I. F. Beeson RN | 1 November 1965 |
| Commander J. T. Tomlinson RN | 1 May 1967 |
| Commander E. D. L. Llewellyn RN | 15 September 1968 |

## Battle Honours

| | |
|---|---|
| Armada 1588 | Zefier 1809 |
| Louisburg 1758 | Burma 1824-26 |
| Quebec 1759 | Norway 1940 |

# Part Nine

# HMAS VOYAGER

## February 1957 -February 1964

*The ill-fated HMAS* Voyager *photographed at Hobart 30 November 1957.* (Russell Priest/L. Rex)

In the late 1940s the Australian Commonwealth Government placed orders for four new destroyers, which were to be a departure from the conventional destroyer in general design, armament and the number of personnel carried. They were to have the striking power of light cruisers, coupled with the latest anti-submarine weapons and detection devices. They were to be Daring-class ships, but they would be built in Australia. In the event the fourth ship, which was to have been named *Waterhen*, was cancelled and dismantled while on the stocks. The other three were completed and the order for the first ship went to the Cockatoo Island Dockyard & Engineering Company Ltd of Sydney, a subsidiary of Vickers Armstrong Shipbuilders. The keel of the ship, which was to become HMAS *Voyager*, was laid on 10 October 1949, but like the

British Darings, building progress was slow. This was mainly due to the severe financial crisis which followed the Second World War, together with shortages of steel and skilled labour. In the event the new destroyer was launched and named *Voyager* on 1 March 1952 by Mrs (later Dame) Pattie Menzies, the wife of the Australian Prime Minister. However, it was almost another five years before, HMAS *Voyager* was commissioned at Sydney, on 12 February 1957, by Captain G. J. B. Crabb DSC RAN.

Like their British counterparts the Australian Darings were armed with six 4·5-inch Mk V guns in three twin turrets. They were also armed with six 40mm anti-aircraft guns in three mountings, one triple 'Limbo' anti-submarine mortar and two sets of 21-inch 'Pentad' torpedo tubes. They were twin-

shaft ships powered by two sets of English Electric geared steam turbines, with the steam being provided by two Foster Wheeler superheat boilers. Altogether the main propulsion machinery developed some 54,000 SHP, giving them a speed of 33 knots and a radius of 3,700 miles at 20 knots. They were manned by a complement of 17 officers and 297 ratings, whose accommodation surpassed anything previously available. The officers were, depending upon seniority, accommodated in single or two- and three-berth cabins. The ratings' messdecks were fitted with three-tiered bunks, each fitted with its own reading light and which folded vertically when not in use to allow for recreation. Catering for ratings was a cafeteria system, each man being served by cooks at the galley serving hatch which was adjacent to the dining hall and separate from the messdecks. The Chief and Petty Officers had a separate dining hall where their meals were served to them by mess men. This meant, however, that there were three separate galleys, with the wardroom galley being directly below the wardroom itself and being served by means of a food hoist. The forward, junior ratings', galley fed 220 men and the after galley 80 CPOs and POs, both in separate sittings. The after galley also incorporated the ship's bakery.

As the 'first of class', *Voyager* underwent an extensive trials and work-up period in the Jervis Bay exercise areas, just south of Sydney. Following this arduous seven-month period *Voyager* underwent three months' maintenance in Sydney, and it was mid-January 1958 before she left, in company with *Warramunga*, to sail via Cairns and Darwin for an eight-month deployment with the Commonwealth Strategic Reserve based at Singapore. In those days, with the Malayan Communist insurgency still very active, the rôle of Australia's Strategic Reserve was to assist with the defence of the Singapore, the Malay Peninsular and the sea lines of communication. The two ships arrived at the Singapore Naval Base on 27 January, and a few weeks later, together with RN ships, *Voyager* was taking part in the annual 'FOTEX' exercise in the South China Sea and the Strait of Malacca, which also included a visit to the island of Penang. During April *Voyager* visited Hong Kong for a three-week self-maintenance period, and again in company with *Warramunga* she visited Manila, Yokohama, Otaru and the Korean naval base at Sasebo. With tensions between China and the breakaway island of Taiwan severely strained, the ships steamed through the Taiwan Strait flying prominent White Ensigns and with ships' companies closed up at Action Stations. The deployment ended on 3 September when they arrived back in Sydney and *Voyager* began a four-month refit period.

On 3 March 1959, after carrying out post-refit trials and a work-up period, she left Sydney for a second deployment to the Far East. This time she made the passage by way of the 'westabout' route via Melbourne, Adelaide and the great Australian Bight. After leaving Adelaide *Voyager* rendezvoused with *Melbourne*, HM Ships *Albion*, *Cheviot*, *Cossack*, three RFAs and HMNZS *Royalist*, to set course for Fremantle. During their passage they took part in a SEATO exercise in the Indian Ocean code-named 'Swanex', which also included Pakistani and US Navy ships. The RAN was well represented with *Voyager*, *Melbourne*, *Tobruk*, *Anzac*, *Queenborough* and *Quiberon*. During the manoeuvres *Voyager* was diverted to Onslow, Western Australia, to land an injured rating, before steaming north to the naval base at Singapore. Once again her arrival on station coincided with the start of the 'FOTEX' exercise, which began on 2 April and included the cruisers *Ceylon* and *Newfoundland*, as well as *Queenborough*, *Quiberon Cheviot*, *Cossack*, *Cardigan Bay*, *St Bride's Bay* and *Alert*. The exercise provided an opportunity for the Australian ships to work up and co-ordinate their weapons efficiency prior to the major multi-national exercise 'Sea Demon'. At the same time *Voyager* had the additional responsibility of acting as consort to *Newfoundland* while was underwent FO2's sea inspection. Her participation was unusual in that she represented a 'British merchantman' which had been captured by pirates and was about to enter 'hostile' Chinese territorial

waters. As the cruiser's boarding parties transferred to the destroyer, *Newfoundland* herself was subjected to air, submarine and shore battery attacks and bombardments. For her ship's company it was an arduous exercise but, apparently, *Voyager*'s personnel recorded that, 'We thoroughly enjoyed ourselves'. Anzac day 1959 was spent in the South China Sea participating in 'Exercise Sea Demon', involving 27 surface ships, three submarines and aircraft from all participating nations. The exercise was co-ordinated by the Flag Officer Commanding the Australian Fleet and it ended with a ceremonial entry into Manila Harbour.

On 30 April *Voyager* left Manila to steam north for Hong Kong, but during the passage she suffered a major mechanical problem in B boiler room when boiler tubes burst, and she was left limping into Hong Kong for repairs. After a long and difficult period in the Crown Colony, which was complicated by the fact that there was a severe water shortage when boiler feed water had to be 'scrounged' from US Navy ships, on 15 June *Voyager* left for Darwin, Cairns and Sydney, where she arrived on 29 June to pay off. Ahead lay a three-month refit, and by 3 July a new ship's company had joined the ship.

It was late October before *Voyager* was at sea again, and for four weeks she carried out post-refit trials off the coast of New South Wales. On 9 October *Melbourne* led *Voyager*, *Quiberon* and *Warramunga* through Sydney Heads and into the harbour where crowds on the bridge gave them a 'ticker-tape' welcome as they made their way to Garden Island. Next day all four ships were opened to the public. Later that month *Voyager* operated with her two sisters *Vampire* and *Vendetta* in the Jervis Bay area, and four days later, during a Families Day, *Voyager* and *Vendetta* operated with *Melbourne* for a flying display and a ceremonial entry into Sydney Harbour. During the remainder of 1959 *Voyager* accompanied *Melbourne* on a visit to New Zealand ports and on exercises with RNZN ships. During this period she visited Milford Sound, Port Lyttleton and Auckland, before returning to Sydney in early December to give leave and to undergo maintenance.

It was early February 1960 before *Voyager* returned to sea, starting with exercises in the Jervis Bay area, before moving on to the Bass Strait and a visit to Hobart. This was followed in early March by the 'Anzac' Joint Maritime Exercise, 'Starglobe', in the Tasman Sea. It was designed to test Australia and New Zealand's sea, air and anti-submarine operations over a long period. At the end of March in company with *Melbourne* and HM Ships *Belfast* and *Cavalier*, *Voyager* set course for Singapore where her first task was to have boiler tubes replaced in what was becoming a troublesome B boiler room. After embarking the tubes at Singapore *Voyager* steamed north to Hong Kong where, with the assistance of Whampoa Dockyard and a great deal of hard of work from the Engineering Department, *Voyager* was able to sail at just before midnight on 3 May to take part in 'Exercise Sea Lion', which involved some 60 ships from all eight SEATO nations. It was reported that *Voyager*'s rôle in the exercise was 'unrewarding', for after all the effort of getting the ship to sea on time she played a very minor role. When it came to the surface and anti-aircraft firings the ship's gunnery radar failed, and the gunners had to use guesswork ranges. Despite this handicap, however, they quickly downed one of the drone targets. During the remainder of May *Voyager* operated in and around Singapore, and on 1 June she left the naval base bound for Sydney. Next day, however, she had to divert to the Indonesian port of Tanjong Priok to land a man suffering from appendicitis, before continuing through the Sunda Strait to Fremantle and Melbourne, eventually arriving at Garden Island, Sydney, on 20 June to begin a five-month refit.

Almost as soon as she had secured alongside the dockyard, work began on making alterations to the bridge superstructure, and on retubing the boilers. It was not until 14 November that she was ready for sea again and for three weeks of post-refit trials and work-up exercises. Finally, on 28 December she sailed for a further deployment with the Commonwealth Strategic Reserve at Singapore. Sailing by way of the Great Australian Bight, with only a brief call at Fremantle for refuelling, the days

HMAS Voyager *seen underway.*                                    *(Royal Australian Navy)*

were spent exercising the ship's company at Defence Stations. On 11 January 1961, *Voyager* arrived at Singapore Naval Base, but almost immediately, in company with the carrier *Hermes* and the frigate *Quickmatch*, she was back at sea heading for Subic Bay and joint exercises with the US Navy. Later in January *Voyager* and *Quickmatch* made a four-day official visit to Bangkok, which ended with a 'Shop Window' display for senior Thai naval officers. In early February *Voyager* rendezvoused with *Hermes* to act as the carrier's planeguard escort during night-flying exercises off Hong Kong, which was followed by a popular 14-day self-maintenance period in Hong Kong dockyard. On 17 February she left to return to Singapore where she prepared for the major Commonwealth naval exercise 'Jet 61' which took place over two weeks in the Indian Ocean. Participating in the manoeuvres were 25 warships from Australia, the United Kingdom, India, Ceylon (Sri Lanka), Pakistan and New Zealand. The exercise ended at the former Royal Navy's fleet anchorage at Trincomalee which, while not an inspiring run ashore, provided

the perfect setting for a combined fleet sailing and pulling regatta. After leaving Trincomalee *Voyager* steamed into the Bay of Bengal to pay a short visit to Viskhapatnam in the Indian State of Andhra Pradesh, before continuing north for a goodwill visit to Calcutta where she negotiated the busy Hooghly River to secure at buoys opposite the city's Fort William and Eden Gardens. During the visit there was a full social and sporting programme, together with numerous invitations from local clubs and associations. When the ship was opened to the public some 2,000 people visited her and, had she been easier to reach, it was thought that many more would have taken the opportunity. From Calcutta *Voyager* returned direct to Singapore where she carried out self maintenance, during which the ship's divers changed the Asdic dome.

In mid-April, together with *Melbourne*, *Queenborough* and *Vendetta*, *Voyager* took part in anti-submarine exercises against the nuclear-powered submarine USS *Sargo* in the Subic Bay exercise areas. This was followed by 'Exercise Pony Express', a SEATO exercise involving 60 ships and

8,000 personnel. For the RAN and RN units the main task was to escort and defend the commando carrier *Bulwark*, carrying the Royal Marines of 42 Commando, from Manila to North Borneo, against attacks from US submarines. The exercise ended on 4 May, and next day *Voyager* handed over to *Vendetta* before setting course for Hong Kong to undergo maintenance and prepare for her annual inspection. In the event this was disrupted by the particularly ferocious typhoon 'Alice', which meant an unscheduled three days at sea riding out the storm. Finally, however, on 23 May *Voyager* left Hong Kong to rendezvous with *Melbourne* and make the voyage, via the Bernardino Strait, Manus and Rabaul, back to Australian waters. After visiting Brisbane *Voyager* steamed south to Jervis Bay where she rendezvoused with *Melbourne, Vampire, Quiberon, Quickmatch, Parramatta, Swan, Barcoo, Kimbla* and the submarines *Tapir* and *Trump*, for a ceremonial entry into Sydney Harbour. A contemporary account of the event records that: 'The weather was bright and clear and there were many spectators. On passing Bradley's Head *Melbourne* hauled out of line and with the Minister for the Navy on board taking the salute, *Voyager* led the ships of the fleet under Sydney Harbour Bridge and round Cockatoo Island, before securing alongside Garden Island's Cruiser Wharf, where families and friends of the ship's company were waiting to greet the ship.' Soon after her arrival *Voyager* began a long refit which kept her out of service for 20 weeks.

On 1 November *Voyager* left the dockyard to commence her work-up in the Jervis Bay exercise areas, before visiting Melbourne for the city's famous Cup Week. On 10 November she joined three British, two New Zealand and four Australian ships for 'Exercise Auckex', a two-phase exercise which began on Australia's east coast and ranged across the Tasman Sea. On completion of the manoeuvres *Voyager* visited Auckland and Lyttleton, and on 8 December she returned to Sydney for the seasonal leave period. The new year of 1962 saw *Voyager* alongside Garden Island Dockyard, and in mid-January she sailed for the

Jervis Bay exercise areas again, remaining in home waters until early March when, with *Melbourne* and *Queenborough*, she sailed by way of the Great Australian Bight, Fremantle and the Sunda Strait to Singapore. Although the 'Confrontation' with Indonesia was still some 12 months away, Indonesia's President Sukarno was already hostile to the proposed Federation of Malaysia, as well as to countries of the SEATO alliance, and so during the passage through the Sunda Strait the ships' companies were closed up at Defence Stations. Fortunately there were no incidents and the three ships arrived at Singapore Naval Base on 8 March.

During the second half of March *Voyager* visited Hong Kong for maintenance, then in early April she arrived at the US naval base of Subic Bay to take part in joint exercises with US Navy ships before steaming into the Sulu Sea and Leyte Gulf to visit the Philippine port of Taeloban. On 16 April she joined the multi-phase SEATO exercise code-named 'Sea Devil', which involved 47 ships, 150 aircraft and 16,000 personnel from Australia, the UK, New Zealand, the USA, Pakistan, Thailand and the Philippines. The exercises were controlled by Rear-Admiral McNichol RAN, flying his flag in *Melbourne*. Also taking part were *Vendetta*, *Queenborough*, and the Royal Navy's fleet carrier *Ark Royal*. During the exercises *Voyager* operated mainly in an anti-submarine role, but a series of accidents marred the overall result, with one man being lost from *Vendetta* and a crew member being lost following an aircraft crash. The exercise concluded on 4 May when *Melbourne, Ark Royal* and USS *Bennington* led a 14-mile long column of ships into Manila Bay. Three days later, in company with *Melbourne, Vendetta, Yarra* and *Parramata*, *Voyager* left the Philippines for Japan and the RAN's biggest goodwill visit to that country. *Voyager* and *Vendetta* visited Nagasaki, Kure and Kobe, before leaving Japanese waters to steam south into the Pacific and the island of Guam. Following this *Voyager* returned, via Samari and Ladava, to Australian waters where she again rendezvoused with *Melbourne* and *Vendetta*. On 21 June she returned to Sydney where leave was given

and the ship underwent maintenance.

On 18 October, under the command of Captain A. A. Willis RAN, *Voyager* put to sea again to carry out her work-up in the Jervis Bay area, and later that month she took part in the SEATO exercise code-named 'Seascape', to evaluate the naval control of merchant shipping. For the remainder of that year she did not stray far from the Jervis Bay exercise areas, and her operational year ended in early December when she returned to Sydney for maintenance and to give leave.

On 2 January 1963 there was another change of command when Captain D. H. Stevens RAN took over from Captain Willis. On 31 January, in company with *Vampire*, *Voyager* left Sydney bound for Singapore. Although the Brunei rebellion, which had broken out on 8 December 1962, had been suppressed, it was clear that diplomatic relations with the Indonesian government of President Sukarno were deteriorating and it was strongly suspected that Indonesia had been the major influence behind the Brunei troubles. Sukarno was vehemently opposed to the British plan for its South-East Asian colonies of Sarawak and North Borneo (Sabah) to join the independent ex-colonies of Malaya and Singapore to form the Federation of Malaysia. The Indonesian argument for sovereignty over Sarawak and North Borneo was based on the fact that both territories, which formed a small part of what was Indonesian Borneo (Kalimantan), had only become British when the island of Borneo was divided up between British and Dutch colonists. Clearly this was not recognised by Britain or by the governments of Singapore and Malaya, and as preparations for the Federation went ahead the scene was set for four years of 'Confrontation' between Indonesia and Malaysia.

*Voyager* and *Vampire* sailed to Singapore by way of Darwin and two days after leaving the port they came under the operational control of the C-in-C Far East Station. On 13 February they arrived alongside the Stores Basin of Singapore Naval Base where they relieved *Queenborough* and *Quiberon* as Australia's presence in the Far East Fleet. After undergoing a short maintenance period *Voyager* and

*Vampire*, together with HMS *Caesar*, sailed for Trincomalee to prepare for the SEATO exercise 'Jet 63' in the Indian Ocean. On her return to Singapore as part of a task group led by *Melbourne*, which also included *Parramata* and *Yarra*, *Voyager* sailed for Hong Kong where she underwent a two-week maintenance period. During her stay in the colony she held an open day and some 12,000 people 'swarmed over the ship'. In mid-April, after exercising in the Hong Kong area, the task group returned to Singapore before taking part in the international exercise code-named 'Sea Serpent' in the South China Sea. This also included the ever-popular banyans on the beaches of Pulau Tioman. Following the exercise *Voyager* and *Vampire* joined a Royal Navy task force for another visit to Hong Kong before sailing in company with HM Ships *Lion* (flag C-in-C, FES) and Caesar and HMNZS *Royalist*, for a visit to Japanese ports. The squadron should also have included the commando carrier *Albion*, but she was urgently required for operations off the coast of North Borneo. After calling at Karatsu on the island of Kyushu, *Voyager* joined *Hermes* and other RN ships off Okinawa for flying operations in the US Navy's exercise areas. On 5 June *Voyager* and *Vampire* paid an official visit to Tokyo, after which they returned to Singapore. During the return passage, however, *Voyager* was forced to put into Subic Bay for urgent boiler repairs, after which she joined *Lion* and *Vampire* to resume her interrupted passage to Singapore.

In early July 1963, after completing a much needed maintenance period, *Voyager* carried out exercises in the South China Sea and Strait of Malacca, and along with the carriers *Ark Royal* and *Hermes*, as well as the submarine *Anchorite*. On 20 July *Voyager* and *Vampire*, having been relieved by *Vendetta* and *Quiberon*, returned via Darwin to the Jervis Bay area where they were subjected to their annual sea inspections. Finally, on 3 August, they entered Sydney Harbour where they were greeted by families and friends. For *Voyager*, however, the visit to her case port was a short one and seven days later she sailed for Melbourne's Williamstown Dockyard to undergo a five-month refit.

The refit ended on 25 January 1964, when *Voyager* made the return passage to Sydney where she spent two weeks alongside at Garden Island. Finally, on 6 February she left Sydney for Jervis Bay again where, with the aircraft carrier *Melbourne*, which had also just completed a refit, she was to carry out work-up exercises. For *Voyager* the exercise programme began on Friday 7 February, when she carried out manoeuvres with *Melbourne*. That night she was ordered to Shoalhaven Bight to recover a target which had broken adrift, a task which *Melbourne*'s divers assisted in. Finally, at 0730 on 9 February, with the target having been taken in tow by an auxiliary, *Voyager* anchored in Jervis Bay. The exercises began again during the forenoon on Monday 10 February, and for *Voyager* these included shore bombardment and anti-submarine exercises with the submarine *Tabard*. On completion of these *Voyager* closed *Melbourne* for a heaving line transfer of mail, which was followed by radio trials between the two ships. During the evening *Melbourne* carried out night-flying exercises off the coast of New South Wales, with *Voyager* acting as her planeguard escort. The main purpose of this was, if necessary, to rescue aircrew personnel from the sea. It was the first time during the work-up that the two ships had been involved in close manoeuvring together and for the purposes of the exercise both vessels were darkened, with only navigation lights showing.

At approximately 2056, when the two ships were some 20 miles south-east of Jervis Bay, they collided with each other. *Melbourne* struck *Voyager*'s port side at the after end of her bridge, heeling her over to an angle of some 50 degrees. There was a huge flash which appeared to come from *Voyager*'s A boiler room, together with the deafening roar of esc-aping steam. The terrific impact pushed the destroyer through the water for several seconds before she broke in two, her forward section passing down *Melbourne*'s port side and the stern section down her starboard side. The forward section floated on its starboard side for five minutes before rolling over and floating keel upwards for another few minutes before it sank. *Voyager*'s after section remained afloat for three hours and it was in this section that most of the 232 survivors had been. There is no doubt that the death toll in the forward section would have been much higher had it not been for Chief Petty Officer J. Rogers who, in the darkness and confusion, organised the evacuation of the cafeteria where there were between 50 and 60 men. Ignoring opportunities to escape himself, he stayed behind to look after those who were unable to get out in time and for his selfless devotion and gallantry he was awarded a posthumous George Cross. There were many acts of great gallantry that night as the rescue operation got into full swing, but in all 82 men lost their lives - 14 officers, including Captain Stevens, 67 sailors and one civilian dockyard employee.

Although *Melbourne*'s stem was badly damaged she suffered no casualties, nor was she in any danger of sinking, and it was her ship's company who recovered the destroyer's survivors from the water. The wreck of HMAS *Voyager* lies in some 600 fathoms of water, 20 nautical miles off Cape Perpendicular, on a bearing of 120 degrees.

## HMAS *Voyager*
## Commanding Officers

| Name: | Date Appointed: |
|---|---|
| Captain G. J. B. Crabb DSC RAN | 27 December 1956 |
| Captain W. J. Dovers DSC RAN | 7 January 1959 |
| Captain R. A. H. Millar RAN | 18 January 1960 |
| Captain D. G. Wells RAN | 21 September 1960 |
| Captain A. A. Willis RAN | 31 July 1962 |
| Captain D. H. Stevens RAN | 2 January 1963 |

## Battle Honours

| | |
|---|---|
| Calabria 1940 | Crete 1941 |
| Libya 1940/41 | Mediterranean 1941 |
| Greece 1941 | Pacific 1945 |

# Part Ten

# HMAS VENDETTA

### November 1958 - October 1979

*HMAS* Vendetta *underway off Sydney in June 1963. In appearance very similar to the RN Darings. Note the small number of portholes in the forward hull.* *(Russell Priest/ J.Freeman)*

The second of the Australian Darings to be commissioned was HMAS *Vendetta*, the contract for which had gone to the Williamstown Naval Dockyard at Melbourne. *Vendetta*'s keel was laid on 4 July 1949, and she was launched on 3 May 1954 by Mrs N. Waller, the widow of the late Captain H. M. L. Waller RAN. He had been lost in February 1942 when in command of the cruiser HMAS *Perth* which was sunk by the Japanese in the Sunda Strait during the final encounters of the Battle of the Java Sea. It was another eight years after her launch before *Vendetta* was in the final stages of fitting out and nearing completion. On 18 July 1958, even before she was commissioned, the destroyer was involved in an accident which, by good fortune, was not more serious. She was moving under the power of her own engines for the first time when the order for 'half astern both engines' was misinterpreted as 'half ahead both engines', with the result that she rammed the gates of the Alfred Graving Dock in which HMAS *Quickmatch*, with many underwater fittings removed, was under refit. With *Vendetta*'s stem firmly embedded in the gate it was only prompt action by the dockyard workers on board, who closed down all watertight doors and hatches and flooded the dry dock in order to equalise the water pressure on both sides of the gate, which narrowly averted a disaster. Repairs to *Vendetta*, meanwhile, took three months and she was finally commissioned under the command of Captain R. J. Robertson DSC RAN on 26 November 1958. After a period of trials and work-up exercises *Vendetta* made an operational cruise of goodwill visits to ports in New Zealand, before

steaming on to New Guinea and Noumea. Later that summer she underwent a short refit at Williamstown Dockyard.

20 October 1959 saw the three Australian Darings, *Vendetta, Vampire* and *Voyager*, together for the first time when they carried out a series of exercises and manoeuvres in the Jervis Bay exercise areas. In November, however, *Vendetta* sailed for Singapore to begin an eight-month deployment with the Far East Fleet. In 1959 the Malayan Emergency was in its final stages[1] and Australia's role in South-East Asia was to support the Royal Navy in defending Malaya's sea lines of communication, and to assist wherever possible in maintaining the internal security of Malaya and Singapore by participating in operations against the Malayan Races Liberation Army. This was ostensibly a force struggling for Independence, but in reality an almost wholly Communist Chinese Organisation which had flourished during the Japanese occupation between 1942 and 1945. During this period with the Far East Fleet *Vendetta* operated closely with the cruiser *Belfast* (flag FO2, FES, Vice-Admiral Varyl Begg) and it is said that Begg was very impressed with the performance of her ship's company. On 18 December she accompanied *Belfast, Quickmatch* and *Cardigan Bay* to Hong Kong where, on Christmas Eve, they entered harbour for seasonal celebrations. In the new year of 1960 the squadron carried out a series of bombardment exercises in the Hong Kong area, before returning to Singapore by way of Sandakan.

In mid-February 1960, in company with Centaur, *Belfast, Quickmatch, Llandaff, Carysfort, Cavendish, Loch Fyne, Alert* (flag C-in-C, FES), the Indian Navy ships *Delhi, Mysore, Godavari, Gomati, Ganga, Kirpan, Kuthar, Khukri, Cauvery,* the Pakistan Naval Ships *Shah Jahan* and *Alamgir,* as well as eight RFAs, *Vendetta* sailed for 'Exercise Jet 60' which began in the Strait of Malacca and continued into the Indian Ocean, with a break at Trincomalee. In May she took part in a second international naval exercise, this time in the South China Sea and the Subic Bay exercise areas. Code-

named 'Sealion' the exercise also involved the aircraft carriers HMAS *Melbourne*, HMS *Albion* and USS *Yorktown*, as well as *Belfast, Cavendish, Caprice* and *Scarborough*. Its primary function was to test SEATO's anti-aircraft defences, but *Vendetta* and BELFAST also undertook a shore bombardment exercise with their main armament. In mid-July *Vendetta* returned to Australian waters where she remained for the rest of the year.

On 19 February 1961 the 13,587-gross ton cargo ship *Runic*, belonging to the Shaw Savill Line, which was on passage between Brisbane and Auckland, went aground on Middleton Reef, some 120 miles north of Lord Howe Island during a severe storm. Attempts to refloat the ship failed and *Vendetta*, which was exercising in Jervis Bay at the time, was ordered to steam with all dispatch the 400 miles to the scene. She arrived off Middleton Reef some 20 hours later, and as a number of tugs were attempting to refloat the stricken ship, *Vendetta* took off three women passengers, the wives of crew members, and nine crewmen who were not required on board. As she could render no further assistance she returned to Sydney with her passengers. In the event *Runic* could not be refloated and she was abandoned.

In mid-March 1961 *Vendetta* left Sydney for her second tour of duty with the Far East Fleet at Singapore. This time she took passage by way of Adelaide and Fremantle, and in early April she arrived alongside the Stores Basin of Singapore Naval Base. No sooner had she arrived on station than she was involved in major fleet exercises with her old friend *Belfast*, as well as *Melbourne, Victorious, Bulwark, Queenborough, Voyager,* HMNZS *Royalist, Carysfort, Cavalier,* and *St Bride's Bay*. The exercises took the fleet into the waters off North Borneo where, as if in anticipation of the coming 'Confrontation', *Bulwark* carried out a full-scale landing of Royal Marines. The exercise continued into the South China Sea, with some welcome relaxation at Pulau Tioman. In May and June she accompanied *Belfast* to Hong Kong and Japan. In July she represented the RAN at Manila for the

---

[1] The Emergency was declared to be finally over on 31 July 1960.

Philippines Independence celebrations, and in October that year she returned to home waters and to a refit at Williamstown Dockyard.

On 1 April 1962 *Vendetta* returned to Singapore for further service with the Far East Fleet, and soon after her arrival she was involved in her first major exercise. Led by aircraft carriers from three of the SEATO nations, *Melbourne, Ark Royal* and USS *Bennington*, the exercise also included ships from New Zealand, Thailand and Pakistan. Code-named 'Sea Devil' the exercise in the South China Sea and the Subic Bay exercise areas, was directed by Rear-Admiral Alan McNicoll, the Flag Officer Commanding the Australian Fleet, and its aim was to strengthen the defensive capabilities of the SEATO Navies when operating together. During the manoeuvres one of *Vendetta*'s ship's company members was lost after falling overboard, and a Sea Vixen and a Skyraider from *Ark Royal* and *Bennington* respectively were lost when they crashed into the sea. Fortunately their crews were rescued. The exercise ended on 3 May when *Melbourne* led a column of ships some 14 miles long into Manila Bay. After visiting Japan *Vendetta* returned to Sydney by way of Guam and Manus Island, and before entering harbour on 21 June she rendezvoused with *Melbourne, Quiberon, Voyager* and *Swan* to make a very impressive entry. After giving leave and undergoing maintenance *Vendetta* sailed for a short visit to Noumea, after which she exercised in waters off Queensland. However, this was cut short when extremely heavy weather prevented HM submarines *Tabard* and *Tapir* from taking part, and during her return passage to Sydney *Vendetta* steamed through the eye of a particularly severe cyclone. During the remainder of 1962 she operated in home waters, and in September with *Melbourne, Vampire, Queenborough* and HM Ships *Tiger, Caprice* and *Loch Killisport* she took part in 'Exercise Tuckerbox 2' in the Jervis Bay exercise areas. Once again unfavourable weather hampered the manoeuvres, and a proposed fleet entry into Sydney Harbour was cancelled. In November *Vendetta* visited Fremantle for the Commonwealth Games, before undergoing a four-month refit.

By this time the political situation in South-East Asia, where Indonesia had begun its policy of 'Confrontation', which saw Indonesian irregular and regular units of the Indonesian Army make armed incursions into North Borneo and Sarawak. The 'Confrontation' lasted until August 1966, and during this period the operational strength of the Far East Fleet was high, with the Australian ships based at Singapore being made available for patrol and escort operations designed to counter any Indonesian attacks. In mid-July 1963 *Vendetta* left Sydney to sail via Townsville and Darwin for another tour of duty at Singapore. She arrived just in time to take part in 'Exercise FOTEX 63' in the South China Sea. Also taking part was the commando carrier *Albion*, which was taking a rare break from operations in Borneo, together with *Ark Royal, Lion, Duchess, Cambrian, Salisbury, Plymouth* and HMNZS *Otago*. Following hard on the heels of this exercise came 'Exercise Sea Dovetail'. *Vendetta* followed this up with visits to 14 ports in five countries, including Japan, culminating in Christmas and New Year in Hong Kong.

The ship returned to Australian waters in February 1964 where she remained until June that year when she was again deployed to South-East Asia. During this deployment she again operated with the RN's Far East Fleet and conducted anti-Indonesian infiltration patrols in the Mersing area on Malaya's east coast. She also took part in 'Exercise Reef Knot', during which she rescued three aircrew from a crashed Gannet aircraft from HMS *Centaur*. *Vendetta*'s deployment ended on 12 December, when she returned to Sydney to undergo a seven-month refit.

In late 1964 the ill-fated United States' intervention in South Vietnam was gathering pace and President Johnson requested a military contribution from both the UK and Australia. As far as Britain was concerned, the Government in London refused to become involved, but in Australia the Prime Minister Sir Robert Menzies saw the Indonesian 'Confrontation' and what was, in effect, the Vietnamese civil war as joint threats to Australia. Thus it was that in May 1965 the first 800

Australian troops left Sydney bound for South Vietnam. It was August that year before *Vendetta* was ready to carry out her post-refit trials and her operational work-up, but when these were completed she returned to Sydney. Her next duty involved her with the Vietnam War when, in company with HMAS *Duchess*, she escorted the troop carrier HMAS *Sydney* carrying 350 Australian troops to South Vietnam. Sailing by way of Manus Island and Subic Bay, the three ships put in at the port of Vung Tau (formerly Cap St Jacques) at the mouth of the Saigon River, some 40 miles from the city, where the troops and their equipment, including armour, artillery, light aircraft and signalling equipment, were disembarked. After leaving Vietnamese waters they steamed south to Singapore where they joined the Far East Fleet. During this deployment *Vendetta* carried out patrols of the Strait of Malacca and there were the usual training exercises. Christmas and New Year were spent at Singapore, and it was 12 March 1966 when *Vendetta* returned to Sydney to give leave and to undergo maintenance.

During the evening of 20 May 1966 the ship was exercising in the Botany Bay area when she received a distress signal from the dredger *W. D. Atlas*, which was in difficulties in a storm just south of Jervis Bay. With high winds and huge waves making the passage very difficult, *Vendetta* battled her way through the mountainous seas to the search area. As she neared the dredger's position *Vendetta* herself was struck by a huge wave and sea water poured into B boiler and engine rooms, resulting in flooded bilges and a complete power failure. To add to the problems the severe weather prevented the changeover of watchkeepers in both machinery spaces. Meanwhile RAN helicopters had managed to rescue four exhausted survivors from the dredger which had foundered and sunk. Despite her own problems *Vendetta* continued to the scene, but after a long search she was only able to recover four bodies from the sea. Of the dredger there was no trace at all. Later that month *Vendetta* escorted the troop carrier *Sydney* as she made another trip to Vung Tau. On 3 November the US Navy's submarine

*Tiru* grounded on the Frederick Reef off the Queensland coast. The tug which attended the scene was unable to shift the submarine, but *Vendetta* assisted with a tandem pull and together they were able to refloat the submarine . As there was no obvious serious damage to *Tiru* she was escorted to Brisbane by *Vendetta* where a full assessment could be made.

During February and March 1967 *Vendetta* underwent a refit, and in the latter half of the year she operated off Australia's east coast. In March 1968, accompanied by *Parramatta*, she was again deployed to Singapore, and she returned home in October that year. In early 1969 *Vendetta* underwent a six-month refit at Sydney's Cockatoo Island Dockyard, during which both propeller shafts were replaced. Her post-refit trials in July that year were disrupted by an electrical fire in the wardroom, and by damage to the ship's generators, and it was September 1969 before *Vendetta* was ready for operational service again. The destroyer's next deployment, which began on 15 September, was unique in the post-1945 Australian Navy in that she became the first 'all-Australian' naval ship to serve in a combat zone. Arriving in Subic Bay on 26 September, she relieved HMAS *Brisbane* as Australia's contribution to the US Navy's Seventh Fleet in Vietnamese waters. During the seven months which followed, *Vendetta* performed well in a role for which she had been designed, that of naval gunfire support for the Army ashore. During her five tours of duty off Vietnam, totalling 93 days in all, *Vendetta* fired 13,295 4·5-inch shells, plus 400 rounds of 40mm ammunition, and in the process steamed some 21,000 nautical miles. She demonstrated the versatility of the Daring-class ships in this role, as, with three turrets, the ship always had at least one turret ready to fire at a moment's notice. Although there were some problems with ammunition supplies and spares, *Vendetta*'s readiness for action, rapid response times and accurate fire won the admiration of the senior officers of the US Navy's Seventh Fleet. Although she spent Christmas and New Year on the gun line, during the deployment her ship's compa-

ny spent well-earned rest periods in Singapore, Hong Kong, Taiwan and at Subic Bay.

In March 1970 Vendetta was relieved by HMAS *Hobart* and after returning to Sydney on 11 April she spent the next four months in home waters. In August, however, she returned to South-East Asia, visiting Colombo, Bombay and Nagasaki. In late October she again escorted HMAS *Sydney* on a trooping voyage to Vung Tau, and in April 1971 she returned to home waters where she remained until 29 September, when she paid off for a modernisation refit at Williamstown Dockyard.

*Vendetta* remained in dockyard hands for some 20 months as she underwent a AUS$10 million refit, during which she was extensively modernised. She was given a new superstructure and an enclosed bridge, new navigation radar and long-range early warning radar. Her communications equipment was renewed and all the messdecks were refurbished and improved. Replacing the superstructure required the largest-ever lift of aluminium superstructure undertaken in an Australian dockyard, with a 45-ton prefabricated structure being hoisted into place. At the same time her old mechanical gunnery fire control system was replaced with a more modern digital system. However, the increasing cost of the refit meant that the proposed fitting of Ikara and Seacat missile systems was abandoned. When *Vendetta* recommissioned at Williamstown on 2 May 1973, after an absence of almost two years, she had a completely new profile. On 26 July, after a series of post-refit trials, she returned to Sydney where she joined her sister *Vampire*.

The months which followed her return to service

*Profiles of the RAN Daring's (*Vampire *and* Vendetta*), pre and post modernisation.*     (Royal Australian Navy)

R.A.N. DARINGS - EXISTING.

R.A.N. DARINGS - AFTER EXTENDED REFIT.

*The Royal Australian Navy Darings, HMA Ships* Vendetta *(08) and* Vampire *(11) seen steaming in company in the mod-1970s after their half life refits which saw major remodelling of their superstructures and the installation of a new electronic gunnery control system.* (Royal Australian Navy)

saw *Vendetta* occupied with her shakedown, work-up exercises and manoeuvres in the Jervis Bay area, then in February 1974 she left Sydney for a four-month deployment with the ANZUK force based at Sembawang Dockyard, Singapore. During her refit the US intervention in Vietnam had ended ignominiously, and at Singapore Britain had withdrawn from the very expensive naval base. Most of the former base was given over to the refitting of merchant ships, but a small corner of the dockyard, the Stores Basin, was maintained jointly by the Australian, New Zealand and British governments. It was here that *Vendetta* was based during the deployment. Sailing by way of Australia's north coast, shortly before calling at Darwin, *Vendetta* rescued the crew of a small coaster which had sunk in the Arafura Sea, and during her Singapore deployment she took part in an amphibious landing exercise and also visited Labuan, Bangkok, Subic Bay, Cebu City and Sandakan, before returning to the ANZUK base for fuel and ammunition. She returned to Sydney in July, having made the home-ward passage by way of Jakarta, Fremantle and Melbourne.

In October 1974 *Vendetta* represented the RAN at Suva for celebrations marking the 100th anniversary of Fiji's cession to Britain, and during the visit she acted as the communications ship for Australia's Prime Minister Mr Gough Whitlam. On her return to Sydney she was dry docked in order to repair badly corroded plating inside her bilge keel. Two months later, in late December, *Vendetta* was one of 13 RAN ships which were ordered to proceed 'with all dispatch' to Darwin. On Christmas Day the capital of the Northern Territories had been hit by 'Cyclone Tracey' which, although not unexpected, was far more severe than had been predicted, with large sections of the city being devastated and 49 people losing their lives. For over two weeks the ship's company from *Vendetta*, and men from other ships, including *Melbourne*, helped to restore wrecked homes, provide power generators and bury tons of rotten food which had spoiled in freezers after electricity supplies had been cut.

Finally, in late January 1975 *Vendetta* arrived back in Sydney.

For six months after her return from Darwin *Vendetta* operated in eastern Australian waters, until early August 1975, when she was part of a task group which sailed for exercises in the Indian Ocean. These were cut short, however, when war broke out in what was then the Portuguese colony of Timor. The fighting between the Revolutionary Front for Independent East Timor (FRETILIN), and the more moderate Democratic Union of Timor (UDT), in which the former gained the upper hand and forced the Portuguese Governor and 800 evacuees to flee to Darwin, led to fears that Australian and other Western citizens trapped by the fighting might be in danger. *Vendetta* and *Vampire* were ordered to remain on stand by in case they were required to evacuate refugees from the war-torn eastern half of Timor (the western half of the island, which had one formed part of the Dutch East Indies,

was part of Indonesia). By mid-September the political situation had eased and *Vendetta* was able to rejoin the Indian Ocean task group, on a deployment which included visits to Singapore and Hong Kong. In December, after her return to Australian waters, began a nine-month refit at Williamstown Naval Dockyard.

The refit ended in September 1976 and the remainder of that year was spent carrying out post-refit trials and work-up exercises. In early January 1977 *Vendetta* sailed for a six-month deployment in South-East Asian waters, followed by exercises in home and New Zealand waters. In late June 1978 she commenced her final overseas deployment which took her on visits to Honiara, Manus Island, Subic Bay, Port Kelang, Surabaya, Penang and Christmas Island. In late October she took part in a major Indian Ocean exercise code-named 'Sandgroper'. In November 1978, while berthed at Sembawang in Singapore, her commanding officer

*The End Of The Line - The decommissioned and stripped former Daring's Vendetta (08) and Duchess (154) tied-up alongside the reserve dolphins in Athol Bight, Sydney in 1980 awaiting disposal.*    *(Vic Jeffery Collection)*

was informed that in order to provide personnel for the new guided missile frigates *Adelaide* and *Canberra*, then under construction in the USA, *Vendetta* would finally pay off in June 1979. Leaving Singapore in late November, she returned home by way of Fremantle, arriving in Sydney in early December.

*Vendetta*'s final six months of operational service began in January 1979, when she took part in Western Australia's 150th Anniversary celebrations at Fremantle. While in Western Australian waters she took part in joint exercises with ships of the Royal Netherlands Navy. She also paid visits to Adelaide, Melbourne, Brisbane and Darwin. Finally, on 28 June 1979, flying a 366-foot paying-off pennant, she entered Port Jackson for the last time and undertook a nostalgic 'tour' of Sydney Harbour before securing alongside at Garden Island. Over the next three months the remaining members of her ship's company de-stored and de-ammunitioned ship, while the dockyard stripped her of equipment. On 9 October 1979, having steamed some 670,952 nautical miles throughout her career, *Vendetta* was paid off.

For over seven years the redundant destroyer languished in the Reserve Fleet in Athol Bay, Sydney, until finally, in January 1987, having been sold to the Ming Hsich Steel Mill, she was towed from Sydney bound for the shipbreaker's yard at Taiwan.

## HMAS *Vendetta*
## Commanding Officers

| Name: | Date Appointed: |
|---|---|
| Captain R. J. Robertson DSC RAN | 5 November 1958 |
| Captain E. J. Peel DSC RAN | 22 June 1959 |
| Captain J. M. Ramsey DSC RAN | 10 January 1961 |
| Captain J. P. Stevenson RAN | 5 October 1962 |
| Commander D. W. Leach RAN | 21 December 1964 |
| Commander P. R. Burnett RAN | 22 August 1966 |
| Commander P. J. Hutson RAN | 1 October 1968 |
| Commander E. E. Johnston RAN | 6 May 1969 |
| Commander M. W. Hudson RAN | 16 June 1970 |
| Commander M. J. Taylor RAN | 30 August 1971 |
| Commander A. G. Ferris RAN | 1973 |
| Commander B. J. G. Dunn RAN | 15 March 1976 |
| Commander M. R. Freeman RAN | 2 January 1978 |

## Battle Honours

| | |
|---|---|
| Libya 1941 | Mediterranean 1941 |
| Matapan 1941 | New Guinea 1943/44 |
| Greece 1941 | Vietnam 1969/70 |

# Part Eleven

# HMAS VAMPIRE

## June 1959 - August 1986

Vampire *fitting out at Cockatoo Island Dockyard, Sydney, New South Wales on 1st November, 1957.*

*(Royal Australian Navy)*

The last of the three Australian Darings to be commissioned was HMAS *Vampire*, the contract for which went to the Cockatoo Island Dockyard Company, Sydney. The first keel plates were laid on 1 July 1952 and she was launched on 27 October 1956 by Lady Slim, the wife of Field Marshal Sir William Slim, who was the Governor General of Australia. Almost three years after her launch, on 23 June 1959, *Vampire* was commissioned into the Royal Australian Navy, and during the weeks that followed she carried out trials and working-up exercises. From October 1959 to March 1960 she exercised with other RAN and with New Zealand ships off Australia's east coast and in the Tasman Sea, and on 29 October 1959 the three Australian Darings operated together for the first time.

In June 1960 *Vampire* left Sydney bound for Singapore and duty with the Royal Navy's Far East Fleet. During this tour of duty she visited Hong Kong, Sandakan and Trincomalee, and took part in a major SEATO exercise in the Indian Ocean. In December that year she returned to Sydney where she underwent an extensive refit which kept her out of commission until April 1961. After recommissioning she spent five months in home waters, during which time she joined *Melbourne*, *Voyager*, *Quiberon*, *Quickmatch* and *Parramatta* for exercises in the Jervis Bay area and a ceremonial entry into Sydney Harbour. In September 1961 she again joined the Far East Fleet, operating out of Singapore and Hong Kong. Soon after arriving on station *Vampire* joined *Belfast*, *Caesar*, *Cavalier*, *Cossack*, *Lincoln* and the submarine *Taciturn* for

exercises in the South China Sea, during which the latter was 'hunted' by the surface ships. During this period there were recreational days at anchor off Pulau Tioman, and in November *Vampire* accompanied *Belfast* and *Cassandra* to Hong Kong. In January 1962 she again joined *Belfast, Cassandra, Cavalier, Lincoln* and *Quickmatch* for a SEATO exercise in the US Navy's exercise areas off Subic Bay. These also included the US Navy cruiser *Los Angeles* which was coming to the end of her operational career. These manoeuvres included visits to the US Naval Base at Subic Bay, and main armament bombardment exercises on the Tabores Gunnery Range. In March, again in company with *Belfast*, as well as *Centaur, Cavalier, Carysfort, Lincoln, Plymouth* and *Rhyl*, INS *Mysore* (ex-HMS *Nigeria*) and *Vikrant* (ex-HMS *Hercules*) she took part in the Indian Ocean 'Exercise Jet 62', which ended at Singapore Naval Base. In April, after a short maintenance period at Singapore, *Vampire* returned to Sydney.

Once again the remaining months of the year were spent closer to home, but in January 1963 she left Sydney for her third tour of duty with the Far East Fleet at Singapore. During this period the 'Confrontation' with Indonesia began, but despite the heightened tension she was able to participate in the SEATO exercise 'Sea Serpent' and also visit Ceylon (Sri Lanka) and Japan. In February *Vampire* acted as planeguard for HMS *Hermes*, the first time since the dark days of April 1942 that two ships bearing these names had operated together. On that occasion, off the coast of Ceylon, Japanese aircraft sank both vessels. *Vampire*'s third deployment to Far Eastern waters ended in July 1963, when she and the ill-fated *Voyager* were relieved by *Vendetta* and *Quiberon*, after which they returned to Sydney. *Vampire* spent the rest of the year refitting

*HMAS* Vampire *seen at Hobart in November 1959. The RAN specific secondary armament can be seen to advantage, as can the lack of portholes in the forward hull* *(Russell Priest/L. Rex)*

*HMAS* Vampire *seen underway in her original 1960s appearance.*　　　　　*(Royal Australian Navy)*

and it was February 1964 before she was at sea again, carrying out training exercises with other RAN ships.

In May 1964 *Vampire* took part in anti-submarine exercises in the Subic Bay area with USS *Sculpin* providing her prey. She also visited Port Moresby and Manus Island, before taking part in 'Exercise Litgas', with RN, RNZN and US Navy ships, including the commando carrier *Bulwark*. On completion of the exercises *Vampire* continued to operate in Asian waters until February 1965 when she returned, via Manus Island, to Australia. After leave and maintenance she steamed north to Manila, exercising en route with the new French frigate *Doudart de Lagree*, following which she escorted HMAS *Sydney* for part of her maiden trooping voyage to Vietnam. Between July and December 1965 *Vampire* underwent another refit at Sydney, and in February 1966 she steamed north to Singapore for another Far Eastern deployment. In late May and early June she took part in 'Exercise Sea Imp', following this up with a visit to Bangkok. However, on 10 June, while transiting the Bangkok

River, she collided with the Danish freighter *Emilie Maersk*. Although *Vampire* suffered some damage to her bow it did not affect her seaworthiness, and upon her return to Singapore she underwent repairs. During this deployment she again escorted HMAS *Sydney* from Manus Island to Vietnam, and for three weeks she was guardship at Tawau in Malaysian Borneo, a coastal town which was particularly vulnerable to Indonesian infiltration. Finally, in August 1966, after visiting Hong Kong, *Vampire*, in company with *Derwent*, returned to Sydney. For the rest of that year she exercised in local waters, underwent a mid-cycle docking period and took part in a four-nation exercise in the Solomon Sea off New Guinea.

In January 1967, in company with HMAS *Duchess*, *Vampire* left Sydney for what was to be a lengthy deployment to the Far East, arriving in Singapore on 19 January. In early February, during a local exercise the South China Sea, she stood by and assisted the Malaysian coaster *Mahra Thevi* which had run aground on the island of Pulau Pemanggil, some ten miles south-east of Tioman

*A 1960s shot of HMAS* Vampire *pounding through a swell in the Southern Ocean.* (Royal Australian Navy)

Island. The month of March was taken up with the SEATO exercise 'Siyasat', as well as visits to Bangkok and Manila. She also escorted HMAS *Sydney* from Manus to Vietnam, and on one occasion from Singapore to Vung Tau. During the remainder of the deployment she participated in 'Exercise Sea Dog' and visited the South Korean ports of Chinhae and Inchon. In September 1967 *Vampire* was the first RAN ship to visit Indonesia following the end of 'Confrontation', which had officially ended in August 1966. The visits came during *Vampire*'s homeward passage when she put into the Indonesian capital Jakarta and the port of Surabaya. Finally, on 19 September 1967, she arrived back in Sydney.

Between the end of September 1967 and May 1969 *Vampire* underwent a long refit, after which she carried out trials and work-up exercises. On 23

March 1969 she left Sydney for another deployment to Far Eastern waters. This time she was accompanied by the frigate *Stuart*, and in June *Vampire* celebrated her tenth birthday, having steamed some 375,000 miles during her service so far. During the deployment *Vampire* visited Hong Kong and Japan, and she underwent maintenance at Singapore. After returning to Sydney on 13 October she remained in local waters. In early 1970 she was involved in junior officers' training, which saw her making goodwill visits to Adelaide, Brisbane and Lord Howe Island. Finally, however, on 23 May 1970, wearing a 400-foot paying-off-pennant, she left Sydney for Williamstown where she was taken over by the naval dockyard to undergo an extended, half-life modernisation refit.

During the 17 months in dockyard hands *Vampire* was fitted with new gun turrets and fire control sys-

tems, new aircraft warning and navigation radar. Major portions of her superstructure were rebuilt and her original funnels were replaced with more modern ones. New masts were fitted and the accommodation for the ship's company was refurbished. On 17 November 1971 *Vampire* was recommissioned at Williamstown, after which she carried out an extensive post-refit trials and work-up exercises, before returning to Sydney in March 1972, ready once again for operational duties.

In August 1972 *Vampire* visited New Zealand, and in October that year she steamed north to Singapore to join the newly-formed ANZUK (Australian, New Zealand, United Kingdom) force which had taken the place of the Far East Fleet following Britain's withdrawal from its Far Eastern military bases. Most of the old naval dockyard, officially opened in 1938, had been taken over by civilian companies, but a small corner centred round what had been the Stores Basin had been retained for use by the ANZUK force. During this deployment she participated in 'Exercise Sea Scorpion', and she returned to Sydney in March 1973. In April that year she sailed into the Pacific Ocean to visit Fiji and Apia, acting as host ship for the Australian Prime Minister during the South Pacific Forum. In September, as well as taking part in 'Exercise Longex 73', which also involved warships from the Royal Navy, US Navy, Royal New Zealand Navy and the Royal Netherlands Navy, *Vampire* also visited New Zealand before returning to Sydney in early October. Later that month she steamed out into Sydney Harbour to secure to No 1 buoy in Farm Cove for the great spectacle of carnival and colour which accompanied the opening of the Sydney Opera House. Over a million people

*An overhead view of HMAS* Vampire *following her 1971 modernisation. She is seen here with an enclosed bridge new funnels and masts and improved radar.* *(Russell Priest/K. Barr)*

crammed the harbour foreshores for the day-long festivities and after the event the destroyer returned to Garden Island to carry out maintenance, which lasted until January 1974.

During 1974 *Vampire* exercised in local waters before beginning a refit which lasted from September that year to May 1975. Later in the year she steamed north for another deployment to the Far East, during which she visited Singapore, Manila, Subic Bay, Hong Kong and Jakarta, before returning to Australia in February 1976. In June and July she visited the West Coast of America, calling at San Francisco and Seattle, and exercising with the US Navy in the Pacific. She returned to Australia via Hawaii, and on 6 August she took part in an impressive Fleet entry into Sydney Harbour.

Apart from acting as 'guard ship' at Melbourne during 'Cup Week' the remainder of 1976 and early

1977 were occupied with local exercises, maintenance and leave periods. During March 1977 *Vampire* acted as escort to the royal yacht *Britannia* during the Queen's Silver Jubilee visit to Australia, which took in Newcastle, Sydney, Melbourne, Adelaide and Fremantle. The arrival in Sydney was considered the highlight of the visit when, on 13 March, she and *Britannia* made a spectacular entry into harbour with a 21-gun salute being fired from the North Head. The hundreds of small boats, yachts and other craft swarming round the harbour created an unforgettable sight on that memorable occasion.

In April 1977, with the royal visit over, she resumed her duties off the coast of eastern Australia, rendering assistance to the junk *Wan Fu* which was en route from Australia to the USA. In June *Vampire* visited Adelaide and this was fol-

*HMAS* Vampire was gifted to the Australian National Maritime Museum, and given a berth in Sydney's Darling Harbour. Today she continues to be a popular tourist attraction. *(Glenn Towler)*

lowed by dry docking at Sydney. In November that year she visited Singapore to take part in a joint RAN, RN and USN exercise, 'Compass 77', which ranged over the South China Sea from northern Malaysia to Subic Bay. During 1978, owing to refitting, trials and work-up exercises, her only overseas duties only took her to New Zealand, but in January 1979 she began a South-East Asian deployment. Her six months in Asian waters included visits to Singapore, Madras, Colombo, Belawan, Manila, Subic Bay, Hong Kong and Japan; in June she returned via Guam to Sydney. *Vampire*'s participation in 'Exercise Kangaroo 3' completed her year and her arrival at Sydney on 6 December 1979 marked the end of her operational career.

In early 1980 *Vampire* underwent a docking period at Sydney prior to assuming a new role as a fleet training ship. As part of the RAN's training squadron, she undertook training cruises mainly in home waters, but occasionally to more distant destinations, such as New Zealand and, in 1983, as part of a larger task group, to Singapore. In 1984 she visited Indonesia and Malaysia and carried out a ten-day maintenance period at Singapore. In April 1986 it was decided that *Vampire* would be decommissioned, and on 24 June, after a final cruise during which she called at Townsville, Suva, Apia and Auckland, she made her last ceremonial entry into Sydney Harbour. A few weeks later, on 13 August, after a 27-year career during which she had steamed some 808,026 nautical miles, she was finally paid off.

Although she was placed in reserve *Vampire* remained in good condition, and a proposal to turn her into a museum ship was accepted. As a result she was gifted to the Australian National Maritime Museum, and given a berth in Sydney's Darling Harbour. Today she continues to be a popular tourist attraction for Australians, and foreign visitors alike, as well as former members of her ship's company. She is also the last surviving example of the 11 RN and RAN Daring-Class destroyers which were designed in the Second World War and built in the 1940s and 1950s.

**HMAS *Vampire*
Commanding Officers**

| Name: | Date Appointed: |
| --- | --- |
| Captain R. G. Robertson RAN | 7 January 1959 |
| Captain D. C. Wells RAN | 20 September 1959 |
| Captain A. M. Synnot RAN | 4 January 1961 |
| Captain G. J. Willis RAN | 19 April 1962 |
| Captain D. J. Hamer RAN | 2 December 1963 |
| Captain J. W. L. Merson RAN | 9 August 1965 |
| Captain N. E. McDonald RAN | 5 December 1966 |
| Captain N. A. Boase RAN | 6 November 1967 |
| Captain J. D. Goble RAN | 5 December 1968 |
| Captain G. J. H. Woolrych RAN | 1 October 1971 |
| Captain G. M. Jude RAN | 19 February 1976 |
| Captain N. E. Lee RAN | 23 May 1977 |
| Captain A. L. Beaumont RAN | 7 July 1978 |

**Battle Honours**

| Calabria 1940 | Libya 1940/41 |
| --- | --- |
| Greece 1941 | Crete 1941 |
| Aegean 1942 | |

# Part Twelve

# HMAS DUCHESS

## May 1964 - October 1977

*A fine 1960s shot of* Duchess *whilst in Royal Australian Navy service.*      *(Royal Australian Navy)*

On Friday 8 May 1964, at Williamstown Naval Dockyard, Melbourne, HMAS *Duchess* was commissioned into the Royal Australian Navy. Her ship's company now consisted of Australian naval personnel and the remaining members of her RN complement travelled by train to Sydney, from where they were flown home. *Duchess* herself remained in refit at Williamstown until September 1964, and in early November she sailed for Sydney to complete her work-up. On 9

January 1965 she sailed for Singapore to join the Far East Fleet, and on her arrival at the naval base found a situation much changed from her last visit. With Indonesia's policy of 'Confrontation', the base was extremely busy and *Duchess* carried out a number of patrols of the Malaysian and Borneo coasts. In March 1965 she returned to Sydney.

By the mid 1960s Australia had become embroiled in the ill-fated Vietnam War and in May 1965, together with *Vendetta*, she escorted HMAS

Duchess *and the carrier* Sydney *refuel on their way to Vietnam, during the ill-fated US-led war in that country.*
*(Royal Australian Navy)*

*Sydney* on the first of the latter's many trooping voyages between Australia and Vung Tau at the mouth of the Saigon River. On completion of this duty *Duchess* returned to Singapore where she joined the Far East Fleet once again. In October she was again assigned as escort to HMAS *Sydney*, which by late 1965 was making regular trooping voyages between Australia and Vietnam. *Duchess* spent Christmas and the New Year of 1966 in Hong Kong which, for the ships' companies, was always a popular venue for the festive season. This was followed by further service in Malaysian waters before, in March 1966, she returned to Sydney where she underwent a mid-year refit. During this period the ship's company was accommodated in the Battle class destroyer, HMAS *Tobruk*, which at that time was in reserve.

On completion of her refit *Duchess*, together with *Vampire*, left for Singapore for another deployment with the Far East Fleet, sailing by way of Cairns and Darwin. On their arrival at Singapore they relieved *Parramatta* and *Stuart*. *Duchess*'s deployment was, following the end of 'Confrontation', more relaxed, but with the conflict having recently

ended, she was again employed on patrols of the Malaysian and Borneo coastline. On 1 March 1967 *Duchess* and *Vampire* were the first ships to hoist the new Australian White Ensign (prior to this RAN ships had worn the White Ensign), and during the deployment *Duchess* visited Bangkok and Hong Kong. In mid-June she returned once again to Sydney.

Following her return home *Duchess* began a major refit which kept her out of service for almost a year, and it was April 1968 when she recommissioned for post-refit trials. These were followed by work-up exercises in home waters, followed by visits to New Zealand ports. During September and October she took part in a major amphibious exercise code-named 'Coral Reef', which also included her two RN sisters *Defender* and *Diamond*, as well as *Hermes*, *Glamorgan*, *Euryalus* and *Grenville*, together with US Navy ships. During this period, while *Duchess* was exercising in the Sulu and Celebes Seas, officials from London and Canberra were actually negotiating *Duchess*'s future. In the event the British Government agreed to extend the loan of *Duchess* to the RAN for a further four years.

On conclusion of 'Coral Sands' *Duchess* left the exercise area to head for Singapore and a further deployment in Asian waters.

After Christmas and New Year in Hong Kong, in January 1969 *Duchess* took part in the fleet exercise 'FOTEX 69' off Penang, in company with *Derwent*, *Hermes*, *Albion*, her sisters *Decoy* and *Diana*, and the frigates *Ajax*, *Aurora*, *Blackpool* and *Cleopatra*. There were short breaks on Langkawi Island, and following a full-scale invasion of Penang, *Duchess* and the rest of the fleet returned to Singapore in the second week of February. During the deployment she also visited India, Pakistan and Ceylon, before returning to Sydney on 18 April. The next six months were occupied in local exercises, leave and maintenance, but in November she returned once again to Singapore. After spending her second successive Christmas and New Year period at Hong Kong, in January 1970 *Duchess* joined a Royal Navy force for 'Exercise Janex 70' in the South China Sea. This involved most ships of the Far East Fleet, including *Fearless*, *Andromeda*, *Galatea*,

*Lynx*, *Nubian*, *Rothesay* and the depot ship *Forth*. The exercise involved an amphibious landing on Malaya's east coast as well as convoy escort duties. This was followed in March by 'Exercise Sea Rover', and this time the commando carrier *Bulwark* was also present. In June *Duchess* was again involved in another major exercise, 'Bersatu Padu', meaning 'total unity' in Malay. Involving ships from five Commonwealth countries, the aim of the joint maritime and air defence exercise was to provide support and training for the Malaysian forces who would take over after Britain's withdrawal from its Far Eastern bases at Singapore. The manoeuvres opened with an amphibious landing on Malaya's east coast and ended with an air defence exercise involving aircraft from the carrier *Melbourne*. Their rôle was to defend the fleet from RAAF aircraft operating from their base at Butterworth near Penang, and RAF aircraft from Singapore. On completion of the exercise *Duchess* accompanied *Melbourne* and *Derwent* to Osaka in Japan, where they represented the RAN at 'Expo

*A fine view of HMAS* Duchess *at Fremantle in April 1969.*                    *(Russell Priest/T. Drake)*

70' which was being held in the city. In June 1970 *Duchess* returned to Sydney to begin an eight-month refit which would keep her out of service until February 1971.

In March 1971, having completed her post-refit trials and work-up, *Duchess* returned to the Far East and during her three-month deployment she visited Hong Kong and Japan before returning to Sydney for a shorter, four-month, refit. Between the end of October 1971 and the end of January 1972 *Duchess* remained in home waters, mainly engaged in exercises in the Jervis Bay area. On 29 January she accompanied other fleet units for a three-month ANZUK deployment to Singapore, based on the now much smaller naval base in the area which used to be known as the Stores Basin. During this period she took part in the major SEATO exercise code-named 'Sea Hawk' which, just as in the 'old days', took place in the South China Sea with banyans on Pulau Tioman. During the return passage to Australia *Duchess* called at the Indonesian naval base at Surabaya on Java's south coast.

In August 1972, with the destroyer's second four-year loan to the RAN having expired, negotiations between the British and Australian Governments were completed, and the RAN purchased *Duchess* outright from Britain. In the event the nominal sum of £150,000 was paid by the Australian Government, but no sooner had the transaction been completed than it was announced that *Duchess* was being withdrawn from front-line service and would be employed as a training ship, replacing *Anzac* in that role. On 3 January 1973, wearing her paying-off-pennant, she left Sydney for Williamstown Naval Dockyard to undergo a refit which would fit her out for her training role. Originally it had been planned that the overhaul would take 12 months, but in the event it was extended to 18 months. The work included the removal of X turret and other fittings, and the construction of new superstructures to provide additional accommodation. In July 1974 she recommissioned as a training ship, and during the three years spent in this role her duties kept her mainly in home waters. She did, however, under-

*A fine view of HMAS* Duchess *in her final configuration as a training ship and still sporting an open bridge. The most noticeable changes were X-turret having been landed and replaced by a classroom and a re-modeled aft stack.*
*(Royal Australian Navy)*

take some cruises to foreign ports. Indeed, prior to paying off on 24 October 1977 she had just completed a cruise to the island of Fiji. After being paid off *Duchess* was laid up in Sydney's Athol Bay for three years, before being sold for scrap. In June 1980 she left Sydney Harbour under tow bound for Taiwan and the ever-hungry steel rolling mills of Asia.

*Leaving Sydney for the last time in June 1980,* Duchess *is under tow and bound for the breaker's yard in Taiwan.*
*(Royal Australian Navy)*

## HMAS *Duchess*
## Commanding Officers

| Name: | Date Appointed: |
| --- | --- |
| Commander I. M. Burnside RAN | 25 May 1964 |
| Commander H. K. Duncan RAN | 22 March 1966 |
| Commander J. A. Robertson RAN | 27 November 1967 |
| Commander P. R. Sinclair RAN | 10 November 1970 |
| Commander J. St B. More RAN | 6 January 1972 |
| Commander D. E. Clinch RAN | 1 March 1974 |
| Commander R. G. Harris RAN | 25 November 1975 |

## Battle Honours

See HMS *Duchess*

# Appendix

# Daring-Class Destroyers

## Technical Data

**Programme**:

Daring-class destroyers ordered under the 1944 wartime construction programme.
Provisional orders placed 20 July 1944
Orders confirmed 24 January 1945: - *Dainty, Daring, Delight, Diamond*.
Orders confirmed 16 February 1945: - *Decoy, Defender, Diana*.
Order confirmed 29 March 1945: - *Duchess*.

**Technical details:**

| | |
|---|---|
| Displacement (standard) | 2,950 tons. |
| Displacement (full load) | 3,580 tons |
| Length Overall | 390 feet |
| Length BP | 366 feet |
| Beam | 43 feet |
| Draught (max) | 17 feet |
| Armament | Six 4.5-inch in twin turrets, fully automatic, radar-controlled. |
| | Two forward, one aft:   Four or six 40mm, semi-automatic Bofors AA. |
| | Ten 21-inch torpedo tubes in two mountings. |
| | Squid anti-submarine mortar. |
| Propulsion Machinery | Two sets of Parsons double reduction geared turbines manufactured by the English Electric Company. Two shafts developing 54,000 SHP, speed 34.75 (designed), 30.5 knots sea speed. |
| | In *Dainty, Defender, Diamond* and *Duchess*, two Foster-Wheeler super heat, oil-fired boilers. In *Daring, Decoy, Delight* and *Diana*, two Babcock & Wilcox superheat boilers. |
| Operational Radius | 1,700 miles at full power and 4,400 miles at 20 knots. |
| Complement | 308 (*Daring* and *Diamond* as leaders): |
| | 297 *Diana*: 295 *Decoy* and *Delight*: 286 *Dainty*: |
| | 278 *Duchess* and *Defender*. |

## Pennant Numbers:

| | |
|---|---|
| *Daring* | D 05 |
| *Diamond* | D 35 |
| *Duchess* | D 154 |
| *Defender* | D 114 |
| *Dainty* | D 108 |
| *Decoy* | D 106 |
| *Delight* | D 119 |
| *Diana* | D 126 |

## Design Notes:

The design originated from the three-turret Battle-class design from which it had been proposed to order two vessels *Vimiera* and *Ypres*, under the 1943 construction programme. These were subsequently cancelled and new orders placed as part of the D-class building programme.

The class was designed to incorporate two units of main propulsion machinery, with higher steam pressures and double reduction steam turbines, in order to secure more efficient propulsion. The machinery arrangement resulted in the vessels being fitted with two funnels.

The designed armament was six, 4.5-inch; eight, 40mm AA guns, and 10, 21-inch torpedo tubes in two mountings of five. The main armament was to have been three Mark VI turrets with a maximum elevation of 85°, two of which were to have been mounted forward in A and B positions and the third on the after shelter deck in X position. The secondary armament was to have consisted of three twin 40mm STAAG AA Mark II mountings, two in the bridge wings and one abaft the after funnel, with two single 40mm AA Bofors Mark VII on the after shelter deck. The 21-inch torpedo tubes were designed in quintuple mountings and four depth charges throwers were to have been fitted at the stern. A Mark VI combined HA/LA director was to have been fitted on the bridge superstructure.

In December 1945, three months after the end of hostilities, orders for eight ships of the class were cancelled and the armament for the eight remaining vessels was modified thus: The twin STAAG mounting abaft the funnel was replaced by a twin 40mm AA Bofors Mark V mounting, and the two single 40mm AA mountings on the after shelter deck were replaced in favour of a MRS I director to provide local control for X 4.5-inch turret. At the stern, in place of the four depth charge throwers, a Squid anti-submarine mortar was fitted.

Electrical installation in *Daring*, *Dainty*, *Defender* and *Delight* was 220-volt DC system, but in *Decoy*, *Diamond*, *Diana* and *Duchess* a 440-volt, three-phase AC system, operating at 60 cycles a second was fitted.

*Diamond*, *Dainty*, *Diana*, *Defender* and *Duchess* were built with all-welded hulls, but the hulls of *Daring*, *Decoy* and *Diana* were of a part-rivetted and part-welded construction. Both *Daring* and *Diamond* were fitted as Leaders.

The construction of the class was protracted and took more than seven years, which meant that, with the advances in weapons technology, by the time they entered service they were quickly becoming outdated. The eight ships required large complements which meant the accommodation for both officers and ratings was cramped. The removal of the torpedo tubes and the building of additional deckhouse space did little to alleviate this state of affairs. With the end of National Service in 1960 manning the Darings became increasingly more difficult, and during the 1960s all of them spent some years laid up in Reserve.

**Appearance Notes:**

The ships were given semi-clipper bows and two funnels, the forward of which was fitted with a cowl and enclosed within the lattice mainmast. The short, slim, after funnel was designed with a ribbed casing. In *Dainty, Defender, Decoy* and *Delight* the after funnel was slightly raked, but in *Daring, Diamond* and *Duchess* it was straight. *Diana* was completed with a larger, raked and streamlined casing for the after funnel, but it was found to obstruct the arcs of the midships 40mm AA mounting and it was removed after only a short period, when she reverted to her original upright funnel. A pole mast for AW RDF was fitted aft on all eight vessels.

In 1959 *Dainty, Daring, Defender* and *Delight* were fitted with a deckhouse in place of the after torpedo tube mounting, and in 1964 an additional deckhouse in place of the forward torpedo tube mounting. It was 1960-61 before *Decoy, Diamond, Diana* and *Duchess* were fitted with a deckhouse in place of the after torpedo tube mounting, and the first three of these were fitted with the additional deckhouse in place of the forward torpedo tube mounting in 1967; in *Duchess* it was 1969.

The large Mark VI director originally fitted on the bridge structure was, in the case of *Decoy, Diamond, Diana* and *Duchess*, replaced by a smaller MRS 3 director in 1960-61. In the case of *Daring, Dainty Defender* and *Delight* the alteration was made during refits in 1964

**Subsidiary Roles:**

| | |
|---|---|
| *Decoy* | Trials ship for Seacat ship-to-air missile system. Based at Devonport. |
| *Defender* | Trials ship for underwater explosive tests by the Naval Constructional Research Establishment, Rosyth, 1972, prior to demolition. |
| *Diamond* | Harbour training ship attached to HMS Sultan, Gosport, and accommodation ship, 1970-1980. |

**Seacat Ship-to-Air Missile System:**

In 1959 it was proposed to install the Seacat ship-to-air guided missile system in *Decoy, Diamond, Diana* and *Duchess*. All were refitted with facilities for the system, with the after quintuple torpedo tube mountings being removed and replaced with a deckhouse upon which the launcher would have been fitted, with the missile handling room directly beneath this. The twin 40mm AA mounting abaft the after funnel was also removed. In 1964, however, it was decided that the Seacat system would only be fitted to newly constructed ships and, purely in her role as a trials ship for the missile system, only *Decoy* was fitted with a quadruple Seacat launcher. In 1963 the launcher was removed from *Decoy* and the deckhouse space was utilised for additional accommodation, as it had been in her sister ships.

## Armament Changes:

1959          *Dainty, Daring, Defender, Delight.*

After quintuple torpedo tube mounting removed and replaced by a deckhouse for additional accommodation.

1960          *Decoy.*

After quintuple torpedo tube mounting removed and replaced by a deckhouse. Twin 40mm AA Mark V abaft funnel removed and replaced by quadruple Seacat ship-to-air missile launcher. Twin 40mm AA STAAG Mark II mountings removed and replaced by two single 40mm AA Bofors Mark IX power mountings on the bridge wings. Mark VI director replaced by MRS 3 combined director.

1960-61       *Diamond, Diana, Duchess.*

After quintuple torpedo tube mounting removed and replaced by a deckhouse. Twin 40mm AA Bofors Mark V abaft the funnel removed. Two twin 40mm AA STAAG Mark II mountings removed from the bridge wings and replaced by two single 40mm AA Bofors Mark IX power mountings. Mark VI director replaced by a MRS 3 combined director.

1963          *Decoy.*

Quadruple Seacat missile launcher removed.

1964          *Dainty, Daring, Defender, Delight.*

Forward quintuple torpedo tube mounting removed and replaced by a deckhouse. Twin 40mm AA STAAG Mark II mountings on bridge wings replaced by two twin 40mm AA Bofors Mark V mountings. Mark VI director replaced by a MRS 3 combined director.

1967          *Decoy, Diamond, Diana.*

Forward quintuple torpedo tube mounting removed and replaced by an accommodation deckhouse.

1968          *Duchess.*

Forward quintuple torpedo tubes removed and replaced by an accommodation deckhouse.

## *Ferré* and *Palacios* - Modernisation:

| | |
|---|---|
| *Ferré* (ex-*Decoy*) | 1970 - 1973 by Cammell Laird Ltd, Birkenhead. |
| *Palacios* (ex-*Diana*) | 1970 - 1973 by Cammell Laird Ltd, Birkenhead. |

## Revised Details:

| | |
|---|---|
| Displacement | 2,966 tons (standard). 3,593 tons (full load) |
| Armament | Six 4.5-inch DP; two 40mm AA; eight Exocet 38MM STS missile launchers; Squid A/S mortar. |

## Design Note:

*Ferré* and *Palacios* were refitted and modernised following their purchase by Peru in October 1969. Their existing armament was retained and eight Exocet 38 MM ship-to-ship missile launchers were fitted on the after shelter deck between the after funnel and the twin 4.5 DP turret. They were installed in groups of four, angled outboard, on the port and starboard sides. The original lattice foremast was replaced by a new plated mast enclosing the forward funnel. New Plessey AWS I radar was fitted and the fire control system was modernised. On the foremast an aerial for air warning radar was fitted.

## Appearance Note:

A new tubular foremast, which encased the forward funnel was fitted in both *Ferré* and *Palacios* and their mainmasts were fitted with a Plessey air warning radar aerial. Their after funnels were fitted with a small, raked cowl and the pole mainmast was stepped forward of X, 4.5-inch turret. MRS I director was removed from the after shelter decks. In 1978 *Palacios* was fitted with a helicopter landing platform and a hangar was also added at this time, but was later removed. The after funnel was given a streamlined casing.

## *Ferré* and *Palacios* - Armament Changes:

1977        *Palacios* (ex-*Diana*)

Squid anti-submarine mortar removed.

1978        *Palacios* (ex-*Diana*)

Twin 4.5-inch DP turret on the after shelter deck and two Exocet STS missile launchers removed and a helicopter landing platform built at the stern.

1979         *Palacios* (*ex-Diana*)

Single 40mm AA Bofors Mark IX on the bridge wings replaced by two 40mm AA Breda mountings.

1980         *Ferre* (ex-*Decoy*)

Single 40mm AA Bofors Mark IX removed from the bridge wings and replaced by two twin 40mm AA Breda mountings. Two Exocet STS missile launchers and the Squid anti-submarine mortar removed.

## Conversion – Duchess:

Between August 1972 and June 1974, at Williamstown Dockyard, Australia, *Duchess* was converted for the rôle of Fleet Training Ship.

## Revised Details:

Armament    Four 4.5-inch DP; two 40mm AA.

## Design Note:

In June 1972, following her purchase outright by the Australian Government, *Duchess* was converted for the rôle of Fleet Training Ship. The twin 4.5-inch turret in X position, and the MRS I close-range barrage fire director were removed from the after shelter deck, together with the Squid anti-submarine mortar from the stern. An enlarged casing was fitted to the after funnel and a deckhouse, for use as classrooms, was built on the after shelter deck.

## Appearance Note:

Main armament all situated forward. Enlarged casing fitted to the after funnel. Deckhouse fitted on after shelter deck.

## Disposal Details:

*Daring*        Sold to Hughes Bolkow & Co Ltd, and arrived at Blyth, Northumberland for demolition 15 September 1971.

*Diamond*     Sold to Shipbreaking (Queenborough) Ltd, and arrived at Queenborough, Kent, for demolition 14 April 1981.

*Duchess*     Paid off at Atholl Bight, Australia, 24 October 1977. Towed to Taiwan for demolition June 1980. Broken up Kaohsiung from August 1980.

*Defender*    Damaged on underwater explosive trials in the Firth of Forth. Sold to J. A. White & Co Ltd, and arrived at Inverkeithing, for demolition 21 July 1972.

*Dainty*       Sold to Thomas Ward & Co Ltd, and arrived at Cairnryan for demolition 15 September 1971.

*Ferré*         Decommissioned during 2005.

*Delight*       Sold to Thomas Ward & Co Ltd, and arrived at Inverkeithing for demolition 26 June 1970.

*Palacios*     Decommissioned July 1993 and scrapped during 1994.


## Australian Daring Class

|  | Builder | Laid Down | Launched | Completed |
|---|---|---|---|---|
| *Vampire* | Cockatoo (Sydney) | 1.7.52 | 27.10.56 | 23.6.59 |
| *Vendetta* | Williamstown Dockyard | 1.7.49 | 3.5.54 | 26.11.58 |
| *Voyager* | Cockatoo (Sydney) | 10.10.49 | 1.3.52 | 12.2.57 |
| *Waterhen* | Williamstown Dockyard | 2.52 | Cancelled and scrapped on slip 1954 | |

While under construction a decision was taken to modify the armament, with the after torpedo tube mounting being omitted and the after shelter deck being extended forward to the after funnel. In place of the four depth charge throwers and depth charges a triple barrelled Limbo anti-submarine mortar was fitted at the after end of the deck with a handling room built at the far end. This installation resulted in the twin 4.5-inch turret in X position being mounted further forward. The two twin 40mm STAAG mounting to have been fitted at the forward end of the shelter deck were omitted.

As completed a total of 6 - 40mm AA were carried, *Voyager*, the lead ship, had two twin STAAG Mk II mountings in the bridge wings and a twin Bofors Mk5 mounting abaft the aft funnel. *Vampire* and

*Vendetta* received two single Bofors Mk7 in the bridge wings and two Bofors Mk5 mountings abaft the after funnel.

All three were fitted with a combined High Angle- Low Angle director on the bridge structure.

*Vampire* and *Vendetta* had two MRS1 Close Range Barrage Fire directors fitted on the centreline, either side of the after funnel.

## Pennant Numbers:

| | |
|---|---|
| *Voyager* | D04 |
| *Vendetta* | D08; 08 |
| *Vampire* | D11; 11 |

## Nomenclature:

All four were named after the Admiralty V and W class destroyers which served with distinction in the Australian 10th Destroyer Flotilla in the Mediterranean during 1941-42.

## Missile Note:

A 1965 proposal to fit Vampire and Vendetta with the Ikara anti-submarine missile system and the removal of the twin 4.5-inch turret on the after shelter deck was abandoned in 1967.

## Subsidiary Rôle:

*Vampire*    Fleet Training Ship 1980-86.

## Armament Changes:

1968        *Vampire*

4 - 4.5-inch DP; 6 - 40mm AA; 5-21-inch TT; Limbo A/S mortar.
Twin 4.5-inch turret in B position landed.

1970        *Vendetta*

6 - 4.5-inch DP; 6 - 40mm AA; Limbo A/S mortar.
Twin 4.5-inch turret in X position on the after shelter deck landed. MRS1 director forward of the after funnel removed.

## Modernisation:

*Vampire*         Williamstown Dockyard 1971-72
*Vendetta*       Williamstown Dockyard 1972-73

## Revised Details:

Displacement:        2960 tons (standard)    3600 tons (full load)
Armament:           6 - 4.5-inch DP, 6 - 40mm AA, Limbo A/S mortar

## Design Note:

Extensive half-life refit and modernisation. The quintuple torpedo tube mounting was removed from *Vampire* and the two twin 4.5-inch turrets were refitted in B and X positions.  The single 40mm Mk7 were retained in the bridge wings and the two twin 40mm Mk5 were sited abaft the after funnel.

The bridge was enclosed and Dutch Signaal WM fire control fitted, with directors fitted on a pedestal on the bridge structure and abaft the after funnel. New funnels were fitted with longer tapered casings. A lighter lattice foremast was fitted and the forward funnel was now visible. A light lattice mast was fitted to the after funnel and a stump mast carrying the early warning LW-02 radar was fitted forward of this funnel.

## Appearance Note:

Twin 4.5-inch turrets in A, B and X positions. Two larger funnels with tapered casings, the fore funnel visible and fitted with a cap. The after funnel fitted with a cowl.
Upperworks built up around the after funnel with a stump mast carrying early warning radar fitted at the fore end.
New enclosed bridge fitted.
Lighter lattice foremast, level with the forecastle break. Light lattice mast stepped on the fore part of the after funnel.

## Armament changes:

1980          *Vampire* ( as Fleet Training Ship)

                6 - 4.5-inch DP; 2 - 40mm AA
                Two twin 40mm AA Mk5 abaft the after funnel and the Limbo A/S mortar landed.

1984        *Vampire*

6 - 4.5-inch DP
Two single 40mm AA Mk7 removed from the bridge wings.

**Loss:**

*Voyager*    Sunk in collision with the aircraft carrier HMAS *Melbourne* during exercises off Jervis Bay, New South Wales, 10.2.64.

**Disposal:**

*Vampire*    Decommissioned 13.8.86. Converted to a Museum Ship 1988.

*Vendetta*    Paid off at Atholl Bight for disposal 8.10.79. Sold for breaking up. Scrapping commenced 11.1.87.